CW00519620

Just The facts101

Textbook Key Facts

Clinical Management of Intestinal Failure

by Cram101

Textbook NOT Included

Table of Contents

Just The Facts101

Exam Prep for

Clinical Management of Intestinal Failure

Just The Facts101 Exam Prep is your link from
the texbook and lecture to your exams.

**Just The Facts101 Exam Preps are unauthorized and comprehensive reviews
of your textbooks.**

All material provided by CTI Publications (c) 2019

Textbook publishers and textbook authors do not particpate in or contribute to these reviews.

Just The Facts101 Exam Prep

Copyright © 2019 by CTI Publications. All rights reserved.

eAIN 442601

Foundations of Business

A business, also known as an enterprise, agency or a firm, is an entity
involved in the provision of goods and/or services to consumers. Businesses are
prevalent in capitalist economies, where most of them are privately owned and
provide goods and services to customers in exchange for other goods, services,
or money.

:: Survey methodology ::

An _____ is a conversation where questions are asked and answers are
given. In common parlance, the word " _____ " refers to a one-on-one
conversation between an _____ er and an _____ ee. The _____ er
asks questions to which the _____ ee responds, usually so information may
be transferred from _____ ee to _____ er . Sometimes, information
can be transferred in both directions. It is a communication, unlike a speech,
which produces a one-way flow of information.

Exam Probability: **Medium**

1. *Answer choices:*
(see index for correct answer)

- a. Self-report study
- b. Data editing
- c. Interview
- d. Swiss Centre of Expertise in the Social Sciences

Guidance: level 1

:: Industrial design ::

In physics and mathematics, the _____ of a mathematical space is informally defined as the minimum number of coordinates needed to specify any point within it. Thus a line has a _____ of one because only one coordinate is needed to specify a point on it for example, the point at 5 on a number line. A surface such as a plane or the surface of a cylinder or sphere has a _____ of two because two coordinates are needed to specify a point on it for example, both a latitude and longitude are required to locate a point on the surface of a sphere. The inside of a cube, a cylinder or a sphere is three- _____ al because three coordinates are needed to locate a point within these spaces.

Exam Probability: **Low**

2. *Answer choices:*
(see index for correct answer)

- a. Transgenerational design
- b. Brand implementation
- c. Dimension
- d. Design 1st

Guidance: level 1

:: ::

Culture is the social behavior and norms found in human societies. Culture is considered a central concept in anthropology, encompassing the range of phenomena that are transmitted through social learning in human societies. _____ universals are found in all human societies; these include expressive forms like art, music, dance, ritual, religion, and technologies like tool usage, cooking, shelter, and clothing. The concept of material culture covers the physical expressions of culture, such as technology, architecture and art, whereas the immaterial aspects of culture such as principles of social organization , mythology, philosophy, literature , and science comprise the intangible _____ heritage of a society.

Exam Probability: **High**

3. *Answer choices:*
(see index for correct answer)

- a. functional perspective
- b. open system

- c. personal values
- d. Cultural

Guidance: level 1

:: Production and manufacturing ::

_____ consists of organization-wide efforts to "install and make permanent climate where employees continuously improve their ability to provide on demand products and services that customers will find of particular value." "Total" emphasizes that departments in addition to production are obligated to improve their operations; "management" emphasizes that executives are obligated to actively manage quality through funding, training, staffing, and goal setting. While there is no widely agreed-upon approach, TQM efforts typically draw heavily on the previously developed tools and techniques of quality control. TQM enjoyed widespread attention during the late 1980s and early 1990s before being overshadowed by ISO 9000, Lean manufacturing, and Six Sigma.

Exam Probability: **Low**

4. *Answer choices:*

(see index for correct answer)

- a. Total quality management
- b. Shifting bottleneck heuristic
- c. Equipment service management and rental
- d. Cellular manufacturing

Guidance: level 1

:: Market research ::

_____ , an acronym for Information through Disguised Experimentation is an annual market research fair conducted by the students of IIM-Lucknow. Students create games and use various other simulated environments to capture consumers' subconscious thoughts. This innovative method of market research removes the sensitization effect that might bias peoples answers to questions. This ensures that the most truthful answers are captured to research questions. The games are designed in such a way that the observers can elicit all the required information just by observing and noting down the behaviour and the responses of the participants.

5. *Answer choices:*
(see index for correct answer)

- a. BrandZ
- b. Viral Marketing Research
- c. Computer-assisted web interviewing
- d. Sagacity segmentation

Guidance: level 1

:: Reputation management ::

_____ or image of a social entity is an opinion about that entity, typically as a result of social evaluation on a set of criteria.

Exam Probability: **Medium**

6. *Answer choices:*
(see index for correct answer)

- a. Reputation
- b. Infamy
- c. ClaimID
- d. TrustRank

Guidance: level 1

:: ::

_____ is the collection of mechanisms, processes and relations by which corporations are controlled and operated. Governance structures and principles identify the distribution of rights and responsibilities among different participants in the corporation and include the rules and procedures for making decisions in corporate affairs. _____ is necessary because of the possibility of conflicts of interests between stakeholders, primarily between shareholders and upper management or among shareholders.

Exam Probability: **High**

7. *Answer choices:*
(see index for correct answer)

- a. Character
- b. hierarchical

- c. open system
- d. co-culture

Guidance: level 1

:: Organizational structure ::

An _____ defines how activities such as task allocation, coordination, and supervision are directed toward the achievement of organizational aims.

Exam Probability: **High**

8. *Answer choices:*
(see index for correct answer)

- a. The Starfish and the Spider
- b. Followership
- c. Organizational structure
- d. Blessed Unrest

Guidance: level 1

:: Alchemical processes ::

In chemistry, a _____ is a special type of homogeneous mixture composed of two or more substances. In such a mixture, a solute is a substance dissolved in another substance, known as a solvent. The mixing process of a _____ happens at a scale where the effects of chemical polarity are involved, resulting in interactions that are specific to solvation. The _____ assumes the phase of the solvent when the solvent is the larger fraction of the mixture, as is commonly the case. The concentration of a solute in a _____ is the mass of that solute expressed as a percentage of the mass of the whole _____ . The term aqueous _____ is when one of the solvents is water.

Exam Probability: **Medium**

9. *Answer choices:*
(see index for correct answer)

- a. Putrefaction
- b. Fixation
- c. Ceration
- d. Solution

Guidance: level 1

An _____ is a good brought into a jurisdiction, especially across a national border, from an external source. The party bringing in the good is called an _____ er. An _____ in the receiving country is an export from the sending country. _____ ation and exportation are the defining financial transactions of international trade.

Exam Probability: **Low**

10. *Answer choices:*
(see index for correct answer)

- a. Third country dumping
- b. Asian Clearing Union
- c. Nordic Innovation
- d. Import

Guidance: level 1

A _____ is a mathematical object used to count, measure, and label. The original examples are the natural _____ s 1, 2, 3, 4, and so forth. A written symbol like "5" that represents a _____ is called a numeral. A numeral system is an organized way to write and manipulate this type of symbol, for example the Hindu–Arabic numeral system allows combinations of numerical digits like "5" and "0" to represent larger _____ s like 50. A numeral in linguistics can refer to a symbol like 5, the words or phrase that names a _____ , like "five hundred", or other words that mean a specific _____ , like "dozen". In addition to their use in counting and measuring, numerals are often used for labels , for ordering , and for codes . In common usage, _____ may refer to a symbol, a word or phrase, or the mathematical object.

Exam Probability: **Medium**

11. *Answer choices:*
(see index for correct answer)

- a. Business service management
- b. Retail design
- c. Number
- d. Shareholder rebellion

:: Business ::

_____ is a trade policy that does not restrict imports or exports; it can also be understood as the free market idea applied to international trade. In government, _____ is predominantly advocated by political parties that hold liberal economic positions while economically left-wing and nationalist political parties generally support protectionism, the opposite of _____ .

Exam Probability: **Low**

12. *Answer choices:*
(see index for correct answer)

- a. Co-creation
- b. Corporate services
- c. Price-based selling
- d. Free trade

:: Business law ::

_____ is where a person's financial liability is limited to a fixed sum, most commonly the value of a person's investment in a company or partnership. If a company with _____ is sued, then the claimants are suing the company, not its owners or investors. A shareholder in a limited company is not personally liable for any of the debts of the company, other than for the amount already invested in the company and for any unpaid amount on the shares in the company, if any. The same is true for the members of a _____ partnership and the limited partners in a limited partnership. By contrast, sole proprietors and partners in general partnerships are each liable for all the debts of the business .

Exam Probability: **Medium**

13. *Answer choices:*
(see index for correct answer)

- a. Limited liability
- b. Forward-looking statement
- c. Duty of fair representation
- d. Forged endorsement

:: Business ::

The seller, or the provider of the goods or services, completes a sale in response to an acquisition, appropriation, requisition or a direct interaction with the buyer at the point of sale. There is a passing of title of the item, and the settlement of a price, in which agreement is reached on a price for which transfer of ownership of the item will occur. The seller, not the purchaser typically executes the sale and it may be completed prior to the obligation of payment. In the case of indirect interaction, a person who sells goods or service on behalf of the owner is known as a _____ man or _____ woman or _____ person, but this often refers to someone selling goods in a store/shop, in which case other terms are also common, including _____ clerk, shop assistant, and retail clerk.

Exam Probability: **High**

14. *Answer choices:*
(see index for correct answer)

- a. Sales
- b. Serviced office broker
- c. Policy capturing
- d. Mavis Amankwah

:: Management ::

_____ is the identification, evaluation, and prioritization of risks followed by coordinated and economical application of resources to minimize, monitor, and control the probability or impact of unfortunate events or to maximize the realization of opportunities.

Exam Probability: **Medium**

15. *Answer choices:*
(see index for correct answer)

- a. Risk management
- b. Economic production quantity

- c. Sensemaking
- d. Force-field analysis

Guidance: level 1

:: Unemployment ::

In economics, a _____ is a business cycle contraction when there is a general decline in economic activity. Macroeconomic indicators such as GDP , investment spending, capacity utilization, household income, business profits, and inflation fall, while bankruptcies and the unemployment rate rise. In the United Kingdom, it is defined as a negative economic growth for two consecutive quarters.

Exam Probability: **High**

16. *Answer choices:*
(see index for correct answer)

- a. Youth unemployment
- b. Technological unemployment
- c. Recession
- d. Misery index

Guidance: level 1

:: Management ::

_____ is a process by which entities review the quality of all factors involved in production. ISO 9000 defines _____ as "A part of quality management focused on fulfilling quality requirements".

Exam Probability: **High**

17. *Answer choices:*
(see index for correct answer)

- a. Event to knowledge
- b. Quality control
- c. Business economics
- d. Opera management

Guidance: level 1

:: ::

An _____ is the production of goods or related services within an economy. The major source of revenue of a group or company is the indicator of its relevant _____ . When a large group has multiple sources of revenue generation, it is considered to be working in different industries. Manufacturing _____ became a key sector of production and labour in European and North American countries during the Industrial Revolution, upsetting previous mercantile and feudal economies. This came through many successive rapid advances in technology, such as the production of steel and coal.

Exam Probability: **Low**

18. *Answer choices:*
(see index for correct answer)

- a. co-culture
- b. empathy
- c. process perspective
- d. Industry

Guidance: level 1

:: Credit cards ::

A _____ is a payment card issued to users to enable the cardholder to pay a merchant for goods and services based on the cardholder's promise to the card issuer to pay them for the amounts plus the other agreed charges. The card issuer creates a revolving account and grants a line of credit to the cardholder, from which the cardholder can borrow money for payment to a merchant or as a cash advance.

Exam Probability: **High**

19. *Answer choices:*
(see index for correct answer)

- a. OnePulse
- b. Negative database
- c. Credit card
- d. Barclaycard

Guidance: level 1

:: Graphic design ::

An _____ is an artifact that depicts visual perception, such as a photograph or other two-dimensional picture, that resembles a subject—usually a physical object—and thus provides a depiction of it. In the context of signal processing, an _____ is a distributed amplitude of color.

Exam Probability: **Medium**

20. *Answer choices:*
(see index for correct answer)

- a. Graphic Exchange
- b. Line art
- c. Image
- d. Graphics

Guidance: level 1

:: Costs ::

In microeconomic theory, the _____ , or alternative cost, of making a particular choice is the value of the most valuable choice out of those that were not taken. In other words, opportunity that will require sacrifices.

Exam Probability: **Medium**

21. *Answer choices:*
(see index for correct answer)

- a. Social cost
- b. Cost of products sold
- c. Opportunity cost
- d. Opportunity cost of capital

Guidance: level 1

:: Corporate crime ::

_____ LLP, based in Chicago, was an American holding company. Formerly one of the "Big Five" accounting firms , the firm had provided auditing, tax, and consulting services to large corporations. By 2001, it had become one of the world's largest multinational companies.

Exam Probability: **Low**

22. *Answer choices:*
(see index for correct answer)

- a. New England Compounding Center
- b. Medco Health Solutions
- c. Langbar International
- d. Arthur Andersen

Guidance: level 1

:: Accounting software ::

_____ is any item or verifiable record that is generally accepted as payment for goods and services and repayment of debts, such as taxes, in a particular country or socio-economic context. The main functions of _____ are distinguished as: a medium of exchange, a unit of account, a store of value and sometimes, a standard of deferred payment. Any item or verifiable record that fulfils these functions can be considered as _____ .

Exam Probability: **High**

23. *Answer choices:*
(see index for correct answer)

- a. BIG4books
- b. Accounting software
- c. Invoiceit
- d. Quicken

Guidance: level 1

:: Production and manufacturing ::

_____ is a set of techniques and tools for process improvement. Though as a shortened form it may be found written as 6S, it should not be confused with the methodology known as 6S .

Exam Probability: **Low**

24. *Answer choices:*
(see index for correct answer)

- a. Production equipment control
- b. Alarm fatigue
- c. Transfer cars
- d. Back-story

Guidance: level 1

:: Stock market ::

The _____ of a corporation is all of the shares into which ownership of the corporation is divided. In American English, the shares are commonly known as " _____ s". A single share of the _____ represents fractional ownership of the corporation in proportion to the total number of shares. This typically entitles the _____ holder to that fraction of the company's earnings, proceeds from liquidation of assets , or voting power, often dividing these up in proportion to the amount of money each _____ holder has invested. Not all _____ is necessarily equal, as certain classes of _____ may be issued for example without voting rights, with enhanced voting rights, or with a certain priority to receive profits or liquidation proceeds before or after other classes of shareholders.

Exam Probability: **High**

25. *Answer choices:*
(see index for correct answer)

- a. Stock
- b. Widow-and-orphan stock
- c. Intermarket analysis
- d. Seeking Alpha

Guidance: level 1

:: Service industries ::

_____ are the economic services provided by the finance industry, which encompasses a broad range of businesses that manage money, including credit unions, banks, credit-card companies, insurance companies, accountancy companies, consumer-finance companies, stock brokerages, investment funds, individual managers and some government-sponsored enterprises. _____ companies are present in all economically developed geographic locations and tend to cluster in local, national, regional and international financial centers such as London, New York City, and Tokyo.

Exam Probability: **Medium**

26. *Answer choices:*
(see index for correct answer)

- a. Inn sign
- b. Association of Special Fares Agents
- c. Maid service
- d. Tourism

Guidance: level 1

:: Business models ::

A _____ is "an autonomous association of persons united voluntarily to meet their common economic, social, and cultural needs and aspirations through a jointly-owned and democratically-controlled enterprise". _____ s may include.

Exam Probability: **Low**

27. *Answer choices:*
(see index for correct answer)

- a. Lemonade stand
- b. Cooperative
- c. Co-operative economics
- d. Praenumeration

Guidance: level 1

:: Materials ::

A _____ , also known as a feedstock, unprocessed material, or primary commodity, is a basic material that is used to produce goods, finished products, energy, or intermediate materials which are feedstock for future finished products. As feedstock, the term connotes these materials are bottleneck assets and are highly important with regard to producing other products. An example of this is crude oil, which is a _____ and a feedstock used in the production of industrial chemicals, fuels, plastics, and pharmaceutical goods; lumber is a _____ used to produce a variety of products including all types of furniture. The term " _____ " denotes materials in minimally processed or unprocessed in states; e.g., raw latex, crude oil, cotton, coal, raw biomass, iron ore, air, logs, or water i.e. "...any product of agriculture, forestry, fishing and any other mineral that is in its natural form or which has undergone the transformation required to prepare it for internationally marketing in substantial volumes."

Exam Probability: **Low**

28. *Answer choices:*
(see index for correct answer)

- a. Agamassan
- b. Materials for use in vacuum
- c. Raw material
- d. Pitch

Guidance: level 1

:: Statistical terminology ::

_____ es can be learned implicitly within cultural contexts. People may develop _____ es toward or against an individual, an ethnic group, a sexual or gender identity, a nation, a religion, a social class, a political party, theoretical paradigms and ideologies within academic domains, or a species. _____ ed means one-sided, lacking a neutral viewpoint, or not having an open mind. _____ can come in many forms and is related to prejudice and intuition.

Exam Probability: **Low**

29. *Answer choices:*
(see index for correct answer)

- a. Permutation test
- b. Bias
- c. Data generating process
- d. Law of large numbers

Guidance: level 1

:: Organizational behavior ::

_____ is the state or fact of exclusive rights and control over property, which may be an object, land/real estate or intellectual property. _____ involves multiple rights, collectively referred to as title, which may be separated and held by different parties.

Exam Probability: **High**

30. *Answer choices:*
(see index for correct answer)

- a. Group behaviour
- b. Ownership
- c. Organizational justice
- d. Administrative Behavior

Guidance: level 1

:: Real estate ::

_____ s serve several societal needs – primarily as shelter from weather, security, living space, privacy, to store belongings, and to comfortably live and work. A _____ as a shelter represents a physical division of the human habitat and the outside .

Exam Probability: **Low**

31. *Answer choices:*
(see index for correct answer)

- a. Building
- b. CMC Group
- c. Estate agent
- d. Monotenure

Guidance: level 1

A _____ is any person who contracts to acquire an asset in return for some form of consideration.

Exam Probability: **Low**

32. *Answer choices:*

(see index for correct answer)

- a. surface-level diversity
- b. functional perspective
- c. open system
- d. Buyer

Guidance: level 1

:: Marketing analytics ::

_____ is a long-term, forward-looking approach to planning with the fundamental goal of achieving a sustainable competitive advantage. Strategic planning involves an analysis of the company's strategic initial situation prior to the formulation, evaluation and selection of market-oriented competitive position that contributes to the company's goals and marketing objectives.

Exam Probability: **Low**

33. *Answer choices:*

(see index for correct answer)

- a. Marketing performance measurement and management
- b. Marketing strategy
- c. Marketing mix modeling
- d. Marketing resource management

Guidance: level 1

:: Insolvency ::

_____ is a legal process through which people or other entities who cannot repay debts to creditors may seek relief from some or all of their debts. In most jurisdictions, _____ is imposed by a court order, often initiated by the debtor.

Exam Probability: **High**

34. *Answer choices:*
(see index for correct answer)

- a. Insolvency
- b. Bankruptcy
- c. Liquidator
- d. United Kingdom insolvency law

Guidance: level 1

:: ::

_____ is a marketing communication that employs an openly sponsored, non-personal message to promote or sell a product, service or idea. Sponsors of _____ are typically businesses wishing to promote their products or services. _____ is differentiated from public relations in that an advertiser pays for and has control over the message. It differs from personal selling in that the message is non-personal, i.e., not directed to a particular individual. _____ is communicated through various mass media, including traditional media such as newspapers, magazines, television, radio, outdoor _____ or direct mail; and new media such as search results, blogs, social media, websites or text messages. The actual presentation of the message in a medium is referred to as an advertisement, or "ad" or advert for short.

Exam Probability: **High**

35. *Answer choices:*
(see index for correct answer)

- a. Advertising
- b. corporate values
- c. surface-level diversity
- d. functional perspective

Guidance: level 1

The _____ is a foundation model for businesses. The _____ has been defined as the "set of marketing tools that the firm uses to pursue its marketing objectives in the target market". Thus the _____ refers to four broad levels of marketing decision, namely: product, price, place, and promotion. Marketing practice has been occurring for millennia, but marketing theory emerged in the early twentieth century. The contemporary _____ , or the 4 Ps, which has become the dominant framework for marketing management decisions, was first published in 1960. In services marketing, an extended _____ is used, typically comprising 7 Ps, made up of the original 4 Ps extended by process, people, and physical evidence. Occasionally service marketers will refer to 8 Ps, comprising these 7 Ps plus performance.

Exam Probability: **High**

36. *Answer choices:*
(see index for correct answer)

- a. Albuquerque Craft Beer Market
- b. Pink money
- c. Marketing mix
- d. Processing fluency theory of aesthetic pleasure

Guidance: level 1

:: Decision theory ::

Within economics the concept of _____ is used to model worth or value, but its usage has evolved significantly over time. The term was introduced initially as a measure of pleasure or satisfaction within the theory of utilitarianism by moral philosophers such as Jeremy Bentham and John Stuart Mill. But the term has been adapted and reapplied within neoclassical economics, which dominates modern economic theory, as a _____ function that represents a consumer's preference ordering over a choice set. As such, it is devoid of its original interpretation as a measurement of the pleasure or satisfaction obtained by the consumer from that choice.

Exam Probability: **High**

37. *Answer choices:*
(see index for correct answer)

- a. Movement pattern analysis
- b. Price of stability
- c. Utility
- d. Ambiguity aversion

Guidance: level 1

:: Financial regulatory authorities of the United States ::

The _____ is the revenue service of the United States federal government. The government agency is a bureau of the Department of the Treasury, and is under the immediate direction of the Commissioner of Internal Revenue, who is appointed to a five-year term by the President of the United States. The IRS is responsible for collecting taxes and administering the Internal Revenue Code, the main body of federal statutory tax law of the United States. The duties of the IRS include providing tax assistance to taxpayers and pursuing and resolving instances of erroneous or fraudulent tax filings. The IRS has also overseen various benefits programs, and enforces portions of the Affordable Care Act.

Exam Probability: **Low**

38. *Answer choices:*
(see index for correct answer)

- a. Federal Reserve Board
- b. Federal Deposit Insurance Corporation
- c. U.S. Securities and Exchange Commission
- d. Internal Revenue Service

Guidance: level 1

:: Security compliance ::

A _____ is a communicated intent to inflict harm or loss on another person. A _____ is considered an act of coercion. _____ s are widely observed in animal behavior, particularly in a ritualized form, chiefly in order to avoid the unnecessary physical violence that can lead to physical damage or the death of both conflicting parties.

Exam Probability: **Low**

39. *Answer choices:*
(see index for correct answer)

- a. North American Electric Reliability Corporation
- b. Month of bugs
- c. Threat
- d. Federal Information Security Management Act of 2002

Guidance: level 1

:: ::

In regulatory jurisdictions that provide for it , _____ is a group of laws and organizations designed to ensure the rights of consumers as well as fair trade, competition and accurate information in the marketplace. The laws are designed to prevent the businesses that engage in fraud or specified unfair practices from gaining an advantage over competitors. They may also provides additional protection for those most vulnerable in society. _____ laws are a form of government regulation that aim to protect the rights of consumers. For example, a government may require businesses to disclose detailed information about products—particularly in areas where safety or public health is an issue, such as food.

Exam Probability: **High**

40. *Answer choices:*

(see index for correct answer)

- a. similarity-attraction theory
- b. hierarchical perspective
- c. Consumer Protection
- d. interpersonal communication

Guidance: level 1

:: Banking ::

A _____ is a financial institution that accepts deposits from the public and creates credit. Lending activities can be performed either directly or indirectly through capital markets. Due to their importance in the financial stability of a country, _____ s are highly regulated in most countries. Most nations have institutionalized a system known as fractional reserve _____ ing under which _____ s hold liquid assets equal to only a portion of their current liabilities. In addition to other regulations intended to ensure liquidity, _____ s are generally subject to minimum capital requirements based on an international set of capital standards, known as the Basel Accords.

Exam Probability: **High**

41. *Answer choices:*
(see index for correct answer)

- a. Bank
- b. Personal account
- c. Tier 1 capital
- d. Standing order

Guidance: level 1

:: Loans ::

In finance, a _____ is the lending of money by one or more individuals, organizations, or other entities to other individuals, organizations etc. The recipient incurs a debt, and is usually liable to pay interest on that debt until it is repaid, and also to repay the principal amount borrowed.

Exam Probability: **High**

42. *Answer choices:*
(see index for correct answer)

- a. Federal Perkins Loan
- b. Loan
- c. Section 502 loans
- d. Hard money loan

Guidance: level 1

:: Telecommunication theory ::

In reliability theory and reliability engineering, the term _____ has the following meanings.

Exam Probability: **Low**

43. *Answer choices:*
(see index for correct answer)

- a. Nyquist rate
- b. Communication physics
- c. Availability
- d. Bias distortion

Guidance: level 1

:: Semiconductor companies ::

_____ Corporation is a Japanese multinational conglomerate corporation headquartered in Konan, Minato, Tokyo. Its diversified business includes consumer and professional electronics, gaming, entertainment and financial services. The company owns the largest music entertainment business in the world, the largest video game console business and one of the largest video game publishing businesses, and is one of the leading manufacturers of electronic products for the consumer and professional markets, and a leading player in the film and television entertainment industry. _____ was ranked 97th on the 2018 Fortune Global 500 list.

Exam Probability: **Medium**

44. *Answer choices:*
(see index for correct answer)

- a. Diodes Incorporated
- b. Sony
- c. ON Semiconductor
- d. GreenPeak Technologies

Guidance: level 1

:: ::

_____ is a means of protection from financial loss. It is a form of risk management, primarily used to hedge against the risk of a contingent or uncertain loss

Exam Probability: **Low**

45. *Answer choices:*
(see index for correct answer)

- a. Insurance
- b. corporate values
- c. personal values
- d. imperative

Guidance: level 1

:: Land value taxation ::

_____, sometimes referred to as dry _____, is the solid surface of Earth that is not permanently covered by water. The vast majority of human activity throughout history has occurred in _____ areas that support agriculture, habitat, and various natural resources. Some life forms have developed from predecessor species that lived in bodies of water.

Exam Probability: **Low**

46. *Answer choices:*
(see index for correct answer)

- a. Land
- b. Lands Valuation Appeal Court
- c. Land value tax
- d. Georgism

Guidance: level 1

:: Summary statistics ::

_____ is the number of occurrences of a repeating event per unit of time. It is also referred to as temporal _____ , which emphasizes the contrast to spatial _____ and angular _____ . The period is the duration of time of one cycle in a repeating event, so the period is the reciprocal of the _____ . For example: if a newborn baby's heart beats at a _____ of 120 times a minute, its period—the time interval between beats—is half a second . _____ is an important parameter used in science and engineering to specify the rate of oscillatory and vibratory phenomena, such as mechanical vibrations, audio signals , radio waves, and light.

Exam Probability: **Medium**

47. *Answer choices:*
(see index for correct answer)

- a. Frequency distribution
- b. Five-number summary
- c. Quantile
- d. Frequency

Guidance: level 1

:: ::

_____ is the means to see, hear, or become aware of something or someone through our fundamental senses. The term _____ derives from the Latin word perceptio, and is the organization, identification, and interpretation of sensory information in order to represent and understand the presented information, or the environment.

Exam Probability: **Medium**

48. *Answer choices:*
(see index for correct answer)

- a. functional perspective
- b. Perception
- c. deep-level diversity
- d. hierarchical perspective

Guidance: level 1

:: Debt ::

_____ is the trust which allows one party to provide money or resources to another party wherein the second party does not reimburse the first party immediately , but promises either to repay or return those resources at a later date. In other words, _____ is a method of making reciprocity formal, legally enforceable, and extensible to a large group of unrelated people.

Exam Probability: **High**

49. *Answer choices:*
(see index for correct answer)

- a. Credit
- b. Debt-lag
- c. Consumer debt
- d. Debit commission

Guidance: level 1

:: Management accounting ::

_____ s are costs that change as the quantity of the good or service that a business produces changes. _____ s are the sum of marginal costs over all units produced. They can also be considered normal costs. Fixed costs and _____ s make up the two components of total cost. Direct costs are costs that can easily be associated with a particular cost object. However, not all _____ s are direct costs. For example, variable manufacturing overhead costs are _____ s that are indirect costs, not direct costs. _____ s are sometimes called unit-level costs as they vary with the number of units produced.

Exam Probability: **High**

50. *Answer choices:*
(see index for correct answer)

- a. Revenue center
- b. Chartered Institute of Management Accountants
- c. Certified Management Accountants of Canada
- d. Spend management

Guidance: level 1

The _____ , now also known as the First _____ , was the transition to new manufacturing processes in Europe and the US, in the period from about 1760 to sometime between 1820 and 1840. This transition included going from hand production methods to machines, new chemical manufacturing and iron production processes, the increasing use of steam power and water power, the development of machine tools and the rise of the mechanized factory system. The _____ also led to an unprecedented rise in the rate of population growth.

Exam Probability: **Medium**

51. *Answer choices:*
(see index for correct answer)

- a. Blast furnace
- b. Line shaft
- c. Industrial Revolution
- d. Bleachfield

Guidance: level 1

A _____ is a wide-ranging taxes, tariff and trade treaty that often includes investment guarantees. It exists when two or more countries agree on terms that helps them trade with each other. The most common _____ s are of the preferential and free trade types are concluded in order to reduce tariffs, quotas and other trade restrictions on items traded between the signatories.

Exam Probability: **Medium**

52. *Answer choices:*
(see index for correct answer)

- a. Trade, Development and Cooperation Agreement
- b. South Asia Free Trade Agreement
- c. Trade agreement
- d. Trans-Pacific Partnership

Guidance: level 1

An _____ is a person who has a position of authority in a hierarchical organization. The term derives from the late Latin from officiarius, meaning "official".

Exam Probability: **Low**

53. *Answer choices:*
(see index for correct answer)

- a. Aeronautical operations technician
- b. Accountant
- c. Officer
- d. Architectural historian

Guidance: level 1

:: ::

_____ is the collection of techniques, skills, methods, and processes used in the production of goods or services or in the accomplishment of objectives, such as scientific investigation. _____ can be the knowledge of techniques, processes, and the like, or it can be embedded in machines to allow for operation without detailed knowledge of their workings. Systems applying _____ by taking an input, changing it according to the system's use, and then producing an outcome are referred to as _____ systems or technological systems.

Exam Probability: **Medium**

54. *Answer choices:*
(see index for correct answer)

- a. cultural
- b. process perspective
- c. information systems assessment
- d. Technology

Guidance: level 1

:: Financial crises ::

A _____ is any of a broad variety of situations in which some financial assets suddenly lose a large part of their nominal value. In the 19th and early 20th centuries, many financial crises were associated with banking panics, and many recessions coincided with these panics. Other situations that are often called financial crises include stock market crashes and the bursting of other financial bubbles, currency crises, and sovereign defaults. Financial crises directly result in a loss of paper wealth but do not necessarily result in significant changes in the real economy .

Exam Probability: **High**

55. *Answer choices:*

(see index for correct answer)

- a. Panic of 1857
- b. Panic of 1866
- c. Currency crisis
- d. Panic of 1847

Guidance: level 1

:: Logistics ::

_____ is generally the detailed organization and implementation of a complex operation. In a general business sense, _____ is the management of the flow of things between the point of origin and the point of consumption in order to meet requirements of customers or corporations. The resources managed in _____ may include tangible goods such as materials, equipment, and supplies, as well as food and other consumable items. The _____ of physical items usually involves the integration of information flow, materials handling, production, packaging, inventory, transportation, warehousing, and often security.

Exam Probability: **Medium**

56. *Answer choices:*

(see index for correct answer)

- a. Medical logistics
- b. Logistics
- c. Distribution resource planning
- d. Global Data Synchronization Network

Guidance: level 1

:: Contract law ::

A _____ is a legally-binding agreement which recognises and governs the rights and duties of the parties to the agreement. A _____ is legally enforceable because it meets the requirements and approval of the law. An agreement typically involves the exchange of goods, services, money, or promises of any of those. In the event of breach of _____ , the law awards the injured party access to legal remedies such as damages and cancellation.

Exam Probability: **Medium**

57. *Answer choices:*
(see index for correct answer)

- a. Beneficial interest
- b. Contract
- c. Franchisor
- d. Option contract

Guidance: level 1

:: Stock market ::

_____ is a form of stock which may have any combination of features not possessed by common stock including properties of both an equity and a debt instrument, and is generally considered a hybrid instrument. _____ s are senior to common stock, but subordinate to bonds in terms of claim and may have priority over common stock in the payment of dividends and upon liquidation. Terms of the _____ are described in the issuing company`s articles of association or articles of incorporation.

Exam Probability: **High**

58. *Answer choices:*
(see index for correct answer)

- a. Mark Twain effect
- b. Common stock
- c. Stock market
- d. Buy side

Guidance: level 1

A _____ is when two or more people come together to discuss one or more topics, often in a formal or business setting, but _____ s also occur in a variety of other environments. Many various types of _____ s exist.

Exam Probability: **Low**

59. *Answer choices:*

(see index for correct answer)

- a. Business process mapping
- b. Meeting
- c. Formula for change
- d. Behavioral risk management

Guidance: level 1

Management

Management is the administration of an organization, whether it is a
business, a not-for-profit organization, or government body. Management
includes the activities of setting the strategy of an organization and
coordinating the efforts of its employees (or of volunteers) to accomplish its
objectives through the application of available resources, such as financial,
natural, technological, and human resources.

:: Organizational structure ::

An _____ defines how activities such as task allocation, coordination,
and supervision are directed toward the achievement of organizational aims.

Exam Probability: **Medium**

1. *Answer choices:*
(see index for correct answer)

- a. Blessed Unrest
- b. Organizational structure
- c. Organization of the New York City Police Department
- d. Automated Bureaucracy

Guidance: level 1

:: ::

In sales, commerce and economics, a _____ is the recipient of a good,
service, product or an idea - obtained from a seller, vendor, or supplier via a
financial transaction or exchange for money or some other valuable
consideration.

Exam Probability: **High**

2. *Answer choices:*
(see index for correct answer)

- a. personal values
- b. Customer
- c. functional perspective
- d. Sarbanes-Oxley act of 2002

Guidance: level 1

:: Market research ::

_____ is an organized effort to gather information about target markets or customers. It is a very important component of business strategy. The term is commonly interchanged with marketing research; however, expert practitioners may wish to draw a distinction, in that marketing research is concerned specifically about marketing processes, while _____ is concerned specifically with markets.

Exam Probability: **Medium**

3. *Answer choices:*
(see index for correct answer)

- a. Situation analysis
- b. Market research
- c. BrandZ
- d. Ad Tracking

Guidance: level 1

:: Information technology management ::

_____ is a collective term for all approaches to prepare , support and help individuals, teams, and organizations in making organizational change. The most common change drivers include: technological evolution, process reviews, crisis, and consumer habit changes; pressure from new business entrants, acquisitions, mergers, and organizational restructuring. It includes methods that redirect or redefine the use of resources, business process, budget allocations, or other modes of operation that significantly change a company or organization. Organizational _____ considers the full organization and what needs to change, while _____ may be used solely to refer to how people and teams are affected by such organizational transition. It deals with many different disciplines, from behavioral and social sciences to information technology and business solutions.

Exam Probability: **High**

4. *Answer choices:*
(see index for correct answer)

- a. Change management
- b. Central Computer and Telecommunications Agency
- c. Storage virtualization
- d. IT baseline protection

Guidance: level 1

:: Cash flow ::

_____ s are narrowly interconnected with the concepts of value, interest rate and liquidity.A _____ that shall happen on a future day tN can be transformed into a _____ of the same value in t0.

Exam Probability: **Medium**

5. *Answer choices:*
(see index for correct answer)

- a. Discounted cash flow
- b. Cash flow forecasting
- c. Free cash flow
- d. Propequity

Guidance: level 1

:: ::

A _____ is a research instrument consisting of a series of questions for the purpose of gathering information from respondents. The _____ was invented by the Statistical Society of London in 1838.

Exam Probability: **Medium**

6. *Answer choices:*
(see index for correct answer)

- a. open system
- b. Questionnaire
- c. cultural
- d. imperative

Guidance: level 1

:: ::

An _____ is a person temporarily or permanently residing in a country other than their native country. In common usage, the term often refers to professionals, skilled workers, or artists taking positions outside their home country, either independently or sent abroad by their employers, who can be companies, universities, governments, or non-governmental organisations. Effectively migrant workers, they usually earn more than they would at home, and less than local employees. However, the term ` _____ ` is also used for retirees and others who have chosen to live outside their native country. Historically, it has also referred to exiles.

Exam Probability: **High**

7. *Answer choices:*
(see index for correct answer)

- a. information systems assessment
- b. similarity-attraction theory
- c. personal values
- d. Expatriate

Guidance: level 1

:: Internet privacy ::

An _____ is a private network accessible only to an organization's staff. Often, a wide range of information and services are available on an organization's internal _____ that are unavailable to the public, unlike the Internet. A company-wide _____ can constitute an important focal point of internal communication and collaboration, and provide a single starting point to access internal and external resources. In its simplest form, an _____ is established with the technologies for local area networks and wide area networks . Many modern _____ s have search engines, user profiles, blogs, mobile apps with notifications, and events planning within their infrastructure.

Exam Probability: **Medium**

8. *Answer choices:*
(see index for correct answer)

- a. Phoning home
- b. Bitmessage
- c. Intranet
- d. ICMP tunnel

Guidance: level 1

:: ::

_____ is the moral stance, political philosophy, ideology, or social outlook that emphasizes the moral worth of the individual. Individualists promote the exercise of one's goals and desires and so value independence and self-reliance and advocate that interests of the individual should achieve precedence over the state or a social group, while opposing external interference upon one's own interests by society or institutions such as the government. _____ is often defined in contrast to totalitarianism, collectivism, and more corporate social forms.

Exam Probability: **Low**

9. *Answer choices:*
(see index for correct answer)

- a. surface-level diversity
- b. imperative
- c. Individualism
- d. Sarbanes-Oxley act of 2002

:: ::

A _____ is a problem offering two possibilities, neither of which is unambiguously acceptable or preferable. The possibilities are termed the horns of the _____ , a clichéd usage, but distinguishing the _____ from other kinds of predicament as a matter of usage.

Exam Probability: **High**

10. *Answer choices:*
(see index for correct answer)

- a. Dilemma
- b. functional perspective
- c. similarity-attraction theory
- d. information systems assessment

:: Teams ::

A _____ usually refers to a group of individuals who work together from different geographic locations and rely on communication technology such as email, FAX, and video or voice conferencing services in order to collaborate. The term can also refer to groups or teams that work together asynchronously or across organizational levels. Powell, Piccoli and Ives define _____ s as "groups of geographically, organizationally and/or time dispersed workers brought together by information and telecommunication technologies to accomplish one or more organizational tasks." According to Ale Ebrahim et. al. , _____ s can also be defined as "small temporary groups of geographically, organizationally and/or time dispersed knowledge workers who coordinate their work predominantly with electronic information and communication technologies in order to accomplish one or more organization tasks."

Exam Probability: **Medium**

11. *Answer choices:*
(see index for correct answer)

- a. Team-building

- b. Virtual team

Guidance: level 1

:: Decision theory ::

A _____ is a deliberate system of principles to guide decisions and achieve rational outcomes. A _____ is a statement of intent, and is implemented as a procedure or protocol. Policies are generally adopted by a governance body within an organization. Policies can assist in both subjective and objective decision making. Policies to assist in subjective decision making usually assist senior management with decisions that must be based on the relative merits of a number of factors, and as a result are often hard to test objectively, e.g. work-life balance _____ . In contrast policies to assist in objective decision making are usually operational in nature and can be objectively tested, e.g. password _____ .

Exam Probability: **Medium**

12. *Answer choices:*
(see index for correct answer)

- a. Subjective expected utility
- b. Policy
- c. Optimal stopping
- d. Bulk Dispatch Lapse

Guidance: level 1

:: Management ::

_____ is a process by which entities review the quality of all factors involved in production. ISO 9000 defines _____ as "A part of quality management focused on fulfilling quality requirements".

Exam Probability: **Medium**

13. *Answer choices:*
(see index for correct answer)

- a. Certified Energy Manager
- b. Dominant design
- c. Plan
- d. Nonconformity

:: Statistical terminology ::

_____ is the ability to avoid wasting materials, energy, efforts, money, and time in doing something or in producing a desired result. In a more general sense, it is the ability to do things well, successfully, and without waste. In more mathematical or scientific terms, it is a measure of the extent to which input is well used for an intended task or function . It often specifically comprises the capability of a specific application of effort to produce a specific outcome with a minimum amount or quantity of waste, expense, or unnecessary effort. _____ refers to very different inputs and outputs in different fields and industries.

Exam Probability: **High**

14. *Answer choices:*
(see index for correct answer)

- a. Neutral vector
- b. Cause of death
- c. Nuisance parameter
- d. Efficiency

:: Business models ::

_____ es are privately owned corporations, partnerships, or sole proprietorships that have fewer employees and/or less annual revenue than a regular-sized business or corporation. Businesses are defined as "small" in terms of being able to apply for government support and qualify for preferential tax policy varies depending on the country and industry. _____ es range from fifteen employees under the Australian Fair Work Act 2009, fifty employees according to the definition used by the European Union, and fewer than five hundred employees to qualify for many U.S. _____ Administration programs. While _____ es can also be classified according to other methods, such as annual revenues, shipments, sales, assets, or by annual gross or net revenue or net profits, the number of employees is one of the most widely used measures.

15. *Answer choices:*
(see index for correct answer)

- a. Small business
- b. 70/20/10 Model
- c. Business Model Canvas
- d. Free-to-play

Guidance: level 1

:: Marketing ::

_____ comes from the Latin neg and otsia referring to businessmen who, unlike the patricians, had no leisure time in their industriousness; it held the meaning of business until the 17th century when it took on the diplomatic connotation as a dialogue between two or more people or parties intended to reach a beneficial outcome over one or more issues where a conflict exists with respect to at least one of these issues. Thus, _____ is a process of combining divergent positions into a joint agreement under a decision rule of unanimity.

16. *Answer choices:*
(see index for correct answer)

- a. Price point
- b. Category management
- c. Negotiation
- d. City marketing

Guidance: level 1

:: ::

According to Torrington, a _____ is usually developed by conducting a job analysis, which includes examining the tasks and sequences of tasks necessary to perform the job. The analysis considers the areas of knowledge and skills needed for the job. A job usually includes several roles. According to Hall, the _____ might be broadened to form a person specification or may be known as "terms of reference". The person/job specification can be presented as a stand-alone document, but in practice it is usually included within the _____ . A _____ is often used by employers in the recruitment process.

Exam Probability: **Low**

17. *Answer choices:*
(see index for correct answer)

- a. process perspective
- b. hierarchical
- c. Character
- d. Job description

Guidance: level 1

:: Management accounting ::

_____ s are costs that change as the quantity of the good or service that a business produces changes. _____ s are the sum of marginal costs over all units produced. They can also be considered normal costs. Fixed costs and _____ s make up the two components of total cost. Direct costs are costs that can easily be associated with a particular cost object. However, not all _____ s are direct costs. For example, variable manufacturing overhead costs are _____ s that are indirect costs, not direct costs. _____ s are sometimes called unit-level costs as they vary with the number of units produced.

Exam Probability: **High**

18. *Answer choices:*
(see index for correct answer)

- a. Variable cost
- b. Direct material usage variance
- c. Total benefits of ownership
- d. Target income sales

:: Belief ::

_____ is the study of general and fundamental questions about existence, knowledge, values, reason, mind, and language. Such questions are often posed as problems to be studied or resolved. The term was probably coined by Pythagoras . Philosophical methods include questioning, critical discussion, rational argument, and systematic presentation. Classic philosophical questions include: Is it possible to know anything and to prove it What is most real Philosophers also pose more practical and concrete questions such as: Is there a best way to live Is it better to be just or unjust Do humans have free will

Exam Probability: **High**

19. *Answer choices:*
(see index for correct answer)

- a. Philosophy
- b. Real life
- c. Intuition
- d. False pleasure

:: Human resource management ::

_____ , also known as management by results , was first popularized by Peter Drucker in his 1954 book The Practice of Management. _____ is the process of defining specific objectives within an organization that management can convey to organization members, then deciding on how to achieve each objective in sequence. This process allows managers to take work that needs to be done one step at a time to allow for a calm, yet productive work environment. This process also helps organization members to see their accomplishments as they achieve each objective, which reinforces a positive work environment and a sense of achievement. An important part of MBO is the measurement and comparison of an employee's actual performance with the standards set. Ideally, when employees themselves have been involved with the goal-setting and choosing the course of action to be followed by them, they are more likely to fulfill their responsibilities. According to George S. Odiorne, the system of _____ can be described as a process whereby the superior and subordinate jointly identify common goals, define each individual's major areas of responsibility in terms of the results expected of him or her, and use these measures as guides for operating the unit and assessing the contribution of each of its members.

Exam Probability: **Low**

20. *Answer choices:*
(see index for correct answer)

- a. Managerial assessment of proficiency
- b. Management by objectives
- c. ROWE
- d. Induction programme

Guidance: level 1

:: ::

_____ is the process of two or more people or organizations working together to complete a task or achieve a goal. _____ is similar to cooperation. Most _____ requires leadership, although the form of leadership can be social within a decentralized and egalitarian group. Teams that work collaboratively often access greater resources, recognition and rewards when facing competition for finite resources.

Exam Probability: **Medium**

21. *Answer choices:*

(see index for correct answer)

- a. corporate values
- b. imperative
- c. surface-level diversity
- d. Sarbanes-Oxley act of 2002

Guidance: level 1

:: Meetings ::

A _____ is a body of one or more persons that is subordinate to a deliberative assembly. Usually, the assembly sends matters into a _____ as a way to explore them more fully than would be possible if the assembly itself were considering them. _____ s may have different functions and their type of work differ depending on the type of the organization and its needs.

Exam Probability: **Low**

22. *Answer choices:*

(see index for correct answer)

- a. Brown bag seminar
- b. Committee
- c. Program book
- d. Carlton Club meeting

Guidance: level 1

:: ::

_____ is the process of making predictions of the future based on past and present data and most commonly by analysis of trends. A commonplace example might be estimation of some variable of interest at some specified future date. Prediction is a similar, but more general term. Both might refer to formal statistical methods employing time series, cross-sectional or longitudinal data, or alternatively to less formal judgmental methods. Usage can differ between areas of application: for example, in hydrology the terms "forecast" and "_____" are sometimes reserved for estimates of values at certain specific future times, while the term "prediction" is used for more general estimates, such as the number of times floods will occur over a long period.

23. *Answer choices:*
(see index for correct answer)

- a. functional perspective
- b. similarity-attraction theory
- c. Forecasting
- d. empathy

Guidance: level 1

:: Project management ::

_____ is a process of setting goals, planning and/or controlling the organizing and leading the execution of any type of activity, such as.

Exam Probability: **High**

24. *Answer choices:*
(see index for correct answer)

- a. Vertical slice
- b. Management process
- c. Pmhub
- d. Hart Mason Index

Guidance: level 1

:: ::

_____ is the assignment of any responsibility or authority to another person to carry out specific activities. It is one of the core concepts of management leadership. However, the person who delegated the work remains accountable for the outcome of the delegated work. _____ empowers a subordinate to make decisions, i.e. it is a shifting of decision-making authority from one organizational level to a lower one. _____ , if properly done, is not fabrication. The opposite of effective _____ is micromanagement, where a manager provides too much input, direction, and review of delegated work. In general, _____ is good and can save money and time, help in building skills, and motivate people. On the other hand, poor _____ might cause frustration and confusion to all the involved parties. Some agents, however, do not favour a _____ and consider the power of making a decision rather burdensome.

25. *Answer choices:*

(see index for correct answer)

- a. Delegation
- b. functional perspective
- c. corporate values
- d. process perspective

Guidance: level 1

:: Classification systems ::

_____ is the practice of comparing business processes and performance metrics to industry bests and best practices from other companies. Dimensions typically measured are quality, time and cost.

Exam Probability: **Medium**

26. *Answer choices:*

(see index for correct answer)

- a. Benchmarking
- b. UNSPSC
- c. TUN
- d. World Health Organisation Composite International Diagnostic Interview

Guidance: level 1

:: Project management ::

A _____ is a source or supply from which a benefit is produced and it has some utility. _____ s can broadly be classified upon their availability—they are classified into renewable and non-renewable _____ s.Examples of non renewable _____ s are coal ,crude oil natural gas nuclear energy etc. Examples of renewable _____ s are air,water,wind,solar energy etc. They can also be classified as actual and potential on the basis of level of development and use, on the basis of origin they can be classified as biotic and abiotic, and on the basis of their distribution, as ubiquitous and localized . An item becomes a _____ with time and developing technology. Typically, _____ s are materials, energy, services, staff, knowledge, or other assets that are transformed to produce benefit and in the process may be consumed or made unavailable. Benefits of _____ utilization may include increased wealth, proper functioning of a system, or enhanced well-being. From a human perspective a natural _____ is anything obtained from the environment to satisfy human needs and wants. From a broader biological or ecological perspective a _____ satisfies the needs of a living organism .

Exam Probability: **Low**

27. *Answer choices:*

(see index for correct answer)

- a. Bill of quantities
- b. Resource
- c. Front-end loading
- d. Test and evaluation master plan

Guidance: level 1

:: Stochastic processes ::

_____ in its modern meaning is a "new idea, creative thoughts, new imaginations in form of device or method". _____ is often also viewed as the application of better solutions that meet new requirements, unarticulated needs, or existing market needs. Such _____ takes place through the provision of more-effective products, processes, services, technologies, or business models that are made available to markets, governments and society. An _____ is something original and more effective and, as a consequence, new, that "breaks into" the market or society. _____ is related to, but not the same as, invention, as _____ is more apt to involve the practical implementation of an invention to make a meaningful impact in the market or society, and not all _____ s require an invention. _____ often manifests itself via the engineering process, when the problem being solved is of a technical or scientific nature. The opposite of _____ is exnovation.

Exam Probability: **High**

28. *Answer choices:*
(see index for correct answer)

- a. Random measure
- b. Zero-order process
- c. Innovation
- d. Brownian excursion

Guidance: level 1

:: Planning ::

_____ is a high level plan to achieve one or more goals under conditions of uncertainty. In the sense of the "art of the general," which included several subsets of skills including tactics, siegecraft, logistics etc., the term came into use in the 6th century C.E. in East Roman terminology, and was translated into Western vernacular languages only in the 18th century. From then until the 20th century, the word "_____" came to denote "a comprehensive way to try to pursue political ends, including the threat or actual use of force, in a dialectic of wills" in a military conflict, in which both adversaries interact.

Exam Probability: **High**

29. *Answer choices:*
(see index for correct answer)

- a. Strategy
- b. Cross-cultural differences in decision-making
- c. Strategic communication
- d. School timetable

Guidance: level 1

:: Labour relations ::

_____ is a field of study that can have different meanings depending on the context in which it is used. In an international context, it is a subfield of labor history that studies the human relations with regard to work – in its broadest sense – and how this connects to questions of social inequality. It explicitly encompasses unregulated, historical, and non-Western forms of labor. Here, _____ define "for or with whom one works and under what rules. These rules determine the type of work, type and amount of remuneration, working hours, degrees of physical and psychological strain, as well as the degree of freedom and autonomy associated with the work."

Exam Probability: **Low**

30. *Answer choices:*
(see index for correct answer)

- a. Eurocadres
- b. Union Wallonne des Entreprises
- c. Labor relations
- d. Inflatable rat

Guidance: level 1

:: Analysis ::

_____ is the process of breaking a complex topic or substance into smaller parts in order to gain a better understanding of it. The technique has been applied in the study of mathematics and logic since before Aristotle , though _____ as a formal concept is a relatively recent development.

Exam Probability: **High**

31. *Answer choices:*
(see index for correct answer)

- a. Water pinch analysis

- b. DESTEP
- c. Analysis
- d. Deviation analysis

Guidance: level 1

:: Management ::

A _____ is a method or technique that has been generally accepted as superior to any alternatives because it produces results that are superior to those achieved by other means or because it has become a standard way of doing things, e.g., a standard way of complying with legal or ethical requirements.

Exam Probability: **High**

32. *Answer choices:*
(see index for correct answer)

- a. Best practice
- b. Main Street Manager
- c. Statistical process control
- d. Records manager

Guidance: level 1

:: Business process ::

A _____ or business method is a collection of related, structured activities or tasks by people or equipment which in a specific sequence produce a service or product for a particular customer or customers. _____ es occur at all organizational levels and may or may not be visible to the customers. A _____ may often be visualized as a flowchart of a sequence of activities with interleaving decision points or as a process matrix of a sequence of activities with relevance rules based on data in the process. The benefits of using _____ es include improved customer satisfaction and improved agility for reacting to rapid market change. Process-oriented organizations break down the barriers of structural departments and try to avoid functional silos.

Exam Probability: **Medium**

33. *Answer choices:*
(see index for correct answer)

- a. Business operations
- b. Business process outsourcing to India
- c. Business process management
- d. Business process reengineering

Guidance: level 1

:: ::

In logic and philosophy, an _____ is a series of statements , called the premises or premisses , intended to determine the degree of truth of another statement, the conclusion. The logical form of an _____ in a natural language can be represented in a symbolic formal language, and independently of natural language formally defined " _____ s" can be made in math and computer science.

Exam Probability: **Medium**

34. *Answer choices:*
(see index for correct answer)

- a. similarity-attraction theory
- b. cultural
- c. Argument
- d. hierarchical

Guidance: level 1

:: ::

In mathematics, a _____ is a relationship between two numbers indicating how many times the first number contains the second. For example, if a bowl of fruit contains eight oranges and six lemons, then the _____ of oranges to lemons is eight to six . Similarly, the _____ of lemons to oranges is 6:8 and the _____ of oranges to the total amount of fruit is 8:14 .

Exam Probability: **Medium**

35. *Answer choices:*
(see index for correct answer)

- a. functional perspective
- b. personal values
- c. Sarbanes-Oxley act of 2002

- d. similarity-attraction theory

Guidance: level 1

:: Organizational theory ::

_____ is the process of creating, retaining, and transferring knowledge within an organization. An organization improves over time as it gains experience. From this experience, it is able to create knowledge. This knowledge is broad, covering any topic that could better an organization. Examples may include ways to increase production efficiency or to develop beneficial investor relations. Knowledge is created at four different units: individual, group, organizational, and inter organizational.

Exam Probability: **Low**

36. *Answer choices:*
(see index for correct answer)

- a. Catfish effect
- b. Employee research
- c. resource dependence
- d. Interaction value analysis

Guidance: level 1

:: Organizational theory ::

A _____ is an organizational theory that claims that there is no best way to organize a corporation, to lead a company, or to make decisions. Instead, the optimal course of action is contingent upon the internal and external situation. A contingent leader effectively applies their own style of leadership to the right situation.

Exam Probability: **Low**

37. *Answer choices:*
(see index for correct answer)

- a. Participatory organization
- b. Network-centric organization
- c. Solid line reporting
- d. Contingency theory

Guidance: level 1

_____ is the magnitude or dimensions of a thing. _____ can be measured as length, width, height, diameter, perimeter, area, volume, or mass.

Exam Probability: **Medium**

38. *Answer choices:*
(see index for correct answer)

- a. Random variate
- b. Treatment group
- c. Kurtosis risk
- d. Size

Guidance: level 1

:: ::

_____ is the collection of mechanisms, processes and relations by which corporations are controlled and operated. Governance structures and principles identify the distribution of rights and responsibilities among different participants in the corporation and include the rules and procedures for making decisions in corporate affairs. _____ is necessary because of the possibility of conflicts of interests between stakeholders, primarily between shareholders and upper management or among shareholders.

Exam Probability: **Medium**

39. *Answer choices:*
(see index for correct answer)

- a. cultural
- b. Corporate governance
- c. co-culture
- d. personal values

Guidance: level 1

:: Marketing ::

_____ or stock control can be broadly defined as "the activity of checking a shop's stock." However, a more focused definition takes into account the more science-based, methodical practice of not only verifying a business' inventory but also focusing on the many related facets of inventory management "within an organisation to meet the demand placed upon that business economically." Other facets of _____ include supply chain management, production control, financial flexibility, and customer satisfaction. At the root of _____, however, is the _____ problem, which involves determining when to order, how much to order, and the logistics of those decisions.

Exam Probability: **Low**

40. *Answer choices:*
(see index for correct answer)

- a. Inventory control
- b. Fourth screen
- c. Customer to customer
- d. Golden sample

Guidance: level 1

:: Management ::

_____ is a set of activities that ensure goals are met in an effective and efficient manner. _____ can focus on the performance of an organization, a department, an employee, or the processes in place to manage particular tasks. _____ standards are generally organized and disseminated by senior leadership at an organization, and by task owners.

Exam Probability: **Medium**

41. *Answer choices:*
(see index for correct answer)

- a. Performance management
- b. Continuous monitoring
- c. Situational crisis communication theory
- d. Sensemaking

Guidance: level 1

:: ::

_____ is the capacity of consciously making sense of things, establishing and verifying facts, applying logic, and changing or justifying practices, institutions, and beliefs based on new or existing information. It is closely associated with such characteristically human activities as philosophy, science, language, mathematics and art, and is normally considered to be a distinguishing ability possessed by humans. _____ , or an aspect of it, is sometimes referred to as rationality.

Exam Probability: **Medium**

42. *Answer choices:*

(see index for correct answer)

- a. personal values
- b. Reason
- c. similarity-attraction theory
- d. Character

Guidance: level 1

:: Game theory ::

To _____ is to make a deal between different parties where each party gives up part of their demand. In arguments, _____ is a concept of finding agreement through communication, through a mutual acceptance of terms—often involving variations from an original goal or desires.

Exam Probability: **High**

43. *Answer choices:*

(see index for correct answer)

- a. Battle of the sexes
- b. Strategic move
- c. Coalition-proof Nash equilibrium
- d. Compromise

Guidance: level 1

:: Types of marketing ::

In microeconomics and management, _____ is an arrangement in which the supply chain of a company is owned by that company. Usually each member of the supply chain produces a different product or service, and the products combine to satisfy a common need. It is contrasted with horizontal integration, wherein a company produces several items which are related to one another. _____ has also described management styles that bring large portions of the supply chain not only under a common ownership, but also into one corporation .

Exam Probability: **High**

44. *Answer choices:*
(see index for correct answer)

- a. Vertical integration
- b. Share of voice
- c. Influencer marketing
- d. Ethical marketing

Guidance: level 1

:: Autonomy ::

In developmental psychology and moral, political, and bioethical philosophy, _____ is the capacity to make an informed, uncoerced decision. Autonomous organizations or institutions are independent or self-governing. _____ can also be defined from a human resources perspective, where it denotes a level of discretion granted to an employee in his or her work. In such cases, _____ is known to generally increase job satisfaction. _____ is a term that is also widely used in the field of medicine — personal _____ is greatly recognized and valued in health care.

Exam Probability: **High**

45. *Answer choices:*
(see index for correct answer)

- a. Autonomy
- b. Urban secession
- c. Autonomous robot
- d. Willpower paradox

Guidance: level 1

:: Human resource management ::

_____ involves improving the effectiveness of organizations and the individuals and teams within them. Training may be viewed as related to immediate changes in organizational effectiveness via organized instruction, while development is related to the progress of longer-term organizational and employee goals. While _____ technically have differing definitions, the two are oftentimes used interchangeably and/or together. _____ has historically been a topic within applied psychology but has within the last two decades become closely associated with human resources management, talent management, human resources development, instructional design, human factors, and knowledge management.

Exam Probability: **High**

46. *Answer choices:*
(see index for correct answer)

- a. Training and development
- b. Job performance
- c. Joint Personnel Administration
- d. Management by observation

Guidance: level 1

:: Marketing ::

_____ is the percentage of a market accounted for by a specific entity. In a survey of nearly 200 senior marketing managers, 67% responded that they found the revenue- "dollar _____" metric very useful, while 61% found "unit _____" very useful.

Exam Probability: **High**

47. *Answer choices:*
(see index for correct answer)

- a. Market share
- b. Mass-market theory
- c. Corporate identity
- d. Enterprise marketing management

Guidance: level 1

:: Strategic alliances ::

A _____ is an agreement between two or more parties to pursue a set of agreed upon objectives needed while remaining independent organizations. A _____ will usually fall short of a legal partnership entity, agency, or corporate affiliate relationship. Typically, two companies form a _____ when each possesses one or more business assets or have expertise that will help the other by enhancing their businesses. _____ s can develop in outsourcing relationships where the parties desire to achieve long-term win-win benefits and innovation based on mutually desired outcomes.

Exam Probability: **Low**

48. *Answer choices:*
(see index for correct answer)

- a. Strategic alliance
- b. Management contract
- c. Bridge Alliance
- d. Cross-licensing

Guidance: level 1

:: ::

In business strategy, _____ is establishing a competitive advantage by having the lowest cost of operation in the industry. _____ is often driven by company efficiency, size, scale, scope and cumulative experience .A _____ strategy aims to exploit scale of production, well-defined scope and other economies , producing highly standardized products, using advanced technology.In recent years, more and more companies have chosen a strategic mix to achieve market leadership. These patterns consist of simultaneous _____ , superior customer service and product leadership. Walmart has succeeded across the world due to its _____ strategy. The company has cut down on exesses at every point of production and thus are able to provide the consumers with quality products at low prices.

Exam Probability: **Low**

49. *Answer choices:*
(see index for correct answer)

- a. interpersonal communication
- b. surface-level diversity
- c. Cost leadership

- d. Sarbanes-Oxley act of 2002

Guidance: level 1

:: ::

A _____ is an organization, usually a group of people or a company, authorized to act as a single entity and recognized as such in law. Early incorporated entities were established by charter . Most jurisdictions now allow the creation of new _____ s through registration.

Exam Probability: **Medium**

50. *Answer choices:*
(see index for correct answer)

- a. process perspective
- b. Corporation
- c. information systems assessment
- d. similarity-attraction theory

Guidance: level 1

:: ::

A _____ or GM is an executive who has overall responsibility for managing both the revenue and cost elements of a company's income statement, known as profit & loss responsibility. A _____ usually oversees most or all of the firm's marketing and sales functions as well as the day-to-day operations of the business. Frequently, the _____ is responsible for effective planning, delegating, coordinating, staffing, organizing, and decision making to attain desirable profit making results for an organization .

Exam Probability: **Medium**

51. *Answer choices:*
(see index for correct answer)

- a. empathy
- b. General manager
- c. imperative
- d. Sarbanes-Oxley act of 2002

Guidance: level 1

In economics, _____ is the assignment of available resources to various uses. In the context of an entire economy, resources can be allocated by various means, such as markets or central planning.

Exam Probability: **Low**

52. *Answer choices:*
(see index for correct answer)

- a. Cost database
- b. Project Management South Africa
- c. Enterprise project management
- d. Effort management

Guidance: level 1

:: Evaluation ::

_____ is the practice of being honest and showing a consistent and uncompromising adherence to strong moral and ethical principles and values.In ethics, _____ is regarded as the honesty and truthfulness or accuracy of one's actions. _____ can stand in opposition to hypocrisy, in that judging with the standards of _____ involves regarding internal consistency as a virtue, and suggests that parties holding within themselves apparently conflicting values should account for the discrepancy or alter their beliefs. The word _____ evolved from the Latin adjective integer, meaning whole or complete. In this context, _____ is the inner sense of "wholeness" deriving from qualities such as honesty and consistency of character. As such, one may judge that others "have _____ " to the extent that they act according to the values, beliefs and principles they claim to hold.

Exam Probability: **Medium**

53. *Answer choices:*
(see index for correct answer)

- a. Academic equivalency evaluation
- b. Teaching and Learning International Survey
- c. Career portfolio
- d. Integrity

:: ::

_____ is the consumption and saving opportunity gained by an entity within a specified timeframe, which is generally expressed in monetary terms. For households and individuals, " _____ is the sum of all the wages, salaries, profits, interest payments, rents, and other forms of earnings received in a given period of time."

Exam Probability: **High**

54. *Answer choices:*
(see index for correct answer)

- a. levels of analysis
- b. hierarchical perspective
- c. information systems assessment
- d. Income

:: ::

_____ or accountancy is the measurement, processing, and communication of financial information about economic entities such as businesses and corporations. The modern field was established by the Italian mathematician Luca Pacioli in 1494. _____ , which has been called the "language of business", measures the results of an organization`s economic activities and conveys this information to a variety of users, including investors, creditors, management, and regulators. Practitioners of _____ are known as accountants. The terms " _____ " and "financial reporting" are often used as synonyms.

Exam Probability: **Low**

55. *Answer choices:*
(see index for correct answer)

- a. hierarchical perspective
- b. information systems assessment
- c. imperative
- d. Accounting

:: Power (social and political) ::

_____ is a form of reverence gained by a leader who has strong interpersonal relationship skills. _____ , as an aspect of personal power, becomes particularly important as organizational leadership becomes increasingly about collaboration and influence, rather than command and control.

Exam Probability: **High**

56. *Answer choices:*
(see index for correct answer)

- a. Hard power
- b. need for power
- c. Referent power

:: Employment ::

_____ is a relationship between two parties, usually based on a contract where work is paid for, where one party, which may be a corporation, for profit, not-for-profit organization, co-operative or other entity is the employer and the other is the employee. Employees work in return for payment, which may be in the form of an hourly wage, by piecework or an annual salary, depending on the type of work an employee does or which sector she or he is working in. Employees in some fields or sectors may receive gratuities, bonus payment or stock options. In some types of _____ , employees may receive benefits in addition to payment. Benefits can include health insurance, housing, disability insurance or use of a gym. _____ is typically governed by _____ laws, regulations or legal contracts.

Exam Probability: **Low**

57. *Answer choices:*
(see index for correct answer)

- a. Employment
- b. Career Development Practitioner
- c. Ontario Disability Employment Network

- d. WorkKeys

Guidance: level 1

:: Management ::

In the field of management, _____ involves the formulation and implementation of the major goals and initiatives taken by an organization's top management on behalf of owners, based on consideration of resources and an assessment of the internal and external environments in which the organization operates.

Exam Probability: **High**

58. *Answer choices:*
(see index for correct answer)

- a. Production flow analysis
- b. Dynamic enterprise modeling
- c. Discovery-driven planning
- d. Strategic management

Guidance: level 1

:: Project management ::

A _____ is a professional in the field of project management. _____ s have the responsibility of the planning, procurement and execution of a project, in any undertaking that has a defined scope, defined start and a defined finish; regardless of industry. _____ s are first point of contact for any issues or discrepancies arising from within the heads of various departments in an organization before the problem escalates to higher authorities. Project management is the responsibility of a _____ . This individual seldom participates directly in the activities that produce the end result, but rather strives to maintain the progress, mutual interaction and tasks of various parties in such a way that reduces the risk of overall failure, maximizes benefits, and minimizes costs.

Exam Probability: **Medium**

59. *Answer choices:*
(see index for correct answer)

- a. Graphical path method
- b. Resource leveling
- c. Critical path drag
- d. Project manager

Guidance: level 1

Business law

Corporate law (also known as business law) is the body of law governing the
rights, relations, and conduct of persons, companies, organizations and
businesses. It refers to the legal practice relating to, or the theory of
corporations. Corporate law often describes the law relating to matters which
derive directly from the life-cycle of a corporation. It thus encompasses the
formation, funding, governance, and death of a corporation.

:: Labour relations ::

_____ is a field of study that can have different meanings depending on
the context in which it is used. In an international context, it is a subfield
of labor history that studies the human relations with regard to work – in its
broadest sense – and how this connects to questions of social inequality. It
explicitly encompasses unregulated, historical, and non-Western forms of labor.
Here, _____ define "for or with whom one works and under what rules.
These rules determine the type of work, type and amount of remuneration,
working hours, degrees of physical and psychological strain, as well as the
degree of freedom and autonomy associated with the work."

Exam Probability: **High**

1. *Answer choices:*
(see index for correct answer)

- a. Union shop
- b. Broad left
- c. Negotiated cartelism
- d. Social dialogue

Guidance: level 1

:: Business law ::

A _____ is a legal right granted by a debtor to a creditor over the debtor's property which enables the creditor to have recourse to the property if the debtor defaults in making payment or otherwise performing the secured obligations. One of the most common examples of a _____ is a mortgage: When person, by the action of an expressed conveyance, pledges by a promise to pay a certain sum of money, with certain conditions, on a said date or dates for a said period, that action on the page with wet ink applied on the part of the one wishing the exchange creates the original funds and negotiable Instrument. That action of pledging conveys a promise binding upon the mortgagee which creates a face value upon the Instrument of the amount of currency being asked for in exchange. It is therein in good faith offered to the Bank in exchange for local currency from the Bank to buy a house. The particular country's Bank Acts usually requires the Banks to deliver such fund bearing negotiable instruments to the Countries Main Bank such as is the case in Canada. This creates a _____ in the land the house sits on for the Bank and they file a caveat at land titles on the house as evidence of that _____ . If the mortgagee fails to pay defaulting in his promise to repay the exchange, the bank then applies to the court to for-close on your property to eventually sell the house and apply the proceeds to the outstanding exchange.

Exam Probability: **Medium**

2. *Answer choices:*

(see index for correct answer)

- a. Limited liability limited partnership
- b. Consumer privacy
- c. Jurisdictional strike
- d. Security interest

Guidance: level 1

:: Business law ::

A _____ is a group of people who jointly supervise the activities of an organization, which can be either a for-profit business, nonprofit organization, or a government agency. Such a board's powers, duties, and responsibilities are determined by government regulations and the organization's own constitution and bylaws. These authorities may specify the number of members of the board, how they are to be chosen, and how often they are to meet.

Exam Probability: **Low**

3. *Answer choices:*

(see index for correct answer)

- a. Whitewash waiver
- b. Firm offer
- c. Enhanced use lease
- d. Board of directors

Guidance: level 1

:: Business law ::

A _____ is a contractual arrangement calling for the lessee to pay the lessor for use of an asset. Property, buildings and vehicles are common assets that are _____ d. Industrial or business equipment is also _____ d.

Exam Probability: **High**

4. *Answer choices:*

(see index for correct answer)

- a. Arbitration award
- b. Industrial relations
- c. Output contract
- d. Lease

Guidance: level 1

:: Legal terms ::

_____ , or exemplary damages, are damages assessed in order to punish the defendant for outrageous conduct and/or to reform or deter the defendant and others from engaging in conduct similar to that which formed the basis of the lawsuit. Although the purpose of _____ is not to compensate the plaintiff, the plaintiff will receive all or some of the _____ award.

Exam Probability: **Low**

5. *Answer choices:*

(see index for correct answer)

- a. Intentional harassment, alarm or distress
- b. Per curiam decision
- c. Punitive damages
- d. Good conduct time

Guidance: level 1

:: Clauses of the United States Constitution ::

The _____ describes an enumerated power listed in the United States Constitution . The clause states that the United States Congress shall have power "To regulate Commerce with foreign Nations, and among the several States, and with the Indian Tribes." Courts and commentators have tended to discuss each of these three areas of commerce as a separate power granted to Congress. It is common to see the individual components of the _____ referred to under specific terms: the Foreign _____ , the Interstate _____ , and the Indian _____ .

Exam Probability: **Low**

6. *Answer choices:*

(see index for correct answer)

- a. Double Jeopardy Clause
- b. Full Faith and Credit Clause
- c. Full faith and credit

Guidance: level 1

:: ::

The U.S. _____ is an independent agency of the United States federal government. The SEC holds primary responsibility for enforcing the federal securities laws, proposing securities rules, and regulating the securities industry, the nation's stock and options exchanges, and other activities and organizations, including the electronic securities markets in the United States.

Exam Probability: **Low**

7. *Answer choices:*

(see index for correct answer)

- a. cultural
- b. personal values
- c. interpersonal communication
- d. hierarchical perspective

Guidance: level 1

:: Forgery ::

_____ is a white-collar crime that generally refers to the false making or material alteration of a legal instrument with the specific intent to defraud anyone . Tampering with a certain legal instrument may be forbidden by law in some jurisdictions but such an offense is not related to _____ unless the tampered legal instrument was actually used in the course of the crime to defraud another person or entity. Copies, studio replicas, and reproductions are not considered forgeries, though they may later become forgeries through knowing and willful misrepresentations.

Exam Probability: **High**

8. *Answer choices:*

(see index for correct answer)

- a. Forgery
- b. Forgery Act
- c. Signature forgery
- d. Forgery Act 1830

Guidance: level 1

:: Criminal procedure ::

_____ is the adjudication process of the criminal law. While _____ differs dramatically by jurisdiction, the process generally begins with a formal criminal charge with the person on trial either being free on bail or incarcerated, and results in the conviction or acquittal of the defendant. _____ can be either in form of inquisitorial or adversarial _____.

Exam Probability: **High**

9. *Answer choices:*
(see index for correct answer)

- a. Exoneration
- b. directed verdict

Guidance: level 1

:: ::

_____ is property that is movable. In common law systems, _____ may also be called chattels or personalty. In civil law systems, _____ is often called movable property or movables – any property that can be moved from one location to another.

Exam Probability: **High**

10. *Answer choices:*
(see index for correct answer)

- a. Sarbanes-Oxley act of 2002
- b. Personal property
- c. levels of analysis
- d. empathy

Guidance: level 1

:: ::

_____ or accountancy is the measurement, processing, and communication of financial information about economic entities such as businesses and corporations. The modern field was established by the Italian mathematician Luca Pacioli in 1494. _____ , which has been called the "language of business", measures the results of an organization's economic activities and conveys this information to a variety of users, including investors, creditors, management, and regulators. Practitioners of _____ are known as accountants. The terms " _____ " and "financial reporting" are often used as synonyms.

Exam Probability: **Medium**

11. *Answer choices:*
(see index for correct answer)

- a. surface-level diversity
- b. personal values
- c. Sarbanes-Oxley act of 2002
- d. similarity-attraction theory

Guidance: level 1

:: Chemical industry ::

The _____ for the Protection of Literary and Artistic Works, usually known as the _____ , is an international agreement governing copyright, which was first accepted in Berne, Switzerland, in 1886.

Exam Probability: **High**

12. *Answer choices:*
(see index for correct answer)

- a. ConverDyn
- b. Chemical plant
- c. Berne Convention
- d. High production volume chemicals

Guidance: level 1

:: Equity (law) ::

An assignment is a legal term used in the context of the law of contract and of property. In both instances, assignment is the process whereby a person, the assignor, transfers rights or benefits to another, the _____ . An assignment may not transfer a duty, burden or detriment without the express agreement of the _____ . The right or benefit being assigned may be a gift or it may be paid for with a contractual consideration such as money.

Exam Probability: **High**

13. *Answer choices:*
(see index for correct answer)

- a. assignor
- b. Assignee

Guidance: level 1

:: ::

_____ is the body of law that governs the activities of administrative agencies of government. Government agency action can include rule making, adjudication, or the enforcement of a specific regulatory agenda. _____ is considered a branch of public law. As a body of law, _____ deals with the decision-making of the administrative units of government that are part of a national regulatory scheme in such areas as police law, international trade, manufacturing, the environment, taxation, broadcasting, immigration and transport. _____ expanded greatly during the twentieth century, as legislative bodies worldwide created more government agencies to regulate the social, economic and political spheres of human interaction.

Exam Probability: **High**

14. *Answer choices:*
(see index for correct answer)

- a. similarity-attraction theory
- b. process perspective
- c. hierarchical perspective
- d. Administrative law

Guidance: level 1

:: Real estate ::

_____ , real estate, realty, or immovable property In English common law refers to landed properties belonging to some person. It include all structures, crops, buildings, machinery, wells, dams, ponds, mines, canals, and roads, among other things. The term is historic, arising from the now-discontinued form of action, which distinguish between _____ disputes and personal property disputes. Personal property was, and continues to refer to all properties that are not real properties.

Exam Probability: **Low**

15. *Answer choices:*
(see index for correct answer)

- a. Slumlord
- b. Real property
- c. Property ladder
- d. Displaced sales

Guidance: level 1

:: ::

_____ s and acquisitions are transactions in which the ownership of companies, other business organizations, or their operating units are transferred or consolidated with other entities. As an aspect of strategic management, M&A can allow enterprises to grow or downsize, and change the nature of their business or competitive position.

Exam Probability: **Low**

16. *Answer choices:*
(see index for correct answer)

- a. co-culture
- b. Merger
- c. hierarchical perspective
- d. process perspective

Guidance: level 1

:: ::

_____ is the collection of mechanisms, processes and relations by which corporations are controlled and operated. Governance structures and principles identify the distribution of rights and responsibilities among different participants in the corporation and include the rules and procedures for making decisions in corporate affairs. _____ is necessary because of the possibility of conflicts of interests between stakeholders, primarily between shareholders and upper management or among shareholders.

Exam Probability: **Low**

17. *Answer choices:*
(see index for correct answer)

- a. similarity-attraction theory
- b. Corporate governance
- c. interpersonal communication
- d. hierarchical

Guidance: level 1

:: ::

_____ is the administration of an organization, whether it is a business, a not-for-profit organization, or government body. _____ includes the activities of setting the strategy of an organization and coordinating the efforts of its employees to accomplish its objectives through the application of available resources, such as financial, natural, technological, and human resources. The term "_____" may also refer to those people who manage an organization.

Exam Probability: **High**

18. *Answer choices:*
(see index for correct answer)

- a. open system
- b. deep-level diversity
- c. process perspective
- d. corporate values

Guidance: level 1

:: Real property law ::

_____ is the judicial process whereby a will is "proved" in a court of law and accepted as a valid public document that is the true last testament of the deceased, or whereby the estate is settled according to the laws of intestacy in the state of residence [or real property] of the deceased at time of death in the absence of a legal will.

Exam Probability: **Low**

19. *Answer choices:*
(see index for correct answer)

- a. Retaliatory eviction
- b. Foreclosure consultant
- c. Massachusetts Land Court
- d. Structural encroachment

Guidance: level 1

:: Majority–minority relations ::

_____ , also known as reservation in India and Nepal, positive discrimination / action in the United Kingdom, and employment equity in Canada and South Africa, is the policy of promoting the education and employment of members of groups that are known to have previously suffered from discrimination. Historically and internationally, support for _____ has sought to achieve goals such as bridging inequalities in employment and pay, increasing access to education, promoting diversity, and redressing apparent past wrongs, harms, or hindrances.

Exam Probability: **Low**

20. *Answer choices:*
(see index for correct answer)

- a. Affirmative action
- b. positive discrimination
- c. cultural Relativism

Guidance: level 1

:: ::

In law, a _____ is a coming together of parties to a dispute, to present information in a tribunal, a formal setting with the authority to adjudicate claims or disputes. One form of tribunal is a court. The tribunal, which may occur before a judge, jury, or other designated trier of fact, aims to achieve a resolution to their dispute.

Exam Probability: **Low**

21. *Answer choices:*
(see index for correct answer)

- a. deep-level diversity
- b. information systems assessment
- c. Trial
- d. Character

Guidance: level 1

:: Patent law ::

A _____ is generally any statement intended to specify or delimit the scope of rights and obligations that may be exercised and enforced by parties in a legally recognized relationship. In contrast to other terms for legally operative language, the term _____ usually implies situations that involve some level of uncertainty, waiver, or risk.

Exam Probability: **High**

22. *Answer choices:*
(see index for correct answer)

- a. Defensive publication
- b. Disclaimer
- c. Biological patent
- d. State of the art

Guidance: level 1

:: Treaties ::

A _____ is an agreement under international law entered into by actors in international law, namely sovereign states and international organizations. A _____ may also be known as an agreement, protocol, covenant, convention, pact, or exchange of letters, among other terms. Regardless of terminology, all of these forms of agreements are, under international law, equally considered treaties and the rules are the same.

Exam Probability: **Low**

23. *Answer choices:*
(see index for correct answer)

- a. Clausula rebus sic stantibus
- b. Secret treaty
- c. Subsidiary alliance
- d. Treaty

Guidance: level 1

:: ::

The _____ of 1933, also known as the 1933 Act, the _____ , the Truth in _____ , the Federal _____ , and the `33 Act, was enacted by the United States Congress on May 27, 1933, during the Great Depression, after the stock market crash of 1929. Legislated pursuant to the Interstate Commerce Clause of the Constitution, it requires every offer or sale of securities that uses the means and instrumentalities of interstate commerce to be registered with the SEC pursuant to the 1933 Act, unless an exemption from registration exists under the law. The term "means and instrumentalities of interstate commerce" is extremely broad and it is virtually impossible to avoid the operation of the statute by attempting to offer or sell a security without using an "instrumentality" of interstate commerce. Any use of a telephone, for example, or the mails would probably be enough to subject the transaction to the statute.

Exam Probability: **High**

24. *Answer choices:*
(see index for correct answer)

- a. cultural
- b. corporate values
- c. open system

- d. Securities Act

Guidance: level 1

:: ::

Competition law is a law that promotes or seeks to maintain market competition by regulating anti-competitive conduct by companies. Competition law is implemented through public and private enforcement. Competition law is known as " _____ law" in the United States for historical reasons, and as "anti-monopoly law" in China and Russia. In previous years it has been known as trade practices law in the United Kingdom and Australia. In the European Union, it is referred to as both _____ and competition law.

Exam Probability: **Low**

25. *Answer choices:*
(see index for correct answer)

- a. Antitrust
- b. open system
- c. cultural
- d. co-culture

Guidance: level 1

:: White-collar criminals ::

_____ refers to financially motivated, nonviolent crime committed by businesses and government professionals. It was first defined by the sociologist Edwin Sutherland in 1939 as "a crime committed by a person of respectability and high social status in the course of their occupation". Typical _____ s could include wage theft, fraud, bribery, Ponzi schemes, insider trading, labor racketeering, embezzlement, cybercrime, copyright infringement, money laundering, identity theft, and forgery. Lawyers can specialize in _____ .

Exam Probability: **Medium**

26. *Answer choices:*
(see index for correct answer)

- a. Du Jun
- b. Tongsun Park

:: Legal doctrines and principles ::

_____ is a doctrine that a party is responsible for acts of their agents. For example, in the United States, there are circumstances when an employer is liable for acts of employees performed within the course of their employment. This rule is also called the master-servant rule, recognized in both common law and civil law jurisdictions.

Exam Probability: **Low**

27. *Answer choices:*
(see index for correct answer)

- a. unconscionable contract
- b. Respondeat superior
- c. Contributory negligence
- d. Caveat emptor

:: Finance ::

A _____ , in the law of the United States, is a contract that governs the relationship between the parties to a kind of financial transaction known as a secured transaction. In a secured transaction, the Grantor assigns, grants and pledges to the grantee a security interest in personal property which is referred to as the collateral. Examples of typical collateral are shares of stock, livestock, and vehicles. A _____ is not used to transfer any interest in real property , only personal property. The document used by lenders to obtain a lien on real property is a mortgage or deed of trust.

Exam Probability: **Low**

28. *Answer choices:*
(see index for correct answer)

- a. Dedicated Portfolio Theory
- b. Security agreement
- c. Weighted-average loan age
- d. Debt-for-nature swap

:: Marketing ::

A _____ is an overall experience of a customer that distinguishes an organization or product from its rivals in the eyes of the customer. _____ s are used in business, marketing, and advertising. Name _____ s are sometimes distinguished from generic or store _____ s.

Exam Probability: **High**

29. *Answer choices:*
(see index for correct answer)

- a. Brand
- b. Non-price competition
- c. Price war
- d. Gold party

:: ::

_____ is the practical authority granted to a legal body to administer justice within a defined field of responsibility, e.g., Michigan tax law. In federations like the United States, areas of _____ apply to local, state, and federal levels; e.g. the court has _____ to apply federal law.

Exam Probability: **Medium**

30. *Answer choices:*
(see index for correct answer)

- a. corporate values
- b. Jurisdiction
- c. process perspective
- d. interpersonal communication

:: Insurance law ::

_____ exists when an insured person derives a financial or other kind of benefit from the continuous existence, without repairment or damage, of the insured object . A person has an _____ in something when loss of or damage to that thing would cause the person to suffer a financial or other kind of loss.Normally, _____ is established by ownership, possession, or direct relationship. For example, people have _____ s in their own homes and vehicles, but not in their neighbors' homes and vehicles, and almost certainly not those of strangers.

Exam Probability: **Medium**

31. *Answer choices:*
(see index for correct answer)

- a. Australian insurance law
- b. Peracomo Inc. v. TELUS Communications Co.
- c. Insurable interest
- d. Assigned risk

Guidance: level 1

:: ::

_____ is an abstract concept of management of complex systems according to a set of rules and trends. In systems theory, these types of rules exist in various fields of biology and society, but the term has slightly different meanings according to context. For example.

Exam Probability: **Medium**

32. *Answer choices:*
(see index for correct answer)

- a. Sarbanes-Oxley act of 2002
- b. Regulation
- c. co-culture
- d. corporate values

Guidance: level 1

:: ::

A _____ , in law, is a set of facts sufficient to justify a right to sue to obtain money, property, or the enforcement of a right against another party. The term also refers to the legal theory upon which a plaintiff brings suit . The legal document which carries a claim is often called a `statement of claim` in English law, or a `complaint` in U.S. federal practice and in many U.S. states. It can be any communication notifying the party to whom it is addressed of an alleged fault which resulted in damages, often expressed in amount of money the receiving party should pay/reimburse.

Exam Probability: **Low**

33. *Answer choices:*
(see index for correct answer)

- a. Cause of action
- b. Sarbanes-Oxley act of 2002
- c. surface-level diversity
- d. imperative

Guidance: level 1

:: Arbitration law ::

The United States Arbitration Act , more commonly referred to as the _____ or FAA, is an act of Congress that provides for judicial facilitation of private dispute resolution through arbitration. It applies in both state courts and federal courts, as was held constitutional in Southland Corp. v. Keating. It applies where the transaction contemplated by the parties "involves" interstate commerce and is predicated on an exercise of the Commerce Clause powers granted to Congress in the U.S. Constitution.

Exam Probability: **Low**

34. *Answer choices:*
(see index for correct answer)

- a. UNCITRAL Model Law on International Commercial Arbitration
- b. James A. Graham
- c. Uniform Arbitration Act
- d. Kompetenz-kompetenz

Guidance: level 1

:: Shareholders ::

A _____ is a payment made by a corporation to its shareholders, usually as a distribution of profits. When a corporation earns a profit or surplus, the corporation is able to re-invest the profit in the business and pay a proportion of the profit as a _____ to shareholders. Distribution to shareholders may be in cash or, if the corporation has a _____ reinvestment plan, the amount can be paid by the issue of further shares or share repurchase. When _____ s are paid, shareholders typically must pay income taxes, and the corporation does not receive a corporate income tax deduction for the _____ payments.

Exam Probability: **High**

35. *Answer choices:*
(see index for correct answer)

- a. UK Shareholders Association
- b. Dividend
- c. Shareholder ownership value
- d. Stock dilution

Guidance: level 1

:: United States corporate law ::

In tort law, a _____ is a legal obligation which is imposed on an individual requiring adherence to a standard of reasonable care while performing any acts that could foreseeably harm others. It is the first element that must be established to proceed with an action in negligence. The claimant must be able to show a _____ imposed by law which the defendant has breached. In turn, breaching a duty may subject an individual to liability. The _____ may be imposed by operation of law between individuals who have no current direct relationship but eventually become related in some manner, as defined by common law .

Exam Probability: **Low**

36. *Answer choices:*
(see index for correct answer)

- a. Dunlop Commission on the Future of Worker-Management Relations: Final Report
- b. Corporate law in the United States
- c. Model Nonprofit Corporation Act

- d. New York Business Corporation Law

Guidance: level 1

:: Promotion and marketing communications ::

In everyday language, _____ refers to exaggerated or false praise. In law, _____ is a promotional statement or claim that expresses subjective rather than objective views, which no "reasonable person" would take literally. _____ serves to "puff up" an exaggerated image of what is being described and is especially featured in testimonials.

Exam Probability: **Low**

37. *Answer choices:*
(see index for correct answer)

- a. Trade literature
- b. Nielsen Broadcast Data Systems
- c. Puffery
- d. Video news release

Guidance: level 1

:: ::

_____ is the act or practice of forbidding something by law; more particularly the term refers to the banning of the manufacture, storage , transportation, sale, possession, and consumption of alcoholic beverages. The word is also used to refer to a period of time during which such bans are enforced.

Exam Probability: **Low**

38. *Answer choices:*
(see index for correct answer)

- a. Character
- b. Prohibition
- c. personal values
- d. hierarchical perspective

Guidance: level 1

A _____ can mean the holder of a license, orin U.S. tort law, a _____ is a person who is on the property of another, despite the fact that the property is not open to the general public, because the owner of the property has allowed the _____ to enter. The status of a visitor as a _____ defines the legal rights of the visitor if they are injured due to the negligence of the property possessor .

Exam Probability: **Medium**

39. *Answer choices:*
(see index for correct answer)

- a. personal values
- b. levels of analysis
- c. cultural
- d. Licensee

Guidance: level 1

:: Consumer theory ::

A _____ is a technical term in psychology, economics and philosophy usually used in relation to choosing between alternatives. For example, someone prefers A over B if they would rather choose A than B.

Exam Probability: **Medium**

40. *Answer choices:*
(see index for correct answer)

- a. Permanent income hypothesis
- b. Price elasticity of demand
- c. Consumer sovereignty
- d. Preference

Guidance: level 1

:: Negotiable instrument law ::

In the United States, The Preservation of Consumers' Claims and Defenses [_____ Rule], formally known as the "Trade Regulation Rule Concerning Preservation of Consumers' Claims and Defenses," protects consumers when merchants sell a consumer's credit contracts to other lenders. Specifically, it preserves consumers' right to assert the same legal claims and defenses against anyone who purchases the credit contract, as they would have against the seller who originally provided the credit. [16 Code of Federal Regulations Part 433]

Exam Probability: **High**

41. *Answer choices:*
(see index for correct answer)

- a. Gold v. Eddy
- b. holder in due course doctrine
- c. Holder in due course
- d. Blank endorsement

Guidance: level 1

:: ::

According to the philosopher Piyush Mathur , "Tangibility is the property that a phenomenon exhibits if it has and/or transports mass and/or energy and/or momentum".

Exam Probability: **Low**

42. *Answer choices:*
(see index for correct answer)

- a. levels of analysis
- b. surface-level diversity
- c. empathy
- d. Tangible

Guidance: level 1

:: Statutory law ::

_____ or statute law is written law set down by a body of legislature or by a singular legislator . This is as opposed to oral or customary law; or regulatory law promulgated by the executive or common law of the judiciary. Statutes may originate with national, state legislatures or local municipalities.

Exam Probability: **Medium**

43. *Answer choices:*
(see index for correct answer)

- a. Statutory Law
- b. incorporation by reference
- c. Statute of repose
- d. ratification

Guidance: level 1

:: Services management and marketing ::

A _____ or servicemark is a trademark used in the United States and several other countries to identify a service rather than a product.

Exam Probability: **Medium**

44. *Answer choices:*
(see index for correct answer)

- a. Internet hosting service
- b. Service delivery framework
- c. Service design
- d. Service climate

Guidance: level 1

:: Business models ::

A _____ , _____ company or daughter company is a company that is owned or controlled by another company, which is called the parent company, parent, or holding company. The _____ can be a company, corporation, or limited liability company. In some cases it is a government or state-owned enterprise. In some cases, particularly in the music and book publishing industries, subsidiaries are referred to as imprints.

Exam Probability: **High**

45. *Answer choices:*
(see index for correct answer)

- a. Sustainable business
- b. Premium business model
- c. Subsidiary
- d. Strategy map

Guidance: level 1

:: ::

Industrial espionage, _____ , corporate spying or corporate espionage is a form of espionage conducted for commercial purposes instead of purely national security. While _____ is conducted or orchestrated by governments and is international in scope, industrial or corporate espionage is more often national and occurs between companies or corporations.

Exam Probability: **High**

46. *Answer choices:*
(see index for correct answer)

- a. hierarchical
- b. deep-level diversity
- c. personal values
- d. co-culture

Guidance: level 1

:: Business law ::

An _____ is a clause in a contract that requires the parties to resolve their disputes through an arbitration process. Although such a clause may or may not specify that arbitration occur within a specific jurisdiction, it always binds the parties to a type of resolution outside the courts, and is therefore considered a kind of forum selection clause.

Exam Probability: **Medium**

47. *Answer choices:*
(see index for correct answer)

- a. Arbitration clause
- b. Industrial relations
- c. Firm offer
- d. Relational contract

Guidance: level 1

:: Contract law ::

An _____ , or simply option, is defined as "a promise which meets the requirements for the formation of a contract and limits the promisor`s power to revoke an offer."

Exam Probability: **High**

48. *Answer choices:*
(see index for correct answer)

- a. Warranty
- b. Option contract
- c. Revocation
- d. Subcontractor

Guidance: level 1

:: ::

In financial markets, a share is a unit used as mutual funds, limited partnerships, and real estate investment trusts. The owner of _____ in the corporation/company is a shareholder of the corporation. A share is an indivisible unit of capital, expressing the ownership relationship between the company and the shareholder. The denominated value of a share is its face value, and the total of the face value of issued _____ represent the capital of a company, which may not reflect the market value of those _____ .

Exam Probability: **High**

49. *Answer choices:*
(see index for correct answer)

- a. corporate values
- b. imperative
- c. Shares
- d. personal values

Guidance: level 1

:: Writs ::

In common law, a _____ is a formal _____ ten order issued by a body with administrative or judicial jurisdiction; in modern usage, this body is generally a court. Warrants, prerogative _____ s, and subpoenas are common types of _____ , but many forms exist and have existed.

Exam Probability: **Low**

50. *Answer choices:*
(see index for correct answer)

- a. Writ of execution
- b. Writ of assistance
- c. Qui tam

Guidance: level 1

:: Legal terms ::

_____ , or non-absolute contributory negligence outside the United States, is a partial legal defense that reduces the amount of damages that a plaintiff can recover in a negligence-based claim, based upon the degree to which the plaintiff's own negligence contributed to cause the injury. When the defense is asserted, the factfinder, usually a jury, must decide the degree to which the plaintiff's negligence and the combined negligence of all other relevant actors all contributed to cause the plaintiff's damages. It is a modification of the doctrine of contributory negligence that disallows any recovery by a plaintiff whose negligence contributed even minimally to causing the damages.

Exam Probability: **Low**

51. *Answer choices:*
(see index for correct answer)

- a. Fuero
- b. Alluvion
- c. Long cause
- d. Comparative negligence

Guidance: level 1

:: ::

_____ , also referred to as orthostasis, is a human position in which the body is held in an upright position and supported only by the feet.

Exam Probability: **High**

52. *Answer choices:*
(see index for correct answer)

- a. surface-level diversity
- b. Standing
- c. information systems assessment
- d. process perspective

Guidance: level 1

:: Communication of falsehoods ::

_____ , calumny, vilification, or traducement is the communication of a false statement that harms the reputation of, depending on the law of the country, an individual, business, product, group, government, religion, or nation.

Exam Probability: **Medium**

53. *Answer choices:*
(see index for correct answer)

- a. Substantial truth
- b. Double bind
- c. Malingering
- d. False allegation of child sexual abuse

Guidance: level 1

:: ::

Credit is the trust which allows one party to provide money or resources to another party wherein the second party does not reimburse the first party immediately , but promises either to repay or return those resources at a later date. In other words, credit is a method of making reciprocity formal, legally enforceable, and extensible to a large group of unrelated people.

Exam Probability: **Low**

54. *Answer choices:*
(see index for correct answer)

- a. empathy
- b. personal values
- c. Consumer credit
- d. similarity-attraction theory

Guidance: level 1

:: Business law ::

A _____ is an arrangement where parties, known as partners, agree to cooperate to advance their mutual interests. The partners in a _____ may be individuals, businesses, interest-based organizations, schools, governments or combinations. Organizations may partner to increase the likelihood of each achieving their mission and to amplify their reach. A _____ may result in issuing and holding equity or may be only governed by a contract.

Exam Probability: **Medium**

55. *Answer choices:*
(see index for correct answer)

- a. Administration
- b. Output contract
- c. Perfection
- d. Refusal to deal

Guidance: level 1

:: American legal terms ::

The phrase "by _____" is a legal term that indicates that a right or liability has been created for a party, irrespective of the intent of that party, because it is dictated by existing legal principles. For example, if a person dies without a will, his or her heirs are determined by _____. Similarly, if a person marries or has a child after his or her will has been executed, the law writes this pretermitted spouse or pretermitted heir into the will if no provision for this situation was specifically included. Adverse possession, in which title to land passes because non-owners have occupied it for a certain period of time, is another important right that vests by _____.

Exam Probability: **High**

56. *Answer choices:*
(see index for correct answer)

- a. Reasonable time
- b. Chilling effect

Guidance: level 1

:: ::

A _____ is the party who initiates a lawsuit before a court. By doing so, the _____ seeks a legal remedy; if this search is successful, the court will issue judgment in favor of the _____ and make the appropriate court order . " _____ " is the term used in civil cases in most English-speaking jurisdictions, the notable exception being England and Wales, where a _____ has, since the introduction of the Civil Procedure Rules in 1999, been known as a "claimant", but that term also has other meanings. In criminal cases, the prosecutor brings the case against the defendant, but the key complaining party is often called the "complainant".

Exam Probability: **Medium**

57. *Answer choices:*
(see index for correct answer)

- a. functional perspective
- b. levels of analysis
- c. hierarchical
- d. Plaintiff

Guidance: level 1

:: ::

_____ is an insurance that covers the whole or a part of the risk of a person incurring medical expenses, spreading the risk over a large number of persons. By estimating the overall risk of health care and health system expenses over the risk pool, an insurer can develop a routine finance structure, such as a monthly premium or payroll tax, to provide the money to pay for the health care benefits specified in the insurance agreement. The benefit is administered by a central organization such as a government agency, private business, or not-for-profit entity.

Exam Probability: **Medium**

58. *Answer choices:*
(see index for correct answer)

- a. deep-level diversity
- b. co-culture
- c. Health insurance
- d. personal values

Guidance: level 1

_____ is "property consisting of land and the buildings on it, along with its natural resources such as crops, minerals or water; immovable property of this nature; an interest vested in this an item of real property, buildings or housing in general. Also: the business of _____ ; the profession of buying, selling, or renting land, buildings, or housing." It is a legal term used in jurisdictions whose legal system is derived from English common law, such as India, England, Wales, Northern Ireland, United States, Canada, Pakistan, Australia, and New Zealand.

Exam Probability: **High**

59. *Answer choices:*
(see index for correct answer)

- a. open system
- b. surface-level diversity
- c. Sarbanes-Oxley act of 2002
- d. Real estate

Guidance: level 1

Finance

Finance is a field that is concerned with the allocation (investment) of assets and liabilities over space and time, often under conditions of risk or uncertainty. Finance can also be defined as the science of money management. Participants in the market aim to price assets based on their risk level, fundamental value, and their expected rate of return. Finance can be split into three sub-categories: public finance, corporate finance and personal finance.

:: Financial economics ::

A _____ is defined to include property of any kind held by an assessee, whether connected with their business or profession or not connected with their business or profession. It includes all kinds of property, movable or immovable, tangible or intangible, fixed or circulating. Thus, land and building, plant and machinery, motorcar, furniture, jewellery, route permits, goodwill, tenancy rights, patents, trademarks, shares, debentures, securities, units, mutual funds, zero-coupon bonds etc. are _____ s.

Exam Probability: **High**

1. *Answer choices:*
(see index for correct answer)

- a. Forward price
- b. Efficient-market hypothesis
- c. Solvency
- d. Capital asset

Guidance: level 1

:: ::

The _____ of a function of a real variable measures the sensitivity to change of the function value with respect to a change in its argument .
_____ s are a fundamental tool of calculus. For example, the _____ of the position of a moving object with respect to time is the object's velocity: this measures how quickly the position of the object changes when time advances.

Exam Probability: **High**

2. *Answer choices:*
(see index for correct answer)

- a. open system
- b. deep-level diversity
- c. Derivative
- d. information systems assessment

Guidance: level 1

:: ::

_____ Corporation was an American energy, commodities, and services company based in Houston, Texas. It was founded in 1985 as a merger between Houston Natural Gas and InterNorth, both relatively small regional companies. Before its bankruptcy on December 3, 2001, _____ employed approximately 29,000 staff and was a major electricity, natural gas, communications and pulp and paper company, with claimed revenues of nearly $101 billion during 2000. Fortune named _____ "America's Most Innovative Company" for six consecutive years.

Exam Probability: **High**

3. *Answer choices:*
(see index for correct answer)

- a. Character
- b. process perspective
- c. surface-level diversity
- d. functional perspective

Guidance: level 1

:: ::

Business is the activity of making one's living or making money by producing or buying and selling products . Simply put, it is "any activity or enterprise entered into for profit. It does not mean it is a company, a corporation, partnership, or have any such formal organization, but it can range from a street peddler to General Motors."

Exam Probability: **Low**

4. *Answer choices:*

(see index for correct answer)

- a. Firm
- b. interpersonal communication
- c. deep-level diversity
- d. corporate values

Guidance: level 1

:: Stock market ::

_____ is a form of corporate equity ownership, a type of security. The terms voting share and ordinary share are also used frequently in other parts of the world; " _____ " being primarily used in the United States. They are known as Equity shares or Ordinary shares in the UK and other Commonwealth realms. This type of share gives the stockholder the right to share in the profits of the company, and to vote on matters of corporate policy and the composition of the members of the board of directors.

Exam Probability: **High**

5. *Answer choices:*

(see index for correct answer)

- a. Chip
- b. Scrip issue
- c. Direct public offering
- d. Common stock

Guidance: level 1

:: Bonds (finance) ::

A _____ is a fund established by an economic entity by setting aside revenue over a period of time to fund a future capital expense, or repayment of a long-term debt.

Exam Probability: **Low**

6. *Answer choices:*
(see index for correct answer)

- a. Arirang bond
- b. Bond option
- c. Dirty price
- d. coupon rate

Guidance: level 1

:: Management accounting ::

In finance, the _____ or net present worth applies to a series of cash flows occurring at different times. The present value of a cash flow depends on the interval of time between now and the cash flow. It also depends on the discount rate. NPV accounts for the time value of money. It provides a method for evaluating and comparing capital projects or financial products with cash flows spread over time, as in loans, investments, payouts from insurance contracts plus many other applications.

Exam Probability: **Medium**

7. *Answer choices:*
(see index for correct answer)

- a. Net present value
- b. Institute of Cost and Management Accountants of Bangladesh
- c. Holding cost
- d. Managerial risk accounting

Guidance: level 1

:: Mutualism (movement) ::

A _____ is a professionally managed investment fund that pools money from many investors to purchase securities. These investors may be retail or institutional in nature.

Exam Probability: **High**

8. *Answer choices:*
(see index for correct answer)

- a. Ayni
- b. United States Federation of Worker Cooperatives
- c. Benefit society
- d. Co-buying

Guidance: level 1

:: Government bonds ::

A _____ or sovereign bond is a bond issued by a national government, generally with a promise to pay periodic interest payments called coupon payments and to repay the face value on the maturity date. The aim of a _____ is to support government spending. _____ s are usually denominated in the country's own currency, in which case the government cannot be forced to default, although it may choose to do so. If a government is close to default on its debt the media often refer to this as a sovereign debt crisis.

Exam Probability: **Low**

9. *Answer choices:*
(see index for correct answer)

- a. Certificate of Annuity
- b. Climate bond
- c. Risk-free bond
- d. Government bond

Guidance: level 1

:: Personal finance ::

_____ is income not spent, or deferred consumption. Methods of _____ include putting money aside in, for example, a deposit account, a pension account, an investment fund, or as cash. _____ also involves reducing expenditures, such as recurring costs. In terms of personal finance, _____ generally specifies low-risk preservation of money, as in a deposit account, versus investment, wherein risk is a lot higher; in economics more broadly, it refers to any income not used for immediate consumption.

Exam Probability: **Low**

10. *Answer choices:*

(see index for correct answer)

- a. Saving
- b. Moneylender
- c. Personal Equity Plan
- d. Asset location

Guidance: level 1

:: Income taxes ::

An _____ is a tax imposed on individuals or entities that varies with respective income or profits . _____ generally is computed as the product of a tax rate times taxable income. Taxation rates may vary by type or characteristics of the taxpayer.

Exam Probability: **Medium**

11. *Answer choices:*

(see index for correct answer)

- a. Income and Corporation Taxes Act 1970
- b. Income Tax Act 1842
- c. Income tax in Spain
- d. Income tax

Guidance: level 1

:: Investment ::

_____ , and investment appraisal, is the planning process used to determine whether an organization's long term investments such as new machinery, replacement of machinery, new plants, new products, and research development projects are worth the funding of cash through the firm's capitalization structure . It is the process of allocating resources for major capital, or investment, expenditures. One of the primary goals of _____ investments is to increase the value of the firm to the shareholders.

Exam Probability: **Medium**

12. *Answer choices:*
(see index for correct answer)

- a. Spell Capital Partners
- b. Indo Premier Investment Management
- c. Capital budgeting
- d. Fund administration

Guidance: level 1

:: Social security ::

_____ is "any government system that provides monetary assistance to people with an inadequate or no income." In the United States, this is usually called welfare or a social safety net, especially when talking about Canada and European countries.

Exam Probability: **High**

13. *Answer choices:*
(see index for correct answer)

- a. Social insurance
- b. Government Service Insurance System
- c. Total Social Security Accounts
- d. Social security

Guidance: level 1

:: Stock market ::

_____ is freedom from, or resilience against, potential harm caused by others. Beneficiaries of _____ may be of persons and social groups, objects and institutions, ecosystems or any other entity or phenomenon vulnerable to unwanted change by its environment.

Exam Probability: **Medium**

14. *Answer choices:*
(see index for correct answer)

- a. Wash trade
- b. Profit warning
- c. Security
- d. Share price

Guidance: level 1

:: Elementary geometry ::

The _____ is the front of an animal's head that features three of the head's sense organs, the eyes, nose, and mouth, and through which animals express many of their emotions. The _____ is crucial for human identity, and damage such as scarring or developmental deformities affects the psyche adversely.

Exam Probability: **Low**

15. *Answer choices:*
(see index for correct answer)

- a. Parallel postulate
- b. Hyperbolic sector
- c. Central angle
- d. Face

Guidance: level 1

:: Costs ::

In economics, _____ is the total economic cost of production and is made up of variable cost, which varies according to the quantity of a good produced and includes inputs such as labour and raw materials, plus fixed cost, which is independent of the quantity of a good produced and includes inputs that cannot be varied in the short term: fixed costs such as buildings and machinery, including sunk costs if any. Since cost is measured per unit of time, it is a flow variable.

Exam Probability: **Medium**

16. *Answer choices:*
(see index for correct answer)

- a. Cost curve
- b. Total cost
- c. Road Logistics Costing in South Africa
- d. Flyaway cost

Guidance: level 1

:: ::

_____ is a means of protection from financial loss. It is a form of risk management, primarily used to hedge against the risk of a contingent or uncertain loss

Exam Probability: **Low**

17. *Answer choices:*
(see index for correct answer)

- a. deep-level diversity
- b. imperative
- c. Insurance
- d. interpersonal communication

Guidance: level 1

:: ::

_____ is the withdrawal from one's position or occupation or from one's active working life. A person may also semi-retire by reducing work hours.

18. *Answer choices:*

(see index for correct answer)

- a. surface-level diversity
- b. deep-level diversity
- c. process perspective
- d. functional perspective

Guidance: level 1

:: Business law ::

A _____ , also known as the sole trader, individual entrepreneurship or proprietorship, is a type of enterprise that is owned and run by one person and in which there is no legal distinction between the owner and the business entity. A sole trader does not necessarily work `alone`—it is possible for the sole trader to employ other people.

Exam Probability: **Low**

19. *Answer choices:*

(see index for correct answer)

- a. Independent contractor
- b. Business license
- c. Forward-looking statement
- d. Retroactive overtime

Guidance: level 1

:: Separation of investment and commercial banking ::

A _____ is a type of bank that provides services such as accepting deposits, making business loans, and offering basic investment products that is operated as a business for profit.

Exam Probability: **Medium**

20. *Answer choices:*

(see index for correct answer)

- a. Commercial bank
- b. Bancassurance
- c. GLBA

- d. Merchant bank

Guidance: level 1

:: Financial accounting ::

_____ is the value of all the non-financial and financial assets owned by an institutional unit or sector minus the value of all its outstanding liabilities. Since financial assets minus outstanding liabilities equal net financial assets, _____ can also be conveniently expressed as non-financial assets plus net financial assets. _____ can apply to companies, individuals, governments or economic sectors such as the sector of financial corporations or to entire countries.

Exam Probability: **Medium**

21. *Answer choices:*
(see index for correct answer)

- a. Net worth
- b. Holding gains
- c. Certified Public Accountants Association
- d. Convenience translation

Guidance: level 1

:: Accounting in the United States ::

_____ is the title of qualified accountants in numerous countries in the English-speaking world. In the United States, the CPA is a license to provide accounting services to the public. It is awarded by each of the 50 states for practice in that state. Additionally, almost every state has passed mobility laws to allow CPAs from other states to practice in their state. State licensing requirements vary, but the minimum standard requirements include passing the Uniform _____ Examination, 150 semester units of college education, and one year of accounting related experience.

Exam Probability: **Low**

22. *Answer choices:*
(see index for correct answer)

- a. Certified Public Accountant
- b. Financial Accounting Foundation

- c. Other comprehensive basis of accounting
- d. Variable interest entity

Guidance: level 1

:: Corporate governance ::

The _____ is the officer of a company that has primary responsibility for managing the company's finances, including financial planning, management of financial risks, record-keeping, and financial reporting. In some sectors, the CFO is also responsible for analysis of data. Some CFOs have the title CFOO for chief financial and operating officer. In the United Kingdom, the typical term for a CFO is finance director . The CFO typically reports to the chief executive officer and the board of directors and may additionally have a seat on the board. The CFO supervises the finance unit and is the chief financial spokesperson for the organization. The CFO directly assists the chief operating officer on all strategic and tactical matters relating to budget management, cost–benefit analysis, forecasting needs, and securing of new funding.

Exam Probability: **High**

23. *Answer choices:*
(see index for correct answer)

- a. InfoSTEP
- b. Digital strategy manager
- c. Frank E. Sheeder III
- d. AS 8015

Guidance: level 1

:: Materials ::

A _____ , also known as a feedstock, unprocessed material, or primary commodity, is a basic material that is used to produce goods, finished products, energy, or intermediate materials which are feedstock for future finished products. As feedstock, the term connotes these materials are bottleneck assets and are highly important with regard to producing other products. An example of this is crude oil, which is a _____ and a feedstock used in the production of industrial chemicals, fuels, plastics, and pharmaceutical goods; lumber is a _____ used to produce a variety of products including all types of furniture. The term " _____ " denotes materials in minimally processed or unprocessed in states; e.g., raw latex, crude oil, cotton, coal, raw biomass, iron ore, air, logs, or water i.e. "...any product of agriculture, forestry, fishing and any other mineral that is in its natural form or which has undergone the transformation required to prepare it for internationally marketing in substantial volumes."

Exam Probability: **Medium**

24. *Answer choices:*
(see index for correct answer)

- a. Raw material
- b. Slag
- c. Agamassan
- d. Sealant

Guidance: level 1

:: Markets (customer bases) ::

In economics, _____ is the economic price for which a good or service is offered in the marketplace. It is of interest mainly in the study of microeconomics. Market value and _____ are equal only under conditions of market efficiency, equilibrium, and rational expectations.

Exam Probability: **High**

25. *Answer choices:*
(see index for correct answer)

- a. Vertical market
- b. Captive market
- c. Two-sided market
- d. Market price

:: Investment ::

The _____ is a measure of an investment's rate of return. The term internal refers to the fact that the calculation excludes external factors, such as the risk-free rate, inflation, the cost of capital, or various financial risks.

Exam Probability: **Medium**

26. *Answer choices:*
(see index for correct answer)

- a. Internal rate of return
- b. Dispersion
- c. Strategic block investing
- d. Price return

:: Budgets ::

A _____ is a financial plan for a defined period, often one year. It may also include planned sales volumes and revenues, resource quantities, costs and expenses, assets, liabilities and cash flows. Companies, governments, families and other organizations use it to express strategic plans of activities or events in measurable terms.

Exam Probability: **Medium**

27. *Answer choices:*
(see index for correct answer)

- a. Budget
- b. Operating budget
- c. Budgeted cost of work scheduled
- d. Black budget

:: ::

In the broadest sense, _____ is any practice which contributes to the sale of products to a retail consumer. At a retail in-store level, _____ refers to the variety of products available for sale and the display of those products in such a way that it stimulates interest and entices customers to make a purchase.

Exam Probability: **Low**

28. *Answer choices:*

(see index for correct answer)

- a. information systems assessment
- b. Merchandising
- c. interpersonal communication
- d. deep-level diversity

Guidance: level 1

:: Financial markets ::

A _____ is a market in which people trade financial securities and derivatives such as futures and options at low transaction costs. Securities include stocks and bonds, and precious metals.

Exam Probability: **Medium**

29. *Answer choices:*

(see index for correct answer)

- a. Convergence trade
- b. Financial market
- c. Lit pool
- d. Advanced Computerized Execution System

Guidance: level 1

:: Money ::

Cash and _____ s are the most liquid current assets found on a business's balance sheet. _____ s are short-term commitments "with temporarily idle cash and easily convertible into a known cash amount". An investment normally counts to be a _____ when it has a short maturity period of 90 days or less, and can be included in the cash and _____ s balance from the date of acquisition when it carries an insignificant risk of changes in the asset value; with more than 90 days maturity, the asset is not considered as cash and _____ s. Equity investments mostly are excluded from _____ s, unless they are essentially _____ s, for instance, if the preferred shares acquired within a short maturity period and with specified recovery date.

Exam Probability: **High**

30. *Answer choices:*
(see index for correct answer)

- a. Key money
- b. Plutus
- c. Automated cash handling
- d. Cash equivalent

Guidance: level 1

:: Banking ::

A _____ is a financial account maintained by a bank for a customer. A _____ can be a deposit account, a credit card account, a current account, or any other type of account offered by a financial institution, and represents the funds that a customer has entrusted to the financial institution and from which the customer can make withdrawals. Alternatively, accounts may be loan accounts in which case the customer owes money to the financial institution.

Exam Probability: **High**

31. *Answer choices:*
(see index for correct answer)

- a. Branch manager
- b. Correlation swap
- c. Bank account
- d. Zombie bank

Guidance: level 1

_____ of something is, in finance, the adding together of interest or different investments over a period of time. It holds specific meanings in accounting, where it can refer to accounts on a balance sheet that represent liabilities and non-cash-based assets used in _____ -based accounting. These types of accounts include, among others, accounts payable, accounts receivable, goodwill, deferred tax liability and future interest expense.

Exam Probability: **Medium**

32. *Answer choices:*
(see index for correct answer)

- a. Cash flow management
- b. Chart of accounts
- c. Account
- d. Share premium

Guidance: level 1

_____ s are costs that change as the quantity of the good or service that a business produces changes. _____ s are the sum of marginal costs over all units produced. They can also be considered normal costs. Fixed costs and _____ s make up the two components of total cost. Direct costs are costs that can easily be associated with a particular cost object. However, not all _____ s are direct costs. For example, variable manufacturing overhead costs are _____ s that are indirect costs, not direct costs. _____ s are sometimes called unit-level costs as they vary with the number of units produced.

Exam Probability: **Medium**

33. *Answer choices:*
(see index for correct answer)

- a. Average per-bit delivery cost
- b. activity based costing
- c. Notional profit
- d. Overhead

:: Financial ratios ::

_____ is the difference between revenue and cost of goods sold divided by revenue. _____ is expressed as a percentage. Generally, it is calculated as the selling price of an item, less the cost of goods sold . _____ is often used interchangeably with Gross Profit, but the terms are different. When speaking about a monetary amount, it is technically correct to use the term Gross Profit; when referring to a percentage or ratio, it is correct to use _____ . In other words, _____ is a percentage value, while Gross Profit is a monetary value.

Exam Probability: **High**

34. *Answer choices:*
(see index for correct answer)

- a. Return on event
- b. AlphaIC
- c. Return on capital employed
- d. Statutory liquidity ratio

:: Management accounting ::

_____ are costs that are not directly accountable to a cost object . _____ may be either fixed or variable. _____ include administration, personnel and security costs. These are those costs which are not directly related to production. Some _____ may be overhead. But some overhead costs can be directly attributed to a project and are direct costs.

Exam Probability: **High**

35. *Answer choices:*
(see index for correct answer)

- a. Resource consumption accounting
- b. Construction accounting
- c. Indirect costs
- d. Pre-determined overhead rate

:: Generally Accepted Accounting Principles ::

An _____ or profit and loss account is one of the financial statements of a company and shows the company's revenues and expenses during a particular period.

Exam Probability: **High**

36. *Answer choices:*

(see index for correct answer)

- a. Write-off
- b. Treasury stock
- c. Fixed investment
- d. Cash method of accounting

Guidance: level 1

:: Financial markets ::

_____ s are monetary contracts between parties. They can be created, traded, modified and settled. They can be cash , evidence of an ownership interest in an entity , or a contractual right to receive or deliver cash .

Exam Probability: **Medium**

37. *Answer choices:*

(see index for correct answer)

- a. Price-weighted
- b. Convergence trade
- c. Ultra-low latency direct market access
- d. Financial instrument

Guidance: level 1

:: Income ::

_____ is a ratio between the net profit and cost of investment resulting from an investment of some resources. A high ROI means the investment's gains favorably to its cost. As a performance measure, ROI is used to evaluate the efficiency of an investment or to compare the efficiencies of several different investments. In purely economic terms, it is one way of relating profits to capital invested. _____ is a performance measure used by businesses to identify the efficiency of an investment or number of different investments.

Exam Probability: **High**

38. *Answer choices:*
(see index for correct answer)

- a. Property investment calculator
- b. Return on investment
- c. Net national income
- d. Family income

Guidance: level 1

:: Insolvency ::

_____ is the process in accounting by which a company is brought to an end in the United Kingdom, Republic of Ireland and United States. The assets and property of the company are redistributed. _____ is also sometimes referred to as winding-up or dissolution, although dissolution technically refers to the last stage of _____ . The process of _____ also arises when customs, an authority or agency in a country responsible for collecting and safeguarding customs duties, determines the final computation or ascertainment of the duties or drawback accruing on an entry.

Exam Probability: **High**

39. *Answer choices:*
(see index for correct answer)

- a. Liquidator
- b. United Kingdom insolvency law
- c. Debt consolidation
- d. Insolvency

Guidance: level 1

_____ is the quantity of three-dimensional space enclosed by a closed surface, for example, the space that a substance or shape occupies or contains. _____ is often quantified numerically using the SI derived unit, the cubic metre. The _____ of a container is generally understood to be the capacity of the container; i. e., the amount of fluid that the container could hold, rather than the amount of space the container itself displaces. Three dimensional mathematical shapes are also assigned _____ s. _____ s of some simple shapes, such as regular, straight-edged, and circular shapes can be easily calculated using arithmetic formulas. _____ s of complicated shapes can be calculated with integral calculus if a formula exists for the shape`s boundary. One-dimensional figures and two-dimensional shapes are assigned zero _____ in the three-dimensional space.

Exam Probability: **Low**

40. *Answer choices:*
(see index for correct answer)

- a. personal values
- b. similarity-attraction theory
- c. deep-level diversity
- d. Volume

Guidance: level 1

:: Accounting terminology ::

Total _____ is a method of Accounting cost which entails the full cost of manufacturing or providing a service. TAC includes not just the costs of materials and labour, but also of all manufacturing overheads . The cost of each cost center can be direct or indirect. The direct cost can be easily identified with individual cost centers. Whereas indirect cost cannot be easily identified with the cost center. The distribution of overhead among the departments is called apportionment.

Exam Probability: **High**

41. *Answer choices:*
(see index for correct answer)

- a. Share premium

- b. Absorption costing
- c. Enterprise liquidity
- d. Adjusting entries

Guidance: level 1

:: ::

In production, research, retail, and accounting, a _____ is the value of money that has been used up to produce something or deliver a service, and hence is not available for use anymore. In business, the _____ may be one of acquisition, in which case the amount of money expended to acquire it is counted as _____ . In this case, money is the input that is gone in order to acquire the thing. This acquisition _____ may be the sum of the _____ of production as incurred by the original producer, and further _____ s of transaction as incurred by the acquirer over and above the price paid to the producer. Usually, the price also includes a mark-up for profit over the _____ of production.

Exam Probability: **Medium**

42. *Answer choices:*
(see index for correct answer)

- a. surface-level diversity
- b. personal values
- c. Cost
- d. corporate values

Guidance: level 1

:: Marketing ::

A _____ is an overall experience of a customer that distinguishes an organization or product from its rivals in the eyes of the customer. _____ s are used in business, marketing, and advertising. Name _____ s are sometimes distinguished from generic or store _____ s.

Exam Probability: **Low**

43. *Answer choices:*
(see index for correct answer)

- a. Postmodern branding

- b. Interactive marketing
- c. Brand
- d. Instant rebate

Guidance: level 1

:: Banking ::

_____ refers to a broad area of finance involving the collection, handling, and usage of cash. It involves assessing market liquidity, cash flow, and investments.

Exam Probability: **Medium**

44. *Answer choices:*
(see index for correct answer)

- a. Clap note
- b. Peer-to-peer banking
- c. Arranger
- d. Bank transaction tax

Guidance: level 1

:: Expense ::

_____ relates to the cost of borrowing money. It is the price that a lender charges a borrower for the use of the lender's money. On the income statement, _____ can represent the cost of borrowing money from banks, bond investors, and other sources. _____ is different from operating expense and CAPEX, for it relates to the capital structure of a company, and it is usually tax-deductible.

Exam Probability: **High**

45. *Answer choices:*
(see index for correct answer)

- a. Tax expense
- b. Interest expense
- c. Expense account
- d. Momentem

Guidance: level 1

:: Inventory ::

It requires a detailed physical count, so that the company knows exactly how many of each goods brought on specific dates remained at year end inventory. When this information is found, the amount of goods are multiplied by their purchase cost at their purchase date, to get a number for the ending inventory cost.

Exam Probability: **Medium**

46. *Answer choices:*
(see index for correct answer)

- a. Reorder point
- b. Perpetual inventory
- c. Cost of goods available for sale
- d. Specific identification

Guidance: level 1

:: Loans ::

In corporate finance, a _____ is a medium- to long-term debt instrument used by large companies to borrow money, at a fixed rate of interest. The legal term " _____ " originally referred to a document that either creates a debt or acknowledges it, but in some countries the term is now used interchangeably with bond, loan stock or note. A _____ is thus like a certificate of loan or a loan bond evidencing the fact that the company is liable to pay a specified amount with interest and although the money raised by the _____ s becomes a part of the company`s capital structure, it does not become share capital. Senior _____ s get paid before subordinate _____ s, and there are varying rates of risk and payoff for these categories.

Exam Probability: **Medium**

47. *Answer choices:*
(see index for correct answer)

- a. Debenture
- b. Loan shark
- c. Industrial loan company
- d. Due-on-sale clause

Guidance: level 1

An _____ is a systematic and independent examination of books, accounts, statutory records, documents and vouchers of an organization to ascertain how far the financial statements as well as non-financial disclosures present a true and fair view of the concern. It also attempts to ensure that the books of accounts are properly maintained by the concern as required by law. _____ ing has become such a ubiquitous phenomenon in the corporate and the public sector that academics started identifying an " _____ Society". The _____ or perceives and recognises the propositions before them for examination, obtains evidence, evaluates the same and formulates an opinion on the basis of his judgement which is communicated through their _____ ing report.

Exam Probability: **High**

48. *Answer choices:*
(see index for correct answer)

- a. imperative
- b. co-culture
- c. similarity-attraction theory
- d. Audit

Guidance: level 1

:: International taxation ::

_____ is the levying of tax by two or more jurisdictions on the same declared income , asset , or financial transaction . Double liability is mitigated in a number of ways, for example.

Exam Probability: **Medium**

49. *Answer choices:*
(see index for correct answer)

- a. Destination principle
- b. Passive foreign investment company
- c. Double taxation
- d. Advance pricing agreement

Guidance: level 1

:: Marketing ::

A _____ is something that is necessary for an organism to live a healthy life. _____ s are distinguished from wants in that, in the case of a _____ , a deficiency causes a clear adverse outcome: a dysfunction or death. In other words, a _____ is something required for a safe, stable and healthy life while a want is a desire, wish or aspiration. When _____ s or wants are backed by purchasing power, they have the potential to become economic demands.

Exam Probability: **Low**

50. *Answer choices:*
(see index for correct answer)

- a. Marketing Week
- b. Editorial calendar
- c. Meta marketing
- d. Markup

Guidance: level 1

:: Inventory ::

_____ is a system of inventory in which updates are made on a periodic basis. This differs from perpetual inventory systems, where updates are made as seen fit.

Exam Probability: **Medium**

51. *Answer choices:*
(see index for correct answer)

- a. Periodic inventory
- b. Inventory bounce
- c. Cost of goods sold
- d. Stock-taking

Guidance: level 1

:: Stock market ::

A _____ , securities exchange or bourse, is a facility where stock brokers and traders can buy and sell securities, such as shares of stock and bonds and other financial instruments. _____ s may also provide for facilities the issue and redemption of such securities and instruments and capital events including the payment of income and dividends. Securities traded on a _____ include stock issued by listed companies, unit trusts, derivatives, pooled investment products and bonds. _____ s often function as "continuous auction" markets with buyers and sellers consummating transactions via open outcry at a central location such as the floor of the exchange or by using an electronic trading platform.

Exam Probability: **High**

52. *Answer choices:*

(see index for correct answer)

- a. GXG Markets
- b. Contract for difference
- c. Stock exchange
- d. Paper valuation

Guidance: level 1

:: Government bonds ::

A _____ , commonly known as a Muni Bond, is a bond issued by a local government or territory, or one of their agencies. It is generally used to finance public projects such as roads, schools, airports and seaports, and infrastructure-related repairs. The term _____ is commonly used in the United States, which has the largest market of such trade-able securities in the world. As of 2011, the _____ market was valued at $3.7 trillion. Potential issuers of _____ s include states, cities, counties, redevelopment agencies, special-purpose districts, school districts, public utility districts, publicly owned airports and seaports, and other governmental entities at or below the state level having more than a de minimis amount of one of the three sovereign powers: the power of taxation, the power of eminent domain or the police power.

Exam Probability: **Low**

53. *Answer choices:*

(see index for correct answer)

- a. Climate bond
- b. Gilt-edged
- c. Sovereign bond
- d. Texas v. White

Guidance: level 1

:: Marketing ::

_____ or stock is the goods and materials that a business holds for the ultimate goal of resale .

Exam Probability: **Medium**

54. *Answer choices:*
(see index for correct answer)

- a. Mass market
- b. Inventory
- c. Customer franchise
- d. BEC

Guidance: level 1

:: ::

An _____ is an asset that lacks physical substance. It is defined in opposition to physical assets such as machinery and buildings. An _____ is usually very hard to evaluate. Patents, copyrights, franchises, goodwill, trademarks, and trade names. The general interpretation also includes software and other intangible computer based assets are all examples of _____ s. _____ s generally—though not necessarily—suffer from typical market failures of non-rivalry and non-excludability.

Exam Probability: **High**

55. *Answer choices:*
(see index for correct answer)

- a. Sarbanes-Oxley act of 2002
- b. deep-level diversity
- c. Intangible asset
- d. hierarchical perspective

Guidance: level 1

A shareholder is an individual or institution that legally owns one or more shares of stock in a public or private corporation. Shareholders may be referred to as members of a corporation. Legally, a person is not a shareholder in a corporation until their name and other details are entered in the corporation's register of shareholders or members.

Exam Probability: **Low**

56. *Answer choices:*
(see index for correct answer)

- a. corporate values
- b. cultural
- c. Sarbanes-Oxley act of 2002
- d. Stockholder

Guidance: level 1

A _____ is a fund into which a sum of money is added during an employee's employment years, and from which payments are drawn to support the person's retirement from work in the form of periodic payments. A _____ may be a "defined benefit plan" where a fixed sum is paid regularly to a person, or a "defined contribution plan" under which a fixed sum is invested and then becomes available at retirement age. _____ s should not be confused with severance pay; the former is usually paid in regular installments for life after retirement, while the latter is typically paid as a fixed amount after involuntary termination of employment prior to retirement.

Exam Probability: **Low**

57. *Answer choices:*
(see index for correct answer)

- a. Pension
- b. surface-level diversity
- c. personal values
- d. similarity-attraction theory

Guidance: level 1

A _____ , publicly-traded company, publicly-held company, publicly-listed company, or public limited company is a corporation whose ownership is dispersed among the general public in many shares of stock which are freely traded on a stock exchange or in over-the-counter markets. In some jurisdictions, public companies over a certain size must be listed on an exchange. A _____ can be listed or unlisted .

Exam Probability: **High**

58. *Answer choices:*
(see index for correct answer)

- a. Creative director
- b. SIMPLE Group
- c. High-net-worth individual
- d. Public company

Guidance: level 1

:: Accounting terminology ::

_____ is a legally enforceable claim for payment held by a business for goods supplied and/or services rendered that customers/clients have ordered but not paid for. These are generally in the form of invoices raised by a business and delivered to the customer for payment within an agreed time frame.

_____ is shown in a balance sheet as an asset. It is one of a series of accounting transactions dealing with the billing of a customer for goods and services that the customer has ordered. These may be distinguished from notes receivable, which are debts created through formal legal instruments called promissory notes.

Exam Probability: **Low**

59. *Answer choices:*
(see index for correct answer)

- a. Share premium
- b. Chart of accounts
- c. Capital appreciation
- d. Mark-to-market

Guidance: level 1

Human resource management

Human resource (HR) management is the strategic approach to the effective management of organization workers so that they help the business gain a competitive advantage. It is designed to maximize employee performance in service of an employer's strategic objectives. HR is primarily concerned with the management of people within organizations, focusing on policies and on systems. HR departments are responsible for overseeing employee-benefits design, employee recruitment, training and development, performance appraisal, and rewarding (e.g., managing pay and benefit systems). HR also concerns itself with organizational change and industrial relations, that is, the balancing of organizational practices with requirements arising from collective bargaining and from governmental laws.

:: United States federal labor legislation ::

The _____ of 1988 is a United States federal law that generally prevents employers from using polygraph tests, either for pre-employment screening or during the course of employment, with certain exemptions.

Exam Probability: **Medium**

1. *Answer choices:*

(see index for correct answer)

- a. Landrum-Griffin Act
- b. Reliable Home Heating Act
- c. Employee Polygraph Protection Act
- d. Federal Emergency Relief Administration

Guidance: level 1

:: Management ::

The term _____ refers to measures designed to increase the degree of autonomy and self-determination in people and in communities in order to enable them to represent their interests in a responsible and self-determined way, acting on their own authority. It is the process of becoming stronger and more confident, especially in controlling one`s life and claiming one`s rights.

_____ as action refers both to the process of self-_____ and to professional support of people, which enables them to overcome their sense of powerlessness and lack of influence, and to recognize and use their resources. To do work with power.

Exam Probability: **Medium**

2. *Answer choices:*
(see index for correct answer)

- a. Project management
- b. Empowerment
- c. Mission critical
- d. Vorstand

Guidance: level 1

:: Employment ::

A _____, a concept developed in contemporary research by organizational scholar Denise Rousseau, represents the mutual beliefs, perceptions and informal obligations between an employer and an employee. It sets the dynamics for the relationship and defines the detailed practicality of the work to be done. It is distinguishable from the formal written contract of employment which, for the most part, only identifies mutual duties and responsibilities in a generalized form.

Exam Probability: **Medium**

3. *Answer choices:*
(see index for correct answer)

- a. Employment Development Department
- b. Shift work sleep disorder
- c. Psychological contract
- d. Academic job market

Guidance: level 1

:: Unemployment ::

_____ is the support service provided by responsible organizations, keen to support individuals who are exiting the business – to help former employees transition to new jobs and help them re-orient themselves in the job market. A consultancy firm usually provides the _____ services which are paid for by the former employer and are achieved usually through practical advice, training materials and workshops. Some companies may offer psychological support.

Exam Probability: **Low**

4. *Answer choices:*
(see index for correct answer)

- a. Texas Workforce Commission
- b. Frictional unemployment
- c. Outplacement
- d. Growth recession

Guidance: level 1

:: Termination of employment ::

The _____ of 1988 is a US labor law which protects employees, their families, and communities by requiring most employers with 100 or more employees to provide 60 calendar-day advance notification of plant closings and mass layoffs of employees, as defined in the Act. In 2001, there were about 2,000 mass layoffs and plant closures which were subject to WARN advance notice requirements and which affected about 660,000 employees.

Exam Probability: **Low**

5. *Answer choices:*
(see index for correct answer)

- a. Notice period
- b. Worker Adjustment and Retraining Notification Act
- c. Termination of Employment Convention, 1982
- d. Letter of resignation

Guidance: level 1

:: ::

The _____ of 1938 29 U.S.C. § 203 is a United States labor law that creates the right to a minimum wage, and "time-and-a-half" overtime pay when people work over forty hours a week. It also prohibits most employment of minors in "oppressive child labor". It applies to employees engaged in interstate commerce or employed by an enterprise engaged in commerce or in the production of goods for commerce, unless the employer can claim an exemption from coverage.

Exam Probability: **Medium**

6. *Answer choices:*

(see index for correct answer)

- a. interpersonal communication
- b. Fair Labor Standards Act
- c. personal values
- d. deep-level diversity

Guidance: level 1

:: Industrial relations ::

_____ or employee satisfaction is a measure of workers' contentedness with their job, whether or not they like the job or individual aspects or facets of jobs, such as nature of work or supervision. _____ can be measured in cognitive , affective , and behavioral components. Researchers have also noted that _____ measures vary in the extent to which they measure feelings about the job . or cognitions about the job .

Exam Probability: **Low**

7. *Answer choices:*

(see index for correct answer)

- a. Industrial violence
- b. Job satisfaction
- c. Injury prevention
- d. European Journal of Industrial Relations

Guidance: level 1

:: Human resource management ::

_____ is athletic training in sports other than the athlete's usual sport. The goal is improving overall performance. It takes advantage of the particular effectiveness of one training method to negate the shortcomings of another.

Exam Probability: **High**

8. *Answer choices:*
(see index for correct answer)

- a. Job sharing
- b. Employment testing
- c. Voluntary redundancy
- d. Cross-training

Guidance: level 1

:: Occupational safety and health ::

A safety data sheet , _____ , or product safety data sheet is a document that lists information relating to occupational safety and health for the use of various substances and products. SDSs are a widely used system for cataloging information on chemicals, chemical compounds, and chemical mixtures. SDS information may include instructions for the safe use and potential hazards associated with a particular material or product, along with spill-handling procedures. SDS formats can vary from source to source within a country depending on national requirements.

Exam Probability: **High**

9. *Answer choices:*
(see index for correct answer)

- a. Kazutaka Kogi
- b. Material safety data sheet
- c. Safe Work Procedure
- d. Wet Bulb Globe Temperature

Guidance: level 1

:: Human resource management ::

_____ are the people who make up the workforce of an organization, business sector, or economy. "Human capital" is sometimes used synonymously with " _____ ", although human capital typically refers to a narrower effect . Likewise, other terms sometimes used include manpower, talent, labor, personnel, or simply people.

Exam Probability: **Medium**

10. *Answer choices:*
(see index for correct answer)

- a. Senior management
- b. Multiculturalism
- c. Incentive program
- d. Selection ratio

Guidance: level 1

:: Outsourcing ::

_____ is the relocation of a business process from one country to another—typically an operational process, such as manufacturing, or supporting processes, such as accounting. Typically this refers to a company business, although state governments may also employ _____ . More recently, technical and administrative services have been offshored.

Exam Probability: **High**

11. *Answer choices:*
(see index for correct answer)

- a. Offshoring
- b. Vested outsourcing
- c. Chinggis Technologies
- d. Website Management Outsourcing

Guidance: level 1

:: Unemployment by country ::

Unemployment benefits are payments made by back authorized bodies to unemployed people. In the United States, benefits are funded by a compulsory governmental insurance system, not taxes on individual citizens. Depending on the jurisdiction and the status of the person, those sums may be small, covering only basic needs, or may compensate the lost time proportionally to the previous earned salary.

Exam Probability: **Low**

12. *Answer choices:*

(see index for correct answer)

- a. Unemployment in Poland
- b. Unemployment insurance
- c. Unemployment in Brazil

Guidance: level 1

:: United States employment discrimination case law ::

_____ , 411 U.S. 792 , is a US employment law case by the United States Supreme Court regarding the burdens and nature of proof in proving a Title VII case and the order in which plaintiffs and defendants present proof. It was the seminal case in the McDonnell Douglas burden-shifting framework.

Exam Probability: **High**

13. *Answer choices:*

(see index for correct answer)

- a. Gross v. FBL Financial Services, Inc.
- b. New York City Transit Authority v. Beazer
- c. Kloeckner v. Solis
- d. Vance v. Ball State University

Guidance: level 1

:: ::

_____ is a belief that hard work and diligence have a moral benefit and an inherent ability, virtue or value to strengthen character and individual abilities. It is a set of values centered on importance of work and manifested by determination or desire to work hard. Social ingrainment of this value is considered to enhance character through hard work that is respective to an individual's field of work.

Exam Probability: **High**

14. *Answer choices:*
(see index for correct answer)

- a. interpersonal communication
- b. hierarchical perspective
- c. Work ethic
- d. Character

Guidance: level 1

:: Employee relations ::

_____ ownership, or employee share ownership, is an ownership interest in a company held by the company's workforce. The ownership interest may be facilitated by the company as part of employees' remuneration or incentive compensation for work performed, or the company itself may be employee owned.

Exam Probability: **Low**

15. *Answer choices:*
(see index for correct answer)

- a. Employee morale
- b. Employee stock
- c. Employee motivation
- d. employee stock ownership

Guidance: level 1

:: Validity (statistics) ::

_____ is a type of evidence that can be gathered to defend the use of a test for predicting other outcomes. It is a parameter used in sociology, psychology, and other psychometric or behavioral sciences. _____ is demonstrated when a test correlates well with a measure that has previously been validated. The two measures may be for the same construct, but more often used for different, but presumably related, constructs.

Exam Probability: **High**

16. *Answer choices:*

(see index for correct answer)

- a. Incremental validity
- b. Concurrent validity
- c. Discriminant validity
- d. Content validity

Guidance: level 1

:: ::

A _____ is an occupation founded upon specialized educational training, the purpose of which is to supply disinterested objective counsel and service to others, for a direct and definite compensation, wholly apart from expectation of other business gain. The term is a truncation of the term "liberal _____ ", which is, in turn, an Anglicization of the French term " _____ libérale". Originally borrowed by English users in the 19th century, it has been re-borrowed by international users from the late 20th, though the class overtones of the term do not seem to survive retranslation: "liberal _____ s" are, according to the European Union's Directive on Recognition of _____ al Qualifications "those practiced on the basis of relevant _____ al qualifications in a personal, responsible and _____ ally independent capacity by those providing intellectual and conceptual services in the interest of the client and the public".

Exam Probability: **High**

17. *Answer choices:*

(see index for correct answer)

- a. Profession
- b. empathy
- c. surface-level diversity

- d. personal values

Guidance: level 1

:: ::

_____ refers to the overall process of attracting, shortlisting, selecting and appointing suitable candidates for jobs within an organization. _____ can also refer to processes involved in choosing individuals for unpaid roles. Managers, human resource generalists and _____ specialists may be tasked with carrying out _____ , but in some cases public-sector employment agencies, commercial _____ agencies, or specialist search consultancies are used to undertake parts of the process. Internet-based technologies which support all aspects of _____ have become widespread.

Exam Probability: **Medium**

18. *Answer choices:*

(see index for correct answer)

- a. similarity-attraction theory
- b. levels of analysis
- c. Sarbanes-Oxley act of 2002
- d. functional perspective

Guidance: level 1

:: Training ::

_____ is a phase of training needs analysis directed at identifying which individuals within an organization should receive training.

Exam Probability: **Low**

19. *Answer choices:*

(see index for correct answer)

- a. Instructor-led training
- b. Endurance training
- c. Person Analysis
- d. Voluntary Protection Program

Guidance: level 1

:: Production and manufacturing ::

_____ is a set of techniques and tools for process improvement. Though as a shortened form it may be found written as 6S, it should not be confused with the methodology known as 6S .

Exam Probability: **Low**

20. *Answer choices:*
(see index for correct answer)

- a. Fieldbus Foundation
- b. Six Sigma
- c. Job shop
- d. Process layout

Guidance: level 1

:: Unemployment ::

The _____ is the negative relationship between the levels of unemployment and wages that arises when these variables are expressed in local terms. According to David Blanchflower and Andrew Oswald , the _____ summarizes the fact that "A worker who is employed in an area of high unemployment earns less than an identical individual who works in a region with low joblessness."

Exam Probability: **Medium**

21. *Answer choices:*
(see index for correct answer)

- a. Unemployment Convention, 1919
- b. Growth recession
- c. Frictional unemployment
- d. Wage curve

Guidance: level 1

:: ::

In business strategy, _____ is establishing a competitive advantage by having the lowest cost of operation in the industry. _____ is often driven by company efficiency, size, scale, scope and cumulative experience .A _____ strategy aims to exploit scale of production, well-defined scope and other economies , producing highly standardized products, using advanced technology.In recent years, more and more companies have chosen a strategic mix to achieve market leadership. These patterns consist of simultaneous _____ , superior customer service and product leadership. Walmart has succeeded across the world due to its _____ strategy. The company has cut down on exesses at every point of production and thus are able to provide the consumers with quality products at low prices.

Exam Probability: **Medium**

22. *Answer choices:*
(see index for correct answer)

- a. process perspective
- b. personal values
- c. open system
- d. deep-level diversity

Guidance: level 1

:: ::

A _____ is the ability to carry out a task with determined results often within a given amount of time, energy, or both. _____ s can often be divided into domain-general and domain-specific _____ s. For example, in the domain of work, some general _____ s would include time management, teamwork and leadership, self-motivation and others, whereas domain-specific _____ s would be used only for a certain job. _____ usually requires certain environmental stimuli and situations to assess the level of _____ being shown and used.

Exam Probability: **Medium**

23. *Answer choices:*
(see index for correct answer)

- a. levels of analysis
- b. imperative
- c. hierarchical

- d. Skill

Guidance: level 1

:: Industrial engineering ::

_____ is the formal process that sits alongside Requirements analysis and focuses on the human elements of the requirements.

Exam Probability: **Low**

24. *Answer choices:*
(see index for correct answer)

- a. Needs analysis
- b. Health systems engineering
- c. Work Measurement
- d. Standard time

Guidance: level 1

:: ::

The causes of _____ are heavily debated. Classical economics, new classical economics, and the Austrian School of economics argued that market mechanisms are reliable means of resolving _____ . These theories argue against interventions imposed on the labor market from the outside, such as unionization, bureaucratic work rules, minimum wage laws, taxes, and other regulations that they claim discourage the hiring of workers. Keynesian economics emphasizes the cyclical nature of _____ and recommends government interventions in the economy that it claims will reduce _____ during recessions. This theory focuses on recurrent shocks that suddenly reduce aggregate demand for goods and services and thus reduce demand for workers. Keynesian models recommend government interventions designed to increase demand for workers; these can include financial stimuli, publicly funded job creation, and expansionist monetary policies. Its namesake economist, John Maynard Keynes, believed that the root cause of _____ is the desire of investors to receive more money rather than produce more products, which is not possible without public bodies producing new money. A third group of theories emphasize the need for a stable supply of capital and investment to maintain full employment. On this view, government should guarantee full employment through fiscal policy, monetary policy and trade policy as stated, for example, in the US Employment Act of 1946, by counteracting private sector or trade investment volatility, and reducing inequality.

Exam Probability: **Medium**

25. *Answer choices:*
(see index for correct answer)

- a. hierarchical perspective
- b. cultural
- c. Unemployment
- d. surface-level diversity

Guidance: level 1

:: Psychometrics ::

In statistics and research, _____ is typically a measure based on the correlations between different items on the same test . It measures whether several items that propose to measure the same general construct produce similar scores. For example, if a respondent expressed agreement with the statements "I like to ride bicycles" and "I've enjoyed riding bicycles in the past", and disagreement with the statement "I hate bicycles", this would be indicative of good _____ of the test.

Exam Probability: **Low**

26. *Answer choices:*
(see index for correct answer)

- a. Computer-Adaptive Sequential Testing
- b. Reproducibility
- c. Multidimensional scaling
- d. Psychometrics

Guidance: level 1

:: ::

_____ , also known as drug abuse, is a patterned use of a drug in which the user consumes the substance in amounts or with methods which are harmful to themselves or others, and is a form of substance-related disorder. Widely differing definitions of drug abuse are used in public health, medical and criminal justice contexts. In some cases criminal or anti-social behaviour occurs when the person is under the influence of a drug, and long term personality changes in individuals may occur as well. In addition to possible physical, social, and psychological harm, use of some drugs may also lead to criminal penalties, although these vary widely depending on the local jurisdiction.

Exam Probability: **Medium**

27. *Answer choices:*
(see index for correct answer)

- a. hierarchical
- b. similarity-attraction theory
- c. Substance abuse
- d. Sarbanes-Oxley act of 2002

Guidance: level 1

The _____ is a labor union in the United States and Canada. Formed in 1903 by the merger of The Team Drivers International Union and The Teamsters National Union, the union now represents a diverse membership of blue-collar and professional workers in both the public and private sectors. The union had approximately 1.3 million members in 2013. Formerly known as the _____, Chauffeurs, Warehousemen and Helpers of America, the IBT is a member of the Change to Win Federation and Canadian Labour Congress.

Exam Probability: **Medium**

28. *Answer choices:*
(see index for correct answer)

- a. Workers United
- b. Art Directors Guild
- c. International Brotherhood of Teamsters
- d. Aircraft Mechanics Fraternal Association

Guidance: level 1

_____ or occupational violence refers to violence, usually in the form of physical abuse or threat, that creates a risk to the health and safety of an employee or multiple employees. The National Institute for Occupational Safety and Health defines worker on worker, personal relationship, customer/client, and criminal intent all as categories of violence in the workplace. These four categories are further broken down into three levels: Level one displays early warning signs of violence, Level two is slightly more violent, and level three is significantly violent. Many workplaces have initiated programs and protocols to protect their workers as the Occupational Health Act of 1970 states that employers must provide an environment in which employees are free of harm or harmful conditions.

Exam Probability: **High**

29. *Answer choices:*
(see index for correct answer)

- a. Workplace conflict

- b. Toxic workplace
- c. Workplace violence
- d. Evaluation

Guidance: level 1

:: Survey methodology ::

A _____ is the procedure of systematically acquiring and recording information about the members of a given population. The term is used mostly in connection with national population and housing _____ es; other common _____ es include agriculture, business, and traffic _____ es. The United Nations defines the essential features of population and housing _____ es as "individual enumeration, universality within a defined territory, simultaneity and defined periodicity", and recommends that population _____ es be taken at least every 10 years. United Nations recommendations also cover _____ topics to be collected, official definitions, classifications and other useful information to co-ordinate international practice.

Exam Probability: **Medium**

30. *Answer choices:*
(see index for correct answer)

- a. American Association for Public Opinion Research
- b. Enterprise feedback management
- c. Census
- d. Swiss Centre of Expertise in the Social Sciences

Guidance: level 1

:: Design of experiments ::

In the design of experiments, treatments are applied to experimental units in the treatment group. In comparative experiments, members of the complementary group, the _____ , receive either no treatment or a standard treatment.

Exam Probability: **Medium**

31. *Answer choices:*
(see index for correct answer)

- a. Control group

- b. One-factor-at-a-time method
- c. Observer-expectancy effect
- d. Nuremberg Code

Guidance: level 1

:: Sociological theories ::

A _____ is a systematic process for determining and addressing needs, or "gaps" between current conditions and desired conditions or "wants". The discrepancy between the current condition and wanted condition must be measured to appropriately identify the need. The need can be a desire to improve current performance or to correct a deficiency.

Exam Probability: **Medium**

32. *Answer choices:*
(see index for correct answer)

- a. social constructionism
- b. comfort zone
- c. Needs assessment
- d. Compliance gaining

Guidance: level 1

:: ::

A _____ is monetary compensation paid by an employer to an employee in exchange for work done. Payment may be calculated as a fixed amount for each task completed , or at an hourly or daily rate , or based on an easily measured quantity of work done.

Exam Probability: **High**

33. *Answer choices:*
(see index for correct answer)

- a. corporate values
- b. Wage
- c. information systems assessment
- d. Character

Guidance: level 1

:: Employment compensation ::

_____ is time off from work that workers can use to stay home to address their health and safety needs without losing pay. Paid _____ is a statutory requirement in many nations. Most European, many Latin American, a few African and a few Asian countries have legal requirements for paid

_____ .

Exam Probability: **Medium**

34. *Answer choices:*
(see index for correct answer)

- a. Pay-for-Performance
- b. Defense Base Act
- c. Anderson v. Mt. Clemens Pottery Co.
- d. Sick leave

Guidance: level 1

:: Employment compensation ::

An _____ is an employee benefit program that assists employees with personal problems and/or work-related problems that may impact their job performance, health, mental and emotional well-being. EAPs generally offer free and confidential assessments, short-term counseling, referrals, and follow-up services for employees and their household members. EAP counselors also work in a consultative role with managers and supervisors to address employee and organizational challenges and needs. Many corporations, academic institution and/or government agencies are active in helping organizations prevent and cope with workplace violence, trauma, and other emergency response situations. There is a variety of support programs offered for employees. Even though EAPs are mainly aimed at work-related problems, there are a variety of programs that can assist with problems outside of the workplace. EAPs have grown over the years, and are more desirable economically and socially.

Exam Probability: **Low**

35. *Answer choices:*
(see index for correct answer)

- a. Profit sharing
- b. Labour law

- c. Australian Fair Pay Commission
- d. Employee assistance program

Guidance: level 1

:: Employment ::

_____ is the probability that an individual will keep his/her job; a job with a high level of _____ is such that a person with the job would have a small chance of losing it.

Exam Probability: **Medium**

36. *Answer choices:*
(see index for correct answer)

- a. Work product
- b. Job security
- c. Intra-company transfer
- d. Hourly worker

Guidance: level 1

:: Employment compensation ::

The formula commonly used by compensation professionals to assess the competitiveness of an employee's pay level involves calculating a "_____". _____ is the short form for Comparative ratio.

Exam Probability: **Low**

37. *Answer choices:*
(see index for correct answer)

- a. Compa-ratio
- b. Stock appreciation right
- c. Lerman ratio
- d. Sick leave

Guidance: level 1

:: Training ::

_____ is teaching, or developing in oneself or others, any skills and knowledge that relate to specific useful competencies. _____ has specific goals of improving one's capability, capacity, productivity and performance. It forms the core of apprenticeships and provides the backbone of content at institutes of technology . In addition to the basic _____ required for a trade, occupation or profession, observers of the labor-market recognize as of 2008 the need to continue _____ beyond initial qualifications: to maintain, upgrade and update skills throughout working life. People within many professions and occupations may refer to this sort of _____ as professional development.

Exam Probability: **High**

38. *Answer choices:*
(see index for correct answer)

- a. Endurance training
- b. Fartlek
- c. Large Group Capacitation
- d. Training

Guidance: level 1

:: Labour law ::

A _____ is a "shop-floor" organization representing workers that functions as a local/firm-level complement to trade unions but is independent of these at least in some countries. _____ s exist with different names in a variety of related forms in a number of European countries, including Britain ; Germany and Austria ; Luxembourg ; the Netherlands and Flanders in Belgium ; Italy ; France ; Wallonia in Belgium and Spain .

Exam Probability: **Medium**

39. *Answer choices:*
(see index for correct answer)

- a. Vesting
- b. Works council
- c. Undue hardship
- d. Bharat Forge Co Ltd v Uttam Manohar Nakate

Guidance: level 1

Some scenarios associate "this kind of planning" with learning "life skills".
_____ s are necessary, or at least useful, in situations where individuals need to know what time they must be at a specific location to receive a specific service, and where people need to accomplish a set of goals within a set time period.

Exam Probability: **Medium**

40. *Answer choices:*
(see index for correct answer)

- a. Punch list
- b. Problem domain analysis
- c. Sequence step algorithm
- d. Site survey

Guidance: level 1

:: Stress ::

_____ means beneficial stress—either psychological, physical , or biochemical/radiological .

Exam Probability: **Low**

41. *Answer choices:*
(see index for correct answer)

- a. Breaking point
- b. Prenatal stress
- c. Defense physiology
- d. Worry

Guidance: level 1

:: Employment compensation ::

Employee stock ownership, or employee share ownership, is an ownership interest in a company held by the company's workforce. The ownership interest may be facilitated by the company as part of employees' remuneration or incentive compensation for work performed, or the company itself may be employee owned.

Exam Probability: **Medium**

42. *Answer choices:*
(see index for correct answer)

- a. Annual enrollment
- b. Annual leave
- c. Golden boot compensation
- d. Employee stock ownership plan

Guidance: level 1

:: Labour relations ::

_____ is a field of study that can have different meanings depending on the context in which it is used. In an international context, it is a subfield of labor history that studies the human relations with regard to work – in its broadest sense – and how this connects to questions of social inequality. It explicitly encompasses unregulated, historical, and non-Western forms of labor. Here, _____ define "for or with whom one works and under what rules. These rules determine the type of work, type and amount of remuneration, working hours, degrees of physical and psychological strain, as well as the degree of freedom and autonomy associated with the work."

Exam Probability: **Low**

43. *Answer choices:*
(see index for correct answer)

- a. Review Body
- b. Negotiated cartelism
- c. Boulwarism
- d. Disciplinary counseling

Guidance: level 1

:: ::

_____ is an experience a person may have when one moves to a cultural environment which is different from one's own; it is also the personal disorientation a person may feel when experiencing an unfamiliar way of life due to immigration or a visit to a new country, a move between social environments, or simply transition to another type of life. One of the most common causes of _____ involves individuals in a foreign environment. _____ can be described as consisting of at least one of four distinct phases: honeymoon, negotiation, adjustment, and adaptation.

Exam Probability: **High**

44. *Answer choices:*
(see index for correct answer)

- a. process perspective
- b. functional perspective
- c. hierarchical
- d. Culture shock

Guidance: level 1

:: ::

_____ involves the development of an action plan designed to motivate and guide a person or group toward a goal. _____ can be guided by goal-setting criteria such as SMART criteria. _____ is a major component of personal-development and management literature.

Exam Probability: **Medium**

45. *Answer choices:*
(see index for correct answer)

- a. hierarchical perspective
- b. Goal setting
- c. information systems assessment
- d. similarity-attraction theory

Guidance: level 1

:: ::

The U.S. _____ is a federal agency that administers and enforces civil rights laws against workplace discrimination. The EEOC investigates discrimination complaints based on an individual`s race, children, national origin, religion, sex, age, disability, sexual orientation, gender identity, genetic information, and retaliation for reporting, participating in, and/or opposing a discriminatory practice.

Exam Probability: **Low**

46. *Answer choices:*
(see index for correct answer)

- a. Sarbanes-Oxley act of 2002
- b. Equal Employment Opportunity Commission
- c. hierarchical
- d. personal values

Guidance: level 1

:: ::

A _____ service is an online platform which people use to build social networks or social relationship with other people who share similar personal or career interests, activities, backgrounds or real-life connections.

Exam Probability: **Low**

47. *Answer choices:*
(see index for correct answer)

- a. corporate values
- b. Social networking
- c. similarity-attraction theory
- d. imperative

Guidance: level 1

:: ::

Educational technology is "the study and ethical practice of facilitating learning and improving performance by creating, using, and managing appropriate technological processes and resources".

48. *Answer choices:*
(see index for correct answer)

- a. surface-level diversity
- b. co-culture
- c. functional perspective
- d. similarity-attraction theory

Guidance: level 1

:: Human resource management ::

_____ means increasing the scope of a job through extending the range of its job duties and responsibilities generally within the same level and periphery. _____ involves combining various activities at the same level in the organization and adding them to the existing job. It is also called the horizontal expansion of job activities. This contradicts the principles of specialisation and the division of labour whereby work is divided into small units, each of which is performed repetitively by an individual worker and the responsibilities are always clear. Some motivational theories suggest that the boredom and alienation caused by the division of labour can actually cause efficiency to fall. Thus, _____ seeks to motivate workers through reversing the process of specialisation. A typical approach might be to replace assembly lines with modular work; instead of an employee repeating the same step on each product, they perform several tasks on a single item. In order for employees to be provided with _____ they will need to be retrained in new fields to understand how each field works.

Exam Probability: **High**

49. *Answer choices:*
(see index for correct answer)

- a. Appreciative inquiry
- b. Job enlargement
- c. Bradford Factor
- d. Health human resources

Guidance: level 1

:: Training ::

_____ is the process of ensuring compliance with laws, regulations, rules, standards, or social norms. By enforcing laws and regulations, governments attempt to effectuate successful implementation of policies.

Exam Probability: **High**

50. *Answer choices:*
(see index for correct answer)

- a. International Society for Performance Improvement
- b. Enforcement
- c. Safety Services Company
- d. Compliance training

Guidance: level 1

:: ::

_____ medicine is an approach to medical practice intended to optimize decision-making by emphasizing the use of evidence from well-designed and well-conducted research. Although all medicine based on science has some degree of empirical support, EBM goes further, classifying evidence by its epistemologic strength and requiring that only the strongest types can yield strong recommendations; weaker types can yield only weak recommendations. The term was originally used to describe an approach to teaching the practice of medicine and improving decisions by individual physicians about individual patients. Use of the term rapidly expanded to include a previously described approach that emphasized the use of evidence in the design of guidelines and policies that apply to groups of patients and populations . It has subsequently spread to describe an approach to decision-making that is used at virtually every level of health care as well as other fields .

Exam Probability: **High**

51. *Answer choices:*
(see index for correct answer)

- a. hierarchical perspective
- b. similarity-attraction theory
- c. Evidence-based
- d. imperative

Guidance: level 1

:: Labor ::

_____ s are workers whose main capital is knowledge. Examples include programmers, physicians, pharmacists, architects, engineers, scientists, design thinkers, public accountants, lawyers, and academics, and any other white-collar workers, whose line of work requires the one to "think for a living".

Exam Probability: **Medium**

52. *Answer choices:*
(see index for correct answer)

- a. Dirty, dangerous and demeaning
- b. Economic activism
- c. Surplus labour
- d. Self-perceived quality-of-life scale

Guidance: level 1

:: Labour law ::

A _____ is a legal contract that is meant to limit the liability of an employer whose employees are romantically involved. An employer may choose to require a _____ when a romantic relationship within the company becomes known, in order to indemnify the company in case the employees` romantic relationship fails, primarily so that one party can`t bring a sexual harassment lawsuit against the company. To that end, the _____ states that the relationship is consensual, and both parties of the relationship must sign it. The _____ may also stipulate rules for acceptable romantic behavior in the workplace.

Exam Probability: **Medium**

53. *Answer choices:*
(see index for correct answer)

- a. The Burke Group
- b. Non-compete clause
- c. Love contract
- d. Victimisation

Guidance: level 1

:: Validity (statistics) ::

In psychometrics, _____ is the extent to which a score on a scale or test predicts scores on some criterion measure.

Exam Probability: **Medium**

54. *Answer choices:*
(see index for correct answer)

- a. Test validity
- b. Content validity
- c. Predictive validity
- d. Incremental validity

Guidance: level 1

:: Employment compensation ::

A _____ is pay and benefits employees receive when they leave employment at a company unwillfully. In addition to their remaining regular pay, it may include some of the following.

Exam Probability: **High**

55. *Answer choices:*
(see index for correct answer)

- a. Severance package
- b. Uninsured employer
- c. Stock appreciation right
- d. Spiff

Guidance: level 1

:: Management ::

_____ or executive pay is composed of the financial compensation and other non-financial awards received by an executive from their firm for their service to the organization. It is typically a mixture of salary, bonuses, shares of or call options on the company stock, benefits, and perquisites, ideally configured to take into account government regulations, tax law, the desires of the organization and the executive, and rewards for performance.

Exam Probability: **Low**

56. *Answer choices:*
(see index for correct answer)

- a. Change advisory board
- b. Managerial hubris
- c. Perth leadership outcome model
- d. Executive compensation

Guidance: level 1

:: Business ethics ::

_____ is a type of harassment technique that relates to a sexual nature and the unwelcome or inappropriate promise of rewards in exchange for sexual favors. _____ includes a range of actions from mild transgressions to sexual abuse or assault. Harassment can occur in many different social settings such as the workplace, the home, school, churches, etc. Harassers or victims may be of any gender.

Exam Probability: **High**

57. *Answer choices:*
(see index for correct answer)

- a. Journal of Business Ethics
- b. Interfaith Center on Corporate Responsibility
- c. Sexual harassment
- d. Marketing ethics

Guidance: level 1

:: Social psychology ::

In social psychology, _____ is the phenomenon of a person exerting less effort to achieve a goal when he or she works in a group than when working alone. This is seen as one of the main reasons groups are sometimes less productive than the combined performance of their members working as individuals, but should be distinguished from the accidental coordination problems that groups sometimes experience.

Exam Probability: **Low**

58. *Answer choices:*

(see index for correct answer)

- a. thought control
- b. coercive persuasion
- c. indoctrination
- d. Social loafing

Guidance: level 1

:: Offshoring ::

Outsourcing is an agreement in which one company hires another company to be responsible for a planned or existing activity that is or could be done internally,and sometimes involves transferring employees and assets from one firm to another.

Exam Probability: **Medium**

59. *Answer choices:*

(see index for correct answer)

- a. Offshore company
- b. Nearshoring
- c. Offshoring Research Network
- d. Layoff

Guidance: level 1

Information systems

Information systems (IS) are formal, sociotechnical, organizational systems
designed to collect, process, store, and distribute information. In a
sociotechnical perspective Information Systems are composed by four components:
technology, process, people and organizational structure.

:: ::

The _____ is the global system of interconnected computer networks
that use the _____ protocol suite to link devices worldwide. It is a
network of networks that consists of private, public, academic, business, and
government networks of local to global scope, linked by a broad array of
electronic, wireless, and optical networking technologies. The _____
carries a vast range of information resources and services, such as the
inter-linked hypertext documents and applications of the World Wide Web ,
electronic mail, telephony, and file sharing.

Exam Probability: **Medium**

1. *Answer choices:*
(see index for correct answer)

- a. surface-level diversity
- b. similarity-attraction theory
- c. Internet
- d. information systems assessment

Guidance: level 1

:: Information science ::

_____ is the resolution of uncertainty; it is that which answers the question of "what an entity is" and thus defines both its essence and nature of its characteristics. _____ relates to both data and knowledge, as data is meaningful _____ representing values attributed to parameters, and knowledge signifies understanding of a concept. _____ is uncoupled from an observer, which is an entity that can access _____ and thus discern what it specifies; _____ exists beyond an event horizon for example. In the case of knowledge, the _____ itself requires a cognitive observer to be obtained.

Exam Probability: **Medium**

2. *Answer choices:*
(see index for correct answer)

- a. Back-of-the-book index
- b. Datafication
- c. Social information architecture
- d. Information

Guidance: level 1

:: Virtual economies ::

_____ Inc. is an American social game developer running social video game services founded in April 2007 and headquartered in San Francisco, California, United States. The company primarily focuses on mobile and social networking platforms. _____ states its mission as "connecting the world through games."

Exam Probability: **Medium**

3. *Answer choices:*
(see index for correct answer)

- a. EverQuest
- b. Gold farming
- c. Zynga
- d. Entropia Universe

Guidance: level 1

:: Management ::

_____ is the identification of an organization's assets , followed by the development, documentation, and implementation of policies and procedures for protecting these assets.

Exam Probability: **Medium**

4. *Answer choices:*

(see index for correct answer)

- a. Risk management
- b. Business rule
- c. Performance indicator
- d. DMSMS

Guidance: level 1

:: Security compliance ::

A _____ is a communicated intent to inflict harm or loss on another person. A _____ is considered an act of coercion. _____ s are widely observed in animal behavior, particularly in a ritualized form, chiefly in order to avoid the unnecessary physical violence that can lead to physical damage or the death of both conflicting parties.

Exam Probability: **Low**

5. *Answer choices:*

(see index for correct answer)

- a. 201 CMR 17.00
- b. North American Electric Reliability Corporation
- c. Threat
- d. Vulnerability

Guidance: level 1

:: ::

A _____ is a system designed to capture, store, manipulate, analyze, manage, and present spatial or geographic data. GIS applications are tools that allow users to create interactive queries , analyze spatial information, edit data in maps, and present the results of all these operations. GIS sometimes refers to geographic information science , the science underlying geographic concepts, applications, and systems.

Exam Probability: **Low**

6. *Answer choices:*
(see index for correct answer)

- a. process perspective
- b. Character
- c. Geographic information system
- d. cultural

Guidance: level 1

:: ::

A database is an organized collection of data, generally stored and accessed electronically from a computer system. Where databases are more complex they are often developed using formal design and modeling techniques.

Exam Probability: **Medium**

7. *Answer choices:*
(see index for correct answer)

- a. co-culture
- b. personal values
- c. imperative
- d. Database management system

Guidance: level 1

:: E-commerce ::

_____ is a subset of electronic commerce that involves social media, online media that supports social interaction, and user contributions to assist online buying and selling of products and services.

8. *Answer choices:*

(see index for correct answer)

- a. Social commerce
- b. POLi Payments
- c. Computer reservations system
- d. Webjet

Guidance: level 1

:: Data management ::

_____ is a form of intellectual property that grants the creator of an original creative work an exclusive legal right to determine whether and under what conditions this original work may be copied and used by others, usually for a limited term of years. The exclusive rights are not absolute but limited by limitations and exceptions to _____ law, including fair use. A major limitation on _____ on ideas is that _____ protects only the original expression of ideas, and not the underlying ideas themselves.

Exam Probability: **Low**

9. *Answer choices:*

(see index for correct answer)

- a. Physical schema
- b. Copyright
- c. DAMA
- d. Core data integration

Guidance: level 1

:: Business planning ::

_____ is an organization's process of defining its strategy, or direction, and making decisions on allocating its resources to pursue this strategy. It may also extend to control mechanisms for guiding the implementation of the strategy. _____ became prominent in corporations during the 1960s and remains an important aspect of strategic management. It is executed by strategic planners or strategists, who involve many parties and research sources in their analysis of the organization and its relationship to the environment in which it competes.

10. *Answer choices:*
(see index for correct answer)

- a. Open Options Corporation
- b. Stakeholder management
- c. Strategic planning
- d. Customer Demand Planning

Guidance: level 1

:: Global Positioning System ::

A _____ is a mechanism for determining the location of an object in space. Technologies for this task exist ranging from worldwide coverage with meter accuracy to workspace coverage with sub-millimetre accuracy.

Exam Probability: **Low**

11. *Answer choices:*
(see index for correct answer)

- a. Receiver autonomous integrity monitoring
- b. Positioning system
- c. High Sensitivity GPS
- d. Earthscope

Guidance: level 1

:: Data interchange standards ::

_____ is the concept of businesses electronically communicating information that was traditionally communicated on paper, such as purchase orders and invoices. Technical standards for EDI exist to facilitate parties transacting such instruments without having to make special arrangements.

Exam Probability: **Low**

12. *Answer choices:*
(see index for correct answer)

- a. Electronic data interchange
- b. Uniform Communication Standard
- c. Common Alerting Protocol
- d. Data Interchange Standards Association

:: E-commerce ::

A _____ is a plastic payment card that can be used instead of cash when making purchases. It is similar to a credit card, but unlike a credit card, the money is immediately transferred directly from the cardholder's bank account when performing a transaction.

Exam Probability: **High**

13. *Answer choices:*
(see index for correct answer)

- a. Want Button
- b. Debit card
- c. Presumed security
- d. Transport Layer Security

:: Ethically disputed business practices ::

_____ is the use of messaging systems to send an unsolicited message , especially advertising, as well as sending messages repeatedly on the same site. While the most widely recognized form of spam is email spam, the term is applied to similar abuses in other media: instant messaging spam, Usenet newsgroup spam, Web search engine spam, spam in blogs, wiki spam, online classified ads spam, mobile phone messaging spam, Internet forum spam, junk fax transmissions, social spam, spam mobile apps, television advertising and file sharing spam. It is named after Spam, a luncheon meat, by way of a Monty Python sketch about a restaurant that has Spam in every dish and where patrons annoyingly chant "Spam!" over and over again.

Exam Probability: **High**

14. *Answer choices:*
(see index for correct answer)

- a. Market saturation
- b. Boiler room
- c. Spamming
- d. Patent privateer

:: Reputation management ::

A _____ is an astronomical object consisting of a luminous spheroid of plasma held together by its own gravity. The nearest _____ to Earth is the Sun. Many other _____ s are visible to the naked eye from Earth during the night, appearing as a multitude of fixed luminous points in the sky due to their immense distance from Earth. Historically, the most prominent _____ s were grouped into constellations and asterisms, the brightest of which gained proper names. Astronomers have assembled _____ catalogues that identify the known _____ s and provide standardized stellar designations. However, most of the estimated 300 sextillion _____ s in the Universe are invisible to the naked eye from Earth, including all _____ s outside our galaxy, the Milky Way.

Exam Probability: **Low**

15. *Answer choices:*

(see index for correct answer)

- a. Star
- b. Lithium Technologies
- c. EigenTrust
- d. Infamy

:: ::

A _____ or data centre is a building, dedicated space within a building, or a group of buildings used to house computer systems and associated components, such as telecommunications and storage systems.

Exam Probability: **High**

16. *Answer choices:*

(see index for correct answer)

- a. Sarbanes-Oxley act of 2002
- b. empathy
- c. functional perspective
- d. imperative

:: Data management ::

_____ , or OLAP , is an approach to answer multi-dimensional analytical queries swiftly in computing. OLAP is part of the broader category of business intelligence, which also encompasses relational databases, report writing and data mining. Typical applications of OLAP include business reporting for sales, marketing, management reporting, business process management , budgeting and forecasting, financial reporting and similar areas, with new applications emerging, such as agriculture. The term OLAP was created as a slight modification of the traditional database term online transaction processing .

Exam Probability: **High**

17. *Answer choices:*
(see index for correct answer)

- a. Government Performance Management
- b. Archive site
- c. Data Reference Model
- d. Online analytical processing

:: Computer file formats ::

_____ is a communication protocol for peer-to-peer file sharing which is used to distribute data and electronic files over the Internet.

Exam Probability: **Low**

18. *Answer choices:*
(see index for correct answer)

- a. Comtrade
- b. BitTorrent
- c. Advanced Audio Coding
- d. Office Open XML file formats

:: E-commerce ::

_____ , cybersecurity or information technology security is the protection of computer systems from theft or damage to their hardware, software or electronic data, as well as from disruption or misdirection of the services they provide.

Exam Probability: **Medium**

19. *Answer choices:*
(see index for correct answer)

- a. Value-added network
- b. UN/CEFACT
- c. RSA
- d. Computer security

Guidance: level 1

:: Strategic management ::

_____ is a management term for an element that is necessary for an organization or project to achieve its mission. Alternative terms are key result area and key success factor .

Exam Probability: **High**

20. *Answer choices:*
(see index for correct answer)

- a. Rule of three
- b. Adversarial purchasing
- c. Strategic business unit
- d. strategy implementation

Guidance: level 1

:: Data management ::

_____ is "data [information] that provides information about other data". Many distinct types of _____ exist, among these descriptive _____ , structural _____ , administrative _____ , reference _____ and statistical _____ .

21. *Answer choices:*

(see index for correct answer)

- a. Tagsistant
- b. Long-lived transaction
- c. H-Store
- d. Metadata

Guidance: level 1

:: Data analysis ::

_____ , also referred to as text data mining, roughly equivalent to text analytics, is the process of deriving high-quality information from text. High-quality information is typically derived through the devising of patterns and trends through means such as statistical pattern learning. _____ usually involves the process of structuring the input text , deriving patterns within the structured data, and finally evaluation and interpretation of the output. 'High quality' in _____ usually refers to some combination of relevance, novelty, and interest. Typical _____ tasks include text categorization, text clustering, concept/entity extraction, production of granular taxonomies, sentiment analysis, document summarization, and entity relation modeling .

22. *Answer choices:*

(see index for correct answer)

- a. Combinatorial data analysis
- b. Relationship square
- c. Text mining
- d. Contingency table

Guidance: level 1

:: ::

_____ consists of tailoring a service or a product to accommodate specific individuals, sometimes tied to groups or segments of individuals. A wide variety of organizations use _____ to improve customer satisfaction, digital sales conversion, marketing results, branding, and improved website metrics as well as for advertising. _____ is a key element in social media and recommender systems.

Exam Probability: **High**

23. *Answer choices:*
(see index for correct answer)

- a. Character
- b. Sarbanes-Oxley act of 2002
- c. Personalization
- d. hierarchical perspective

Guidance: level 1

:: Marketing ::

_____ is the percentage of a market accounted for by a specific entity. In a survey of nearly 200 senior marketing managers, 67% responded that they found the revenue- "dollar _____ " metric very useful, while 61% found "unit _____ " very useful.

Exam Probability: **Low**

24. *Answer choices:*
(see index for correct answer)

- a. Chaotics
- b. Market share
- c. Bluetooth advertising
- d. Franchising

Guidance: level 1

:: Domain name system ::

The _____ is a hierarchical and decentralized naming system for computers, services, or other resources connected to the Internet or a private network. It associates various information with domain names assigned to each of the participating entities. Most prominently, it translates more readily memorized domain names to the numerical IP addresses needed for locating and identifying computer services and devices with the underlying network protocols. By providing a worldwide, distributed directory service, the _____ has been an essential component of the functionality of the Internet since 1985.

Exam Probability: **Medium**

25. *Answer choices:*
(see index for correct answer)

- a. Global Name Registry
- b. Vanity domain
- c. Domain Name System
- d. Registrar-Lock

Guidance: level 1

:: E-commerce ::

Electronic governance or e-governance is the application of information and communication technology for delivering government services, exchange of information, communication transactions, integration of various stand-alone systems and services between _____ , government-to-business , government-to-government , government-to-employees as well as back-office processes and interactions within the entire government framework. Through e-governance, government services are made available to citizens in a convenient, efficient, and transparent manner. The three main target groups that can be distinguished in governance concepts are government, citizens, andbusinesses/interest groups. In e-governance, there are no distinct boundaries.

Exam Probability: **High**

26. *Answer choices:*
(see index for correct answer)

- a. PayXpert
- b. Storefront

- c. USAePay
- d. Government-to-citizen

Guidance: level 1

:: ::

Within the Internet, _____ s are formed by the rules and procedures of the _____ System . Any name registered in the DNS is a _____ . _____ s are used in various networking contexts and for application-specific naming and addressing purposes. In general, a _____ represents an Internet Protocol resource, such as a personal computer used to access the Internet, a server computer hosting a web site, or the web site itself or any other service communicated via the Internet. In 2017, 330.6 million _____ s had been registered.

Exam Probability: **Medium**

27. *Answer choices:*
(see index for correct answer)

- a. imperative
- b. hierarchical perspective
- c. surface-level diversity
- d. Domain name

Guidance: level 1

:: Computer networking ::

_____ is a method of grouping data that is transmitted over a digital network into packets. Packets are made of a header and a payload. Data in the header are used by networking hardware to direct the packet to its destination where the payload is extracted and used by application software. _____ is the primary basis for data communications in computer networks worldwide.

Exam Probability: **High**

28. *Answer choices:*
(see index for correct answer)

- a. Packet switching
- b. Network equipment provider
- c. Wireless Andrew

- d. Switch virtual interface

Guidance: level 1

:: Search engine optimization ::

_____ is an algorithm used by Google Search to rank web pages in their search engine results. _____ was named after Larry Page, one of the founders of Google. _____ is a way of measuring the importance of website pages. According to Google.

Exam Probability: **High**

29. *Answer choices:*
(see index for correct answer)

- a. PageTraffic
- b. PM Digital
- c. Google Hummingbird
- d. Trademark stuffing

Guidance: level 1

:: Virtual economies ::

_____ is an online virtual world, developed and owned by the San Francisco-based firm Linden Lab and launched on June 23, 2003. By 2013, _____ had approximately one million regular users; at the end of 2017 active user count totals "between 800,000 and 900,000". In many ways, _____ is similar to massively multiplayer online role-playing games; however, Linden Lab is emphatic that their creation is not a game: "There is no manufactured conflict, no set objective".

Exam Probability: **Low**

30. *Answer choices:*
(see index for correct answer)

- a. Cataclysm: Dark Days Ahead
- b. Elite: Dangerous
- c. Cabal Online
- d. Second Life

Guidance: level 1

An _____ is a type of computer communications protocol or cryptographic protocol specifically designed for transfer of authentication data between two entities. It allows the receiving entity to authenticate the connecting entity as well as authenticate itself to the connecting entity by declaring the type of information needed for authentication as well as syntax. It is the most important layer of protection needed for secure communication within computer networks.

Exam Probability: **Low**

31. *Answer choices:*
(see index for correct answer)

- a. Authentication protocol
- b. NTLMSSP
- c. IEEE 802.1X
- d. SPNEGO

Guidance: level 1

:: Content management systems ::

_____ is the textual, visual, or aural content that is encountered as part of the user experience on websites. It may include—among other things—text, images, sounds, videos, and animations.

Exam Probability: **Medium**

32. *Answer choices:*
(see index for correct answer)

- a. PrestaShop
- b. Pluck
- c. Elcom Technology
- d. Enterprise report management

Guidance: level 1

:: Network management ::

_____ is the process of administering and managing computer networks. Services provided by this discipline include fault analysis, performance management, provisioning of networks and maintaining the quality of service. Software that enables network administrators to perform their functions is called _____ software.

Exam Probability: **Low**

33. *Answer choices:*
(see index for correct answer)

- a. Rollover cable
- b. Managed object
- c. Multi Router Traffic Grapher
- d. Network management

Guidance: level 1

:: ::

_____ LLC is an American multinational technology company that specializes in Internet-related services and products, which include online advertising technologies, search engine, cloud computing, software, and hardware. It is considered one of the Big Four technology companies, alongside Amazon, Apple and Facebook.

Exam Probability: **High**

34. *Answer choices:*
(see index for correct answer)

- a. information systems assessment
- b. similarity-attraction theory
- c. Google
- d. surface-level diversity

Guidance: level 1

:: Data modeling languages ::

An entity–relationship model describes interrelated things of interest in a specific domain of knowledge. A basic ER model is composed of entity types and specifies relationships that can exist between entities .

Exam Probability: **High**

35. *Answer choices:*
(see index for correct answer)

- a. Standard Generalized Markup Language
- b. Interface description language
- c. Entity-relationship
- d. TREX

Guidance: level 1

:: Internet advertising ::

_____ is software that aims to gather information about a person or organization, sometimes without their knowledge, that may send such information to another entity without the consumer's consent, that asserts control over a device without the consumer's knowledge, or it may send such information to another entity with the consumer's consent, through cookies.

Exam Probability: **Medium**

36. *Answer choices:*
(see index for correct answer)

- a. Spyware
- b. Article marketing
- c. Automated bid managers
- d. Type-in traffic

Guidance: level 1

:: Networking hardware ::

A network interface controller is a computer hardware component that connects a computer to a computer network.

Exam Probability: **Low**

37. *Answer choices:*

(see index for correct answer)

- a. Ethernet hub
- b. Network interface card
- c. bridging

Guidance: level 1

:: Supply chain management terms ::

In business and finance, _____ is a system of organizations, people, activities, information, and resources involved in moving a product or service from supplier to customer. _____ activities involve the transformation of natural resources, raw materials, and components into a finished product that is delivered to the end customer. In sophisticated _____ systems, used products may re-enter the _____ at any point where residual value is recyclable. _____ s link value chains.

Exam Probability: **Medium**

38. *Answer choices:*

(see index for correct answer)

- a. Final assembly schedule
- b. inventory management
- c. Supply chain
- d. Consumables

Guidance: level 1

:: Management ::

_____ is the kind of knowledge that is difficult to transfer to another person by means of writing it down or verbalizing it. For example, that London is in the United Kingdom is a piece of explicit knowledge that can be written down, transmitted, and understood by a recipient. However, the ability to speak a language, ride a bicycle, knead dough, play a musical instrument, or design and use complex equipment requires all sorts of knowledge that is not always known explicitly, even by expert practitioners, and which is difficult or impossible to explicitly transfer to other people.

Exam Probability: **Low**

39. *Answer choices:*

(see index for correct answer)

- a. Tacit knowledge
- b. Performance indicator
- c. Radical transparency
- d. PhD in management

Guidance: level 1

:: E-commerce ::

_____ is a type of performance-based marketing in which a business rewards one or more affiliates for each visitor or customer brought by the affiliate's own marketing efforts.

Exam Probability: **Medium**

40. *Answer choices:*

(see index for correct answer)

- a. Cart32
- b. Eurocheque
- c. Tor
- d. Affiliate marketing

Guidance: level 1

:: Data quality ::

_____ is the maintenance of, and the assurance of the accuracy and consistency of, data over its entire life-cycle, and is a critical aspect to the design, implementation and usage of any system which stores, processes, or retrieves data. The term is broad in scope and may have widely different meanings depending on the specific context even under the same general umbrella of computing. It is at times used as a proxy term for data quality, while data validation is a pre-requisite for _____ . _____ is the opposite of data corruption. The overall intent of any _____ technique is the same: ensure data is recorded exactly as intended and upon later retrieval, ensure the data is the same as it was when it was originally recorded. In short, _____ aims to prevent unintentional changes to information. _____ is not to be confused with data security, the discipline of protecting data from unauthorized parties.

41. *Answer choices:*

(see index for correct answer)

- a. Data Quality Campaign
- b. Link rot
- c. Data corruption
- d. One-for-one checking

Guidance: level 1

:: Information technology organisations ::

The Internet Corporation for Assigned Names and Numbers is a nonprofit organization responsible for coordinating the maintenance and procedures of several databases related to the namespaces and numerical spaces of the Internet, ensuring the network's stable and secure operation. _____ performs the actual technical maintenance work of the Central Internet Address pools and DNS root zone registries pursuant to the Internet Assigned Numbers Authority function contract. The contract regarding the IANA stewardship functions between _____ and the National Telecommunications and Information Administration of the United States Department of Commerce ended on October 1, 2016, formally transitioning the functions to the global multistakeholder community.

Exam Probability: **High**

42. *Answer choices:*

(see index for correct answer)

- a. ICANN
- b. UNIGIS
- c. Logic Programming Associates
- d. ICT Hub

Guidance: level 1

:: Cloud storage ::

_____ was an online backup service for both Windows and macOS users. Linux support was made available in Q3, 2014. In 2007 _____ was acquired by EMC, and in 2013 _____ was included in the EMC Backup Recovery Systems division's product list.On September 7, 2016, Dell Inc. acquired EMC Corporation to form Dell Technologies, restructuring the original Dell Inc. as a subsidiary of Dell Technologies.. On March 19, 2018 Carbonite acquired _____ from Dell for $148.5 million in cash and in 2019 shut down the service, incorporating _____'s clients into its own online backup service programs.

Exam Probability: **Low**

43. *Answer choices:*
(see index for correct answer)

- a. Mozy
- b. Scality
- c. Free Haven Project
- d. IASO Backup

Guidance: level 1

:: Internet privacy ::

An _____ is a private network accessible only to an organization's staff. Often, a wide range of information and services are available on an organization's internal _____ that are unavailable to the public, unlike the Internet. A company-wide _____ can constitute an important focal point of internal communication and collaboration, and provide a single starting point to access internal and external resources. In its simplest form, an _____ is established with the technologies for local area networks and wide area networks . Many modern _____ s have search engines, user profiles, blogs, mobile apps with notifications, and events planning within their infrastructure.

Exam Probability: **High**

44. *Answer choices:*
(see index for correct answer)

- a. Intranet
- b. DoNotTrackMe
- c. Local shared object

- d. Web storage

Guidance: level 1

:: Automatic identification and data capture ::

_____ is the trademark for a type of matrix barcode first designed in 1994 for the automotive industry in Japan. A barcode is a machine-readable optical label that contains information about the item to which it is attached. In practice, _____ s often contain data for a locator, identifier, or tracker that points to a website or application. A _____ uses four standardized encoding modes to store data efficiently; extensions may also be used.

Exam Probability: **Medium**

45. *Answer choices:*
(see index for correct answer)

- a. Psion Teklogix
- b. Optical braille recognition
- c. Burst transmission
- d. QR code

Guidance: level 1

:: E-commerce ::

_____ is the activity of buying or selling of products on online services or over the Internet. Electronic commerce draws on technologies such as mobile commerce, electronic funds transfer, supply chain management, Internet marketing, online transaction processing, electronic data interchange , inventory management systems, and automated data collection systems.

Exam Probability: **Low**

46. *Answer choices:*
(see index for correct answer)

- a. Cart32
- b. Silent commerce
- c. Seja online
- d. Cyber Black Friday

Guidance: level 1

_____ , Inc. is an American company based in Reston, Virginia, United States that operates a diverse array of network infrastructure, including two of the Internet's thirteen root nameservers, the authoritative registry for the .com, .net, and .name generic top-level domains and the .cc and .tv country-code top-level domains, and the back-end systems for the .jobs, .gov, and .edu top-level domains. _____ also offers a range of security services, including managed DNS, distributed denial-of-service attack mitigation and cyber-threat reporting.

Exam Probability: **Medium**

47. *Answer choices:*
(see index for correct answer)

- a. Verisign
- b. Drop registrar
- c. DNS blocking
- d. Getaddrinfo

Guidance: level 1

_____ tools or technological protection measures are a set of access control technologies for restricting the use of proprietary hardware and copyrighted works. DRM technologies try to control the use, modification, and distribution of copyrighted works , as well as systems within devices that enforce these policies.

Exam Probability: **High**

48. *Answer choices:*
(see index for correct answer)

- a. Digital rights management
- b. Compliance and Robustness
- c. Hardware restriction
- d. Software protection dongle

Guidance: level 1

:: Asset ::

In financial accounting, an _____ is any resource owned by the business. Anything tangible or intangible that can be owned or controlled to produce value and that is held by a company to produce positive economic value is an _____ . Simply stated, _____ s represent value of ownership that can be converted into cash . The balance sheet of a firm records the monetary value of the _____ s owned by that firm. It covers money and other valuables belonging to an individual or to a business.

Exam Probability: **Medium**

49. *Answer choices:*
(see index for correct answer)

- a. Current asset
- b. Fixed asset

Guidance: level 1

:: Remote administration software ::

_____ is a protocol used on the Internet or local area network to provide a bidirectional interactive text-oriented communication facility using a virtual terminal connection. User data is interspersed in-band with _____ control information in an 8-bit byte oriented data connection over the Transmission Control Protocol .

Exam Probability: **Low**

50. *Answer choices:*
(see index for correct answer)

- a. Remote Utilities
- b. LogMeIn
- c. Sub7
- d. Telnet

Guidance: level 1

:: Data security ::

In information technology, a _____ , or data _____ , or the process of backing up, refers to the copying into an archive file of computer data that is already in secondary storage—so that it may be used to restore the original after a data loss event. The verb form is "back up", whereas the noun and adjective form is " _____ ".

Exam Probability: **High**

51. *Answer choices:*
(see index for correct answer)

- a. Backup
- b. Password fatigue
- c. National Industrial Security Program
- d. Virtual private database

Guidance: level 1

:: ::

A _____ , sometimes called a passcode, is a memorized secret used to confirm the identity of a user. Using the terminology of the NIST Digital Identity Guidelines, the secret is memorized by a party called the claimant while the party verifying the identity of the claimant is called the verifier. When the claimant successfully demonstrates knowledge of the _____ to the verifier through an established authentication protocol, the verifier is able to infer the claimant's identity.

Exam Probability: **High**

52. *Answer choices:*
(see index for correct answer)

- a. Character
- b. empathy
- c. Password
- d. hierarchical

Guidance: level 1

:: Data management ::

Given organizations' increasing dependency on information technology to run their operations, Business continuity planning covers the entire organization, and Disaster recovery focuses on IT.

Exam Probability: **Low**

53. *Answer choices:*
(see index for correct answer)

- a. Storage area network
- b. Virtual facility
- c. Dynamic knowledge repository
- d. Automatic data processing equipment

Guidance: level 1

:: Data analysis ::

_____ is a process of inspecting, cleansing, transforming, and modeling data with the goal of discovering useful information, informing conclusions, and supporting decision-making. _____ has multiple facets and approaches, encompassing diverse techniques under a variety of names, and is used in different business, science, and social science domains. In today's business world, _____ plays a role in making decisions more scientific and helping businesses operate more effectively.

Exam Probability: **High**

54. *Answer choices:*
(see index for correct answer)

- a. Synqera
- b. Missing data
- c. Data analysis
- d. Statistical assumption

Guidance: level 1

:: E-commerce ::

Electronic governance or e-governance is the application of information and communication technology for delivering government services, exchange of information, communication transactions, integration of various stand-alone systems and services between government-to-citizen , _____ , government-to-government , government-to-employees as well as back-office processes and interactions within the entire government framework. Through e-governance, government services are made available to citizens in a convenient, efficient, and transparent manner. The three main target groups that can be distinguished in governance concepts are government, citizens, andbusinesses/interest groups. In e-governance, there are no distinct boundaries.

Exam Probability: **Medium**

55. *Answer choices:*
(see index for correct answer)

- a. Supply chain attack
- b. MOL AccessPortal
- c. Government-to-business
- d. Net settlement

Guidance: level 1

:: History of human–computer interaction ::

A _____ , plural mice, is a small rodent characteristically having a pointed snout, small rounded ears, a body-length scaly tail and a high breeding rate. The best known _____ species is the common house _____ . It is also a popular pet. In some places, certain kinds of field mice are locally common. They are known to invade homes for food and shelter.

Exam Probability: **Medium**

56. *Answer choices:*
(see index for correct answer)

- a. Touchpad
- b. The Mother of All Demos
- c. Mouse
- d. Electronic Document System

Guidance: level 1

_____ is the technology by which a process or procedure is performed with minimal human assistance. _____ or automatic control is the use of various control systems for operating equipment such as machinery, processes in factories, boilers and heat treating ovens, switching on telephone networks, steering and stabilization of ships, aircraft and other applications and vehicles with minimal or reduced human intervention.

Exam Probability: **Low**

57. *Answer choices:*

(see index for correct answer)

- a. EtherCAT
- b. PieP
- c. CODESYS
- d. Sequential function chart

Guidance: level 1

_____ are safeguards or countermeasures to avoid, detect, counteract, or minimize security risks to physical property, information, computer systems, or other assets.

Exam Probability: **Low**

58. *Answer choices:*

(see index for correct answer)

- a. Titan Rain
- b. Separation of duties
- c. Alternative compensation system
- d. Security information and event management

Guidance: level 1

:: ::

The _____ is a unit of digital information that most commonly consists of eight bits, representing a binary number. Historically, the _____ was the number of bits used to encode a single character of text in a computer and for this reason it is the smallest addressable unit of memory in many computer architectures.

Exam Probability: **Low**

59. *Answer choices:*
(see index for correct answer)

- a. information systems assessment
- b. Byte
- c. personal values
- d. deep-level diversity

Guidance: level 1

Marketing

Marketing is the study and management of exchange relationships. Marketing is the business process of creating relationships with and satisfying customers. With its focus on the customer, marketing is one of the premier components of business management.

Marketing is defined by the American Marketing Association as "the activity, set of institutions, and processes for creating, communicating, delivering, and exchanging offerings that have value for customers, clients, partners, and society at large."

:: ::

Business is the activity of making one's living or making money by producing or buying and selling products . Simply put, it is "any activity or enterprise entered into for profit. It does not mean it is a company, a corporation, partnership, or have any such formal organization, but it can range from a street peddler to General Motors."

Exam Probability: **Low**

1. *Answer choices:*
(see index for correct answer)

- a. Firm
- b. co-culture
- c. corporate values
- d. levels of analysis

Guidance: level 1

:: ::

Distribution is one of the four elements of the marketing mix. Distribution is the process of making a product or service available for the consumer or business user who needs it. This can be done directly by the producer or service provider, or using indirect channels with distributors or intermediaries. The other three elements of the marketing mix are product, pricing, and promotion.

Exam Probability: **Low**

2. *Answer choices:*

(see index for correct answer)

- a. cultural
- b. personal values
- c. levels of analysis
- d. Character

Guidance: level 1

:: Information technology ::

_____ is the use of computers to store, retrieve, transmit, and manipulate data, or information, often in the context of a business or other enterprise. IT is considered to be a subset of information and communications technology . An _____ system is generally an information system, a communications system or, more specifically speaking, a computer system – including all hardware, software and peripheral equipment – operated by a limited group of users.

Exam Probability: **High**

3. *Answer choices:*

(see index for correct answer)

- a. Information technology
- b. ISO/IEC JTC 1/SC 23
- c. United States v. Ivanov
- d. CineGrid

Guidance: level 1

:: Survey methodology ::

A _____ is the procedure of systematically acquiring and recording information about the members of a given population. The term is used mostly in connection with national population and housing _____ es; other common _____ es include agriculture, business, and traffic _____ es. The United Nations defines the essential features of population and housing _____ es as "individual enumeration, universality within a defined territory, simultaneity and defined periodicity", and recommends that population _____ es be taken at least every 10 years. United Nations recommendations also cover _____ topics to be collected, official definitions, classifications and other useful information to co-ordinate international practice.

Exam Probability: **High**

4. *Answer choices:*
(see index for correct answer)

- a. Self-report study
- b. Total survey error
- c. Census
- d. Coverage error

Guidance: level 1

:: Basic financial concepts ::

_____ is a sustained increase in the general price level of goods and services in an economy over a period of time. When the general price level rises, each unit of currency buys fewer goods and services; consequently, _____ reflects a reduction in the purchasing power per unit of money a loss of real value in the medium of exchange and unit of account within the economy. The measure of _____ is the _____ rate, the annualized percentage change in a general price index, usually the consumer price index, over time. The opposite of _____ is deflation.

Exam Probability: **Medium**

5. *Answer choices:*
(see index for correct answer)

- a. Future-oriented
- b. Present value of benefits
- c. Leverage cycle

- d. Inflation

Guidance: level 1

:: Types of marketing ::

_____ was first defined as a form of marketing developed from direct response marketing campaigns which emphasizes customer retention and satisfaction, rather than a focus on sales transactions.

Exam Probability: **Medium**

6. *Answer choices:*
(see index for correct answer)

- a. Figure of merit
- b. Vertical disintegration
- c. Relationship marketing
- d. Z-CARD

Guidance: level 1

:: Marketing ::

A _____ is a group of customers within a business's serviceable available market at which a business aims its marketing efforts and resources. A _____ is a subset of the total market for a product or service. The _____ typically consists of consumers who exhibit similar characteristics and are considered most likely to buy a business's market offerings or are likely to be the most profitable segments for the business to service.

Exam Probability: **High**

7. *Answer choices:*
(see index for correct answer)

- a. Neuromarketing
- b. Market environment
- c. Target market
- d. Market segmentation index

Guidance: level 1

:: ::

In logic and philosophy, an _____ is a series of statements , called the premises or premisses , intended to determine the degree of truth of another statement, the conclusion. The logical form of an _____ in a natural language can be represented in a symbolic formal language, and independently of natural language formally defined " _____ s" can be made in math and computer science.

Exam Probability: **High**

8. *Answer choices:*

(see index for correct answer)

- a. Argument
- b. open system
- c. functional perspective
- d. co-culture

Guidance: level 1

:: Brand management ::

Marketing communications uses different marketing channels and tools in combination: Marketing communication channels focus on any way a business communicates a message to its desired market, or the market in general. A marketing communication tool can be anything from: advertising, personal selling, direct marketing, sponsorship, communication, and promotion to public relations.

Exam Probability: **High**

9. *Answer choices:*

(see index for correct answer)

- a. Purple Cow: Transform Your Business by Being Remarkable
- b. Westinghouse Licensing Corporation
- c. Web 2.0
- d. Integrated marketing

Guidance: level 1

:: Management ::

A _____ is an idea of the future or desired result that a person or a group of people envisions, plans and commits to achieve. People endeavor to reach _____ s within a finite time by setting deadlines.

Exam Probability: **Low**

10. *Answer choices:*
(see index for correct answer)

- a. Goal
- b. Top development
- c. Resource breakdown structure
- d. Investment control

Guidance: level 1

:: Marketing techniques ::

The _____ or unique selling point is a marketing concept first proposed as a theory to explain a pattern in successful advertising campaigns of the early 1940s. The USP states that such campaigns made unique propositions to customers that convinced them to switch brands. The term was developed by television advertising pioneer Rosser Reeves of Ted Bates & Company. Theodore Levitt, a professor at Harvard Business School, suggested that, "Differentiation is one of the most important strategic and tactical activities in which companies must constantly engage." The term has been used to describe one's "personal brand" in the marketplace. Today, the term is used in other fields or just casually to refer to any aspect of an object that differentiates it from similar objects.

Exam Probability: **High**

11. *Answer choices:*
(see index for correct answer)

- a. Celebrity branding
- b. Unique selling proposition
- c. Elevator pitch
- d. Flyposting

Guidance: level 1

:: Business ::

In commerce, _____ is the product of an interaction between an organization and a customer over the duration of their relationship. This interaction is made up of three parts: the customer journey, the brand touchpoints the customer interacts with, and the environments the _____ s during their experience. A good _____ means that the individual's experience during all points of contact matches the individual's expectations. Gartner asserts the importance of managing the customer's experience.

Exam Probability: **High**

12. *Answer choices:*
(see index for correct answer)

- a. Business directory
- b. Resource slack
- c. Kingdomality
- d. Customer experience

Guidance: level 1

:: ::

_____ is the production of products for use or sale using labour and machines, tools, chemical and biological processing, or formulation. The term may refer to a range of human activity, from handicraft to high tech, but is most commonly applied to industrial design, in which raw materials are transformed into finished goods on a large scale. Such finished goods may be sold to other manufacturers for the production of other, more complex products, such as aircraft, household appliances, furniture, sports equipment or automobiles, or sold to wholesalers, who in turn sell them to retailers, who then sell them to end users and consumers.

Exam Probability: **High**

13. *Answer choices:*
(see index for correct answer)

- a. co-culture
- b. Manufacturing
- c. similarity-attraction theory
- d. hierarchical

Guidance: level 1

A _____ exists when a specific person or enterprise is the only supplier of a particular commodity. This contrasts with a monopsony which relates to a single entity's control of a market to purchase a good or service, and with oligopoly which consists of a few sellers dominating a market. Monopolies are thus characterized by a lack of economic competition to produce the good or service, a lack of viable substitute goods, and the possibility of a high _____ price well above the seller's marginal cost that leads to a high _____ profit. The verb monopolise or monopolize refers to the process by which a company gains the ability to raise prices or exclude competitors. In economics, a _____ is a single seller. In law, a _____ is a business entity that has significant market power, that is, the power to charge overly high prices. Although monopolies may be big businesses, size is not a characteristic of a _____ . A small business may still have the power to raise prices in a small industry .

Exam Probability: **Medium**

14. *Answer choices:*
(see index for correct answer)

- a. Privatization
- b. Cost per procedure
- c. National Competition Policy
- d. Monopoly

Guidance: level 1

In finance, an _____ is the rate at which one currency will be exchanged for another. It is also regarded as the value of one country's currency in relation to another currency. For example, an interbank _____ of 114 Japanese yen to the United States dollar means that ¥114 will be exchanged for each US$1 or that US$1 will be exchanged for each ¥114. In this case it is said that the price of a dollar in relation to yen is ¥114, or equivalently that the price of a yen in relation to dollars is $1/114.

Exam Probability: **Low**

15. *Answer choices:*

(see index for correct answer)

- a. Exchange rate
- b. Neomercantilism
- c. DataArt
- d. Dollar hegemony

Guidance: level 1

:: ::

_____ is the collection of techniques, skills, methods, and processes used in the production of goods or services or in the accomplishment of objectives, such as scientific investigation. _____ can be the knowledge of techniques, processes, and the like, or it can be embedded in machines to allow for operation without detailed knowledge of their workings. Systems applying _____ by taking an input, changing it according to the system's use, and then producing an outcome are referred to as _____ systems or technological systems.

Exam Probability: **High**

16. *Answer choices:*
(see index for correct answer)

- a. cultural
- b. personal values
- c. deep-level diversity
- d. process perspective

Guidance: level 1

:: Marketing ::

A _____ is the quantity of payment or compensation given by one party to another in return for one unit of goods or services.. A _____ is influenced by both production costs and demand for the product. A _____ may be determined by a monopolist or may be imposed on the firm by market conditions.

Exam Probability: **Medium**

17. *Answer choices:*

(see index for correct answer)

- a. Price
- b. Customer lifetime value
- c. Price on application
- d. Digital native

Guidance: level 1

:: Consumer behaviour ::

Convenient procedures, products and services are those intended to increase ease in accessibility, save resources and decrease frustration. A modern _____ is a labor-saving device, service or substance which make a task easier or more efficient than a traditional method. _____ is a relative concept, and depends on context. For example, automobiles were once considered a _____, yet today are regarded as a normal part of life.

Exam Probability: **Low**

18. *Answer choices:*

(see index for correct answer)

- a. Consumer confusion
- b. Convenience
- c. VALS
- d. Shopping while black

Guidance: level 1

:: Consumer theory ::

_____ is the quantity of a good that consumers are willing and able to purchase at various prices during a given period of time.

Exam Probability: **Medium**

19. *Answer choices:*

(see index for correct answer)

- a. Elasticity of substitution
- b. Convex preferences
- c. Consumer choice
- d. Time-based pricing

Guidance: level 1

:: Marketing ::

_____ is the percentage of a market accounted for by a specific entity. In a survey of nearly 200 senior marketing managers, 67% responded that they found the revenue- "dollar _____ " metric very useful, while 61% found "unit _____ " very useful.

Exam Probability: **High**

20. *Answer choices:*
(see index for correct answer)

- a. Marketing operations
- b. Breakthrough Moments
- c. Movement marketing
- d. Market share

Guidance: level 1

:: Management ::

_____ is the process of thinking about the activities required to achieve a desired goal. It is the first and foremost activity to achieve desired results. It involves the creation and maintenance of a plan, such as psychological aspects that require conceptual skills. There are even a couple of tests to measure someone's capability of _____ well. As such, _____ is a fundamental property of intelligent behavior. An important further meaning, often just called " _____ " is the legal context of permitted building developments.

Exam Probability: **High**

21. *Answer choices:*
(see index for correct answer)

- a. Reval
- b. Process capability
- c. Enterprise smart grid
- d. Continuous-flow manufacturing

Guidance: level 1

:: ::

_____ are interactive computer-mediated technologies that facilitate the creation and sharing of information, ideas, career interests and other forms of expression via virtual communities and networks. The variety of stand-alone and built-in _____ services currently available introduces challenges of definition; however, there are some common features.

Exam Probability: **Medium**

22. *Answer choices:*
(see index for correct answer)

- a. co-culture
- b. open system
- c. levels of analysis
- d. interpersonal communication

Guidance: level 1

:: Retailing ::

A _____ is a retail establishment offering a wide range of consumer goods in different product categories known as "departments". In modern major cities, the _____ made a dramatic appearance in the middle of the 19th century, and permanently reshaped shopping habits, and the definition of service and luxury. Similar developments were under way in London , in Paris and in New York .

Exam Probability: **Medium**

23. *Answer choices:*
(see index for correct answer)

- a. Retail
- b. Omni-channel Retailing
- c. Retail Systems Research
- d. Shoppable Windows

Guidance: level 1

:: Direct marketing ::

_____ is a method of direct marketing in which a salesperson solicits prospective customers to buy products or services, either over the phone or through a subsequent face to face or Web conferencing appointment scheduled during the call. _____ can also include recorded sales pitches programmed to be played over the phone via automatic dialing.

Exam Probability: **Medium**

24. *Answer choices:*
(see index for correct answer)

- a. Ginsu
- b. Book of the Month Club
- c. Cold calling
- d. Telemarketing

Guidance: level 1

:: ::

A _____ is the process of presenting a topic to an audience. It is typically a demonstration, introduction, lecture, or speech meant to inform, persuade, inspire, motivate, or to build good will or to present a new idea or product. The term can also be used for a formal or ritualized introduction or offering, as with the _____ of a debutante. _____ s in certain formats are also known as keynote address.

Exam Probability: **Low**

25. *Answer choices:*
(see index for correct answer)

- a. hierarchical
- b. Presentation
- c. co-culture
- d. personal values

Guidance: level 1

:: Business ::

The seller, or the provider of the goods or services, completes a sale in response to an acquisition, appropriation, requisition or a direct interaction with the buyer at the point of sale. There is a passing of title of the item, and the settlement of a price, in which agreement is reached on a price for which transfer of ownership of the item will occur. The seller, not the purchaser typically executes the sale and it may be completed prior to the obligation of payment. In the case of indirect interaction, a person who sells goods or service on behalf of the owner is known as a salesman or saleswoman or salesperson, but this often refers to someone _____ goods in a store/shop, in which case other terms are also common, including salesclerk, shop assistant, and retail clerk.

Exam Probability: **High**

26. *Answer choices:*
(see index for correct answer)

- a. Citizenship for life
- b. Sales
- c. Crowdsourcing
- d. Retail design

Guidance: level 1

:: Stock market ::

The _____ of a corporation is all of the shares into which ownership of the corporation is divided. In American English, the shares are commonly known as " _____ s". A single share of the _____ represents fractional ownership of the corporation in proportion to the total number of shares. This typically entitles the _____ holder to that fraction of the company's earnings, proceeds from liquidation of assets , or voting power, often dividing these up in proportion to the amount of money each _____ holder has invested. Not all _____ is necessarily equal, as certain classes of _____ may be issued for example without voting rights, with enhanced voting rights, or with a certain priority to receive profits or liquidation proceeds before or after other classes of shareholders.

Exam Probability: **Medium**

27. *Answer choices:*
(see index for correct answer)

- a. International Retail Service
- b. Delivery versus payment
- c. Trader
- d. Stock

Guidance: level 1

:: ::

_____ is change in the heritable characteristics of biological populations over successive generations. These characteristics are the expressions of genes that are passed on from parent to offspring during reproduction. Different characteristics tend to exist within any given population as a result of mutation, genetic recombination and other sources of genetic variation. _____ occurs when _____ ary processes such as natural selection and genetic drift act on this variation, resulting in certain characteristics becoming more common or rare within a population. It is this process of _____ that has given rise to biodiversity at every level of biological organisation, including the levels of species, individual organisms and molecules.

Exam Probability: **High**

28. *Answer choices:*
(see index for correct answer)

- a. Character
- b. process perspective
- c. empathy
- d. Evolution

Guidance: level 1

:: Manufacturing ::

A _____ is a building for storing goods. _____ s are used by manufacturers, importers, exporters, wholesalers, transport businesses, customs, etc. They are usually large plain buildings in industrial parks on the outskirts of cities, towns or villages.

Exam Probability: **High**

29. *Answer choices:*

(see index for correct answer)

- a. Manufacturing engineering
- b. Microfactory
- c. Demand flow technology
- d. Warehouse

Guidance: level 1

:: ::

In production, research, retail, and accounting, a _____ is the value of money that has been used up to produce something or deliver a service, and hence is not available for use anymore. In business, the _____ may be one of acquisition, in which case the amount of money expended to acquire it is counted as _____ . In this case, money is the input that is gone in order to acquire the thing. This acquisition _____ may be the sum of the _____ of production as incurred by the original producer, and further _____ s of transaction as incurred by the acquirer over and above the price paid to the producer. Usually, the price also includes a mark-up for profit over the _____ of production.

Exam Probability: **Low**

30. *Answer choices:*
(see index for correct answer)

- a. cultural
- b. empathy
- c. hierarchical
- d. hierarchical perspective

Guidance: level 1

:: Television commercials ::

_____ is a phenomenon whereby something new and somehow valuable is formed. The created item may be intangible or a physical object .

Exam Probability: **Low**

31. *Answer choices:*
(see index for correct answer)

- a. World History. Bank Imperial

- b. Pipes
- c. Gorilla
- d. Yeh Dil Maange More!

Guidance: level 1

:: Television commercials ::

_____ is a characteristic that distinguishes physical entities that have biological processes, such as signaling and self-sustaining processes, from those that do not, either because such functions have ceased , or because they never had such functions and are classified as inanimate. Various forms of _____ exist, such as plants, animals, fungi, protists, archaea, and bacteria. The criteria can at times be ambiguous and may or may not define viruses, viroids, or potential synthetic _____ as "living". Biology is the science concerned with the study of _____ .

Exam Probability: **Low**

32. *Answer choices:*
(see index for correct answer)

- a. Creativity
- b. Terry Tate: Office Linebacker
- c. Reassuringly Expensive
- d. Life

Guidance: level 1

:: ::

An _____ is a systematic and independent examination of books, accounts, statutory records, documents and vouchers of an organization to ascertain how far the financial statements as well as non-financial disclosures present a true and fair view of the concern. It also attempts to ensure that the books of accounts are properly maintained by the concern as required by law. _____ ing has become such a ubiquitous phenomenon in the corporate and the public sector that academics started identifying an " _____ Society". The _____ or perceives and recognises the propositions before them for examination, obtains evidence, evaluates the same and formulates an opinion on the basis of his judgement which is communicated through their _____ ing report.

33. *Answer choices:*

(see index for correct answer)

- a. process perspective
- b. levels of analysis
- c. Audit
- d. Sarbanes-Oxley act of 2002

Guidance: level 1

:: Competition (economics) ::

_____ arises whenever at least two parties strive for a goal which cannot be shared: where one's gain is the other's loss .

Exam Probability: **Low**

34. *Answer choices:*

(see index for correct answer)

- a. Economic forces
- b. Competition
- c. Transfer pricing
- d. Currency competition

Guidance: level 1

:: ::

A _____ is a professional who provides expert advice in a particular area such as security , management, education, accountancy, law, human resources, marketing , finance, engineering, science or any of many other specialized fields.

Exam Probability: **Medium**

35. *Answer choices:*

(see index for correct answer)

- a. levels of analysis
- b. process perspective
- c. co-culture
- d. Consultant

Guidance: level 1

:: Types of marketing ::

_____ is "marketing on a worldwide scale reconciling or taking commercial advantage of global operational differences, similarities and opportunities in order to meet global objectives".

Exam Probability: **Low**

36. *Answer choices:*
(see index for correct answer)

- a. Global marketing
- b. Guerrilla marketing
- c. Close Range Marketing
- d. Social pull marketing

Guidance: level 1

:: Project management ::

Contemporary business and science treat as a _____ any undertaking, carried out individually or collaboratively and possibly involving research or design, that is carefully planned to achieve a particular aim.

Exam Probability: **High**

37. *Answer choices:*
(see index for correct answer)

- a. Project manufacturing
- b. Team performance management
- c. Dependency
- d. Project

Guidance: level 1

:: ::

_____ is a process whereby a person assumes the parenting of another, usually a child, from that person's biological or legal parent or parents.

Legal _____ s permanently transfers all rights and responsibilities, along with filiation, from the biological parent or parents.

Exam Probability: **Medium**

38. *Answer choices:*
(see index for correct answer)

- a. hierarchical
- b. open system
- c. Adoption
- d. similarity-attraction theory

Guidance: level 1

:: ::

_____ , also referred to as orthostasis, is a human position in which the body is held in an upright position and supported only by the feet.

Exam Probability: **High**

39. *Answer choices:*
(see index for correct answer)

- a. process perspective
- b. empathy
- c. functional perspective
- d. similarity-attraction theory

Guidance: level 1

:: ::

Market segmentation is the activity of dividing a broad consumer or business market, normally consisting of existing and potential customers, into sub-groups of consumers based on some type of shared characteristics. In dividing or segmenting markets, researchers typically look for common characteristics such as shared needs, common interests, similar lifestyles or even similar demographic profiles. The overall aim of segmentation is to identify high yield segments – that is, those segments that are likely to be the most profitable or that have growth potential – so that these can be selected for special attention .

Exam Probability: **Low**

40. *Answer choices:*
(see index for correct answer)

- a. personal values
- b. levels of analysis
- c. surface-level diversity
- d. Market segments

Guidance: level 1

:: Evaluation methods ::

_____ is a scientific method of observation to gather non-numerical data. This type of research "refers to the meanings, concepts definitions, characteristics, metaphors, symbols, and description of things" and not to their "counts or measures." This research answers why and how a certain phenomenon may occur rather than how often. _____ approaches are employed across many academic disciplines, focusing particularly on the human elements of the social and natural sciences; in less academic contexts, areas of application include qualitative market research, business, service demonstrations by non-profits, and journalism.

Exam Probability: **High**

41. *Answer choices:*
(see index for correct answer)

- a. Reference class forecasting
- b. Qualitative research
- c. Logic model
- d. Random digit dialing

:: Financial economics ::

In management, business value is an informal term that includes all forms of value that determine the health and well-being of the firm in the long run. Business value expands concept of value of the firm beyond economic value to include other forms of value such as employee value, _____ , supplier value, channel partner value, alliance partner value, managerial value, and societal value. Many of these forms of value are not directly measured in monetary terms.

Exam Probability: **Low**

42. *Answer choices:*
(see index for correct answer)

- a. Pricing schedule
- b. Forward price
- c. Customer value
- d. Cyclical asymmetry

:: Decision theory ::

A _____ is a deliberate system of principles to guide decisions and achieve rational outcomes. A _____ is a statement of intent, and is implemented as a procedure or protocol. Policies are generally adopted by a governance body within an organization. Policies can assist in both subjective and objective decision making. Policies to assist in subjective decision making usually assist senior management with decisions that must be based on the relative merits of a number of factors, and as a result are often hard to test objectively, e.g. work-life balance _____ . In contrast policies to assist in objective decision making are usually operational in nature and can be objectively tested, e.g. password _____ .

Exam Probability: **High**

43. *Answer choices:*
(see index for correct answer)

- a. Decision aids

- b. Rete algorithm
- c. Policy
- d. Distinction bias

Guidance: level 1

:: Supply chain management ::

The _____ is a barcode symbology that is widely used in the United States, Canada, United Kingdom, Australia, New Zealand, in Europe and other countries for tracking trade items in stores.

Exam Probability: **Medium**

44. *Answer choices:*
(see index for correct answer)

- a. Transportation management system
- b. ISO/PAS 28000
- c. Procurement
- d. Revenue Technology Services

Guidance: level 1

:: Investment ::

In finance, the benefit from an _____ is called a return. The return may consist of a gain realised from the sale of property or an _____ , unrealised capital appreciation , or _____ income such as dividends, interest, rental income etc., or a combination of capital gain and income. The return may also include currency gains or losses due to changes in foreign currency exchange rates.

Exam Probability: **Low**

45. *Answer choices:*
(see index for correct answer)

- a. Investment broker
- b. Asian option
- c. Value averaging
- d. Relative return

Guidance: level 1

An _____ is the production of goods or related services within an economy. The major source of revenue of a group or company is the indicator of its relevant _____ . When a large group has multiple sources of revenue generation, it is considered to be working in different industries. Manufacturing _____ became a key sector of production and labour in European and North American countries during the Industrial Revolution, upsetting previous mercantile and feudal economies. This came through many successive rapid advances in technology, such as the production of steel and coal.

Exam Probability: **Medium**

46. *Answer choices:*
(see index for correct answer)

- a. co-culture
- b. cultural
- c. Industry
- d. levels of analysis

Guidance: level 1

:: Production and manufacturing ::

_____ consists of organization-wide efforts to "install and make permanent climate where employees continuously improve their ability to provide on demand products and services that customers will find of particular value." "Total" emphasizes that departments in addition to production are obligated to improve their operations; "management" emphasizes that executives are obligated to actively manage quality through funding, training, staffing, and goal setting. While there is no widely agreed-upon approach, TQM efforts typically draw heavily on the previously developed tools and techniques of quality control. TQM enjoyed widespread attention during the late 1980s and early 1990s before being overshadowed by ISO 9000, Lean manufacturing, and Six Sigma.

Exam Probability: **Medium**

47. *Answer choices:*
(see index for correct answer)

- a. Zero Defects

- b. Master production schedule
- c. Total Quality Management
- d. Cycle time variation

Guidance: level 1

:: Income ::

_____ is a ratio between the net profit and cost of investment resulting from an investment of some resources. A high ROI means the investment's gains favorably to its cost. As a performance measure, ROI is used to evaluate the efficiency of an investment or to compare the efficiencies of several different investments. In purely economic terms, it is one way of relating profits to capital invested. _____ is a performance measure used by businesses to identify the efficiency of an investment or number of different investments.

Exam Probability: **High**

48. *Answer choices:*
(see index for correct answer)

- a. Meetup fee
- b. Return on investment
- c. IRD asset
- d. Gratuity

Guidance: level 1

:: Credit cards ::

The _____ Company, also known as Amex, is an American multinational financial services corporation headquartered in Three World Financial Center in New York City. The company was founded in 1850 and is one of the 30 components of the Dow Jones Industrial Average. The company is best known for its charge card, credit card, and traveler's cheque businesses.

Exam Probability: **Low**

49. *Answer choices:*
(see index for correct answer)

- a. American Express
- b. Credit Saison

- c. Kisan Credit Card
- d. The Everything Card

Guidance: level 1

:: ::

In business and engineering, new _____ covers the complete process of bringing a new product to market. A central aspect of NPD is product design, along with various business considerations. New _____ is described broadly as the transformation of a market opportunity into a product available for sale. The product can be tangible or intangible , though sometimes services and other processes are distinguished from "products." NPD requires an understanding of customer needs and wants, the competitive environment, and the nature of the market.Cost, time and quality are the main variables that drive customer needs. Aiming at these three variables, innovative companies develop continuous practices and strategies to better satisfy customer requirements and to increase their own market share by a regular development of new products. There are many uncertainties and challenges which companies must face throughout the process. The use of best practices and the elimination of barriers to communication are the main concerns for the management of the NPD .

Exam Probability: **High**

50. *Answer choices:*
(see index for correct answer)

- a. deep-level diversity
- b. Product development
- c. co-culture
- d. hierarchical perspective

Guidance: level 1

:: ::

In _____ relations and communication science, _____ s are groups of individual people, and the _____ is the totality of such groupings. This is a different concept to the sociological concept of the Öffentlichkeit or _____ sphere. The concept of a _____ has also been defined in political science, psychology, marketing, and advertising. In _____ relations and communication science, it is one of the more ambiguous concepts in the field. Although it has definitions in the theory of the field that have been formulated from the early 20th century onwards, it has suffered in more recent years from being blurred, as a result of conflation of the idea of a _____ with the notions of audience, market segment, community, constituency, and stakeholder.

Exam Probability: **Medium**

51. *Answer choices:*

(see index for correct answer)

- a. Public
- b. levels of analysis
- c. functional perspective
- d. Sarbanes-Oxley act of 2002

Guidance: level 1

:: ::

_____ is a marketing communication that employs an openly sponsored, non-personal message to promote or sell a product, service or idea. Sponsors of _____ are typically businesses wishing to promote their products or services. _____ is differentiated from public relations in that an advertiser pays for and has control over the message. It differs from personal selling in that the message is non-personal, i.e., not directed to a particular individual. _____ is communicated through various mass media, including traditional media such as newspapers, magazines, television, radio, outdoor _____ or direct mail; and new media such as search results, blogs, social media, websites or text messages. The actual presentation of the message in a medium is referred to as an advertisement, or "ad" or advert for short.

Exam Probability: **Low**

52. *Answer choices:*

(see index for correct answer)

- a. information systems assessment
- b. Advertising
- c. functional perspective
- d. deep-level diversity

Guidance: level 1

:: Public relations ::

_____ is the public visibility or awareness for any product, service or company. It may also refer to the movement of information from its source to the general public, often but not always via the media. The subjects of _____ include people , goods and services, organizations, and works of art or entertainment.

Exam Probability: **Low**

53. *Answer choices:*
(see index for correct answer)

- a. Sexed up
- b. Public diplomacy
- c. Corporate Representatives for Ethical Wikipedia Engagement
- d. Press videoconferencing

Guidance: level 1

:: Advertising by type ::

_____ or advertising war is an advertisement in which a particular product, or service, specifically mentions a competitor by name for the express purpose of showing why the competitor is inferior to the product naming it. Also referred to as "knocking copy", it is loosely defined as advertising where "the advertised brand is explicitly compared with one or more competing brands and the comparison is obvious to the audience."

Exam Probability: **Medium**

54. *Answer choices:*
(see index for correct answer)

- a. Aerial advertising
- b. Comparative advertising
- c. Parody advertisement
- d. Out-of-home advertising

:: ::

According to the philosopher Piyush Mathur , "Tangibility is the property that a phenomenon exhibits if it has and/or transports mass and/or energy and/or momentum".

Exam Probability: **Medium**

55. *Answer choices:*

- a. Character
- b. Tangible
- c. imperative
- d. hierarchical

:: Materials ::

A _____ , also known as a feedstock, unprocessed material, or primary commodity, is a basic material that is used to produce goods, finished products, energy, or intermediate materials which are feedstock for future finished products. As feedstock, the term connotes these materials are bottleneck assets and are highly important with regard to producing other products. An example of this is crude oil, which is a _____ and a feedstock used in the production of industrial chemicals, fuels, plastics, and pharmaceutical goods; lumber is a _____ used to produce a variety of products including all types of furniture. The term " _____ " denotes materials in minimally processed or unprocessed in states; e.g., raw latex, crude oil, cotton, coal, raw biomass, iron ore, air, logs, or water i.e. "...any product of agriculture, forestry, fishing and any other mineral that is in its natural form or which has undergone the transformation required to prepare it for internationally marketing in substantial volumes."

Exam Probability: **Medium**

56. *Answer choices:*

- a. Raw material

- b. Lute
- c. Superhard material
- d. Latex

Guidance: level 1

:: ::

In law, an _____ is the process in which cases are reviewed, where parties request a formal change to an official decision. _____ s function both as a process for error correction as well as a process of clarifying and interpreting law. Although appellate courts have existed for thousands of years, common law countries did not incorporate an affirmative right to _____ into their jurisprudence until the 19th century.

Exam Probability: **Medium**

57. *Answer choices:*
(see index for correct answer)

- a. similarity-attraction theory
- b. Appeal
- c. cultural
- d. empathy

Guidance: level 1

:: Marketing techniques ::

_____ is the activity of dividing a broad consumer or business market, normally consisting of existing and potential customers, into sub-groups of consumers based on some type of shared characteristics. In dividing or segmenting markets, researchers typically look for common characteristics such as shared needs, common interests, similar lifestyles or even similar demographic profiles. The overall aim of segmentation is to identify high yield segments – that is, those segments that are likely to be the most profitable or that have growth potential – so that these can be selected for special attention .

Exam Probability: **High**

58. *Answer choices:*
(see index for correct answer)

- a. market segment
- b. Seeding trial
- c. Horizontal marketing system
- d. Aaker Model

Guidance: level 1

:: ::

A _____ is an organization, usually a group of people or a company, authorized to act as a single entity and recognized as such in law. Early incorporated entities were established by charter . Most jurisdictions now allow the creation of new _____ s through registration.

Exam Probability: **Medium**

59. *Answer choices:*
(see index for correct answer)

- a. interpersonal communication
- b. process perspective
- c. Corporation
- d. similarity-attraction theory

Guidance: level 1

Manufacturing

Manufacturing is the production of merchandise for use or sale using labor and machines, tools, chemical and biological processing, or formulation. The term may refer to a range of human activity, from handicraft to high tech, but is most commonly applied to industrial design , in which raw materials are transformed into finished goods on a large scale. Such finished goods may be sold to other manufacturers for the production of other, more complex products, such as aircraft, household appliances, furniture, sports equipment or automobiles, or sold to wholesalers, who in turn sell them to retailers, who then sell them to end users and consumers.

:: Promotion and marketing communications ::

The _____ of American Manufacturers, now ThomasNet, is an online platform for supplier discovery and product sourcing in the US and Canada. It was once known as the "big green books" and "Thomas Registry", and was a multi-volume directory of industrial product information covering 650,000 distributors, manufacturers and service companies within 67,000-plus industrial categories that is now published on ThomasNet.

Exam Probability: **Medium**

1. *Answer choices:*
(see index for correct answer)

- a. Thomas Register
- b. CollarCard
- c. Shop fitting
- d. Nielsen Broadcast Data Systems

Guidance: level 1

:: ::

In sales, commerce and economics, a _____ is the recipient of a good, service, product or an idea - obtained from a seller, vendor, or supplier via a financial transaction or exchange for money or some other valuable consideration.

Exam Probability: **Low**

2. *Answer choices:*
(see index for correct answer)

- a. Character
- b. empathy
- c. Customer
- d. hierarchical perspective

Guidance: level 1

:: Data management ::

_____ is the ability of a physical product to remain functional, without requiring excessive maintenance or repair, when faced with the challenges of normal operation over its design lifetime. There are several measures of _____ in use, including years of life, hours of use, and number of operational cycles. In economics, goods with a long usable life are referred to as durable goods.

Exam Probability: **High**

3. *Answer choices:*
(see index for correct answer)

- a. Data integration
- b. Core Data
- c. Content migration
- d. Durability

Guidance: level 1

:: Data management ::

_____ refers to a data-driven improvement cycle used for improving, optimizing and stabilizing business processes and designs. The _____ improvement cycle is the core tool used to drive Six Sigma projects. However, _____ is not exclusive to Six Sigma and can be used as the framework for other improvement applications.

Exam Probability: **Medium**

4. *Answer choices:*

(see index for correct answer)

- a. DMAIC
- b. Content migration
- c. Information integration
- d. Rainbow Storage

Guidance: level 1

:: Process management ::

_____ is a statistics package developed at the Pennsylvania State University by researchers Barbara F. Ryan, Thomas A. Ryan, Jr., and Brian L. Joiner in 1972. It began as a light version of OMNITAB 80, a statistical analysis program by NIST. Statistical analysis software such as _____ automates calculations and the creation of graphs, allowing the user to focus more on the analysis of data and the interpretation of results. It is compatible with other _____ , Inc. software.

Exam Probability: **Low**

5. *Answer choices:*

(see index for correct answer)

- a. Conformance checking
- b. Business process discovery
- c. Minitab
- d. Hazard analysis and critical control points

Guidance: level 1

:: Risk analysis ::

Supply-chain risk management is "the implementation of strategies to manage both everyday and exceptional risks along the supply chain based on continuous risk assessment with the objective of reducing vulnerability and ensuring continuity".

Exam Probability: **Medium**

6. *Answer choices:*
(see index for correct answer)

- a. Singleton
- b. Supply chain risk management
- c. Fault tree analysis
- d. Event tree

Guidance: level 1

:: Decision theory ::

_____ is a method developed in Japan beginning in 1966 to help transform the voice of the customer into engineering characteristics for a product. Yoji Akao, the original developer, described QFD as a "method to transform qualitative user demands into quantitative parameters, to deploy the functions forming quality, and to deploy methods for achieving the design quality into subsystems and component parts, and ultimately to specific elements of the manufacturing process." The author combined his work in quality assurance and quality control points with function deployment used in value engineering.

Exam Probability: **High**

7. *Answer choices:*
(see index for correct answer)

- a. Belief structure
- b. Price of stability
- c. Quality function deployment
- d. Two-moment decision model

Guidance: level 1

:: Project management ::

In economics and business decision-making, a sunk cost is a cost that has already been incurred and cannot be recovered.

Exam Probability: **Medium**

8. *Answer choices:*

(see index for correct answer)

- a. Commissioning management systems
- b. Scrumedge
- c. Sunk costs
- d. Resource allocation

Guidance: level 1

:: ::

_____ refers to the confirmation of certain characteristics of an object, person, or organization. This confirmation is often, but not always, provided by some form of external review, education, assessment, or audit. Accreditation is a specific organization's process of _____ . According to the National Council on Measurement in Education, a _____ test is a credentialing test used to determine whether individuals are knowledgeable enough in a given occupational area to be labeled "competent to practice" in that area.

Exam Probability: **Low**

9. *Answer choices:*

(see index for correct answer)

- a. process perspective
- b. hierarchical perspective
- c. Certification
- d. similarity-attraction theory

Guidance: level 1

:: ::

A _____ consists of an orchestrated and repeatable pattern of business activity enabled by the systematic organization of resources into processes that transform materials, provide services, or process information. It can be depicted as a sequence of operations, the work of a person or group, the work of an organization of staff, or one or more simple or complex mechanisms.

Exam Probability: **Medium**

10. *Answer choices:*
(see index for correct answer)

- a. Workflow
- b. Sarbanes-Oxley act of 2002
- c. Character
- d. interpersonal communication

Guidance: level 1

:: Procurement ::

Purchasing is the formal process of buying goods and services. The _____ can vary from one organization to another, but there are some common key elements.

Exam Probability: **Medium**

11. *Answer choices:*
(see index for correct answer)

- a. Purchasing Managers Index
- b. Request price quotation
- c. Swiss challenge
- d. Central billing

Guidance: level 1

:: Alchemical processes ::

In chemistry, a _____ is a special type of homogeneous mixture composed of two or more substances. In such a mixture, a solute is a substance dissolved in another substance, known as a solvent. The mixing process of a _____ happens at a scale where the effects of chemical polarity are involved, resulting in interactions that are specific to solvation. The _____ assumes the phase of the solvent when the solvent is the larger fraction of the mixture, as is commonly the case. The concentration of a solute in a _____ is the mass of that solute expressed as a percentage of the mass of the whole _____ . The term aqueous _____ is when one of the solvents is water.

Exam Probability: **Medium**

12. *Answer choices:*
(see index for correct answer)

- a. Fermentation
- b. Projection
- c. Corporification
- d. Putrefying bacteria

Guidance: level 1

:: Infographics ::

The _____ is a form used to collect data in real time at the location where the data is generated. The data it captures can be quantitative or qualitative. When the information is quantitative, the _____ is sometimes called a tally sheet.

Exam Probability: **High**

13. *Answer choices:*
(see index for correct answer)

- a. Check sheet
- b. Baby on board
- c. U.S. Route shield
- d. Archaeological illustration

Guidance: level 1

:: Production and manufacturing ::

_____ is a systematic method to improve the "value" of goods or products and services by using an examination of function. Value, as defined, is the ratio of function to cost. Value can therefore be manipulated by either improving the function or reducing the cost. It is a primary tenet of _____ that basic functions be preserved and not be reduced as a consequence of pursuing value improvements.

Exam Probability: **Medium**

14. *Answer choices:*
(see index for correct answer)

- a. Value engineering
- b. Miniaturization
- c. Piece work
- d. Digital materialization

Guidance: level 1

:: Natural resources ::

_____ s are resources that exist without actions of humankind. This includes all valued characteristics such as magnetic, gravitational, electrical properties and forces etc. On Earth it includes sunlight, atmosphere, water, land along with all vegetation, crops and animal life that naturally subsists upon or within the heretofore identified characteristics and substances.

Exam Probability: **Medium**

15. *Answer choices:*
(see index for correct answer)

- a. Natural resource
- b. Ferrallitisation
- c. Ecosystem Health
- d. QEMSCAN

Guidance: level 1

:: Production and manufacturing ::

_____ is a comprehensive and rigorous industrial process by which a previously sold, leased, used, worn or non-functional product or part is returned to a 'like-new' or 'better-than-new' condition, from both a quality and performance perspective, through a controlled, reproducible and sustainable process.

Exam Probability: **Medium**

16. *Answer choices:*
(see index for correct answer)

- a. Fixed position assembly
- b. Remanufacturing
- c. International Automotive Task Force
- d. EFQM Excellence Model

Guidance: level 1

:: Business planning ::

_____ is an organization's process of defining its strategy, or direction, and making decisions on allocating its resources to pursue this strategy. It may also extend to control mechanisms for guiding the implementation of the strategy. _____ became prominent in corporations during the 1960s and remains an important aspect of strategic management. It is executed by strategic planners or strategists, who involve many parties and research sources in their analysis of the organization and its relationship to the environment in which it competes.

Exam Probability: **Low**

17. *Answer choices:*
(see index for correct answer)

- a. operational planning
- b. Exit planning
- c. Strategic planning
- d. Customer Demand Planning

Guidance: level 1

:: ::

An _____ is, most an organized examination or formal evaluation exercise. In engineering activities _____ involves the measurements, tests, and gauges applied to certain characteristics in regard to an object or activity. The results are usually compared to specified requirements and standards for determining whether the item or activity is in line with these targets, often with a Standard _____ Procedure in place to ensure consistent checking. _____ s are usually non-destructive.

Exam Probability: **High**

18. *Answer choices:*
(see index for correct answer)

- a. personal values
- b. corporate values
- c. empathy
- d. Inspection

Guidance: level 1

:: Product management ::

_____ is the state of being which occurs when an object, service, or practice is no longer wanted even though it may still be in good working order; however, the international standard EN62402 _____ Management - Application Guide defines _____ as being the "transition from availability of products by the original manufacturer or supplier to unavailability". _____ frequently occurs because a replacement has become available that has, in sum, more advantages compared to the disadvantages incurred by maintaining or repairing the original. Obsolete also refers to something that is already disused or discarded, or antiquated. Typically, _____ is preceded by a gradual decline in popularity.

Exam Probability: **High**

19. *Answer choices:*
(see index for correct answer)

- a. Obsolescence
- b. Rapid prototyping
- c. Technology acceptance model
- d. Trademark distinctiveness

Guidance: level 1

_____ is the creation of a whole that is greater than the simple sum of its parts. The term _____ comes from the Attic Greek word sea synergia from synergos, , meaning "working together".

Exam Probability: **Low**

20. *Answer choices:*
(see index for correct answer)

- a. Diseconomies of scale
- b. Sectoral output
- c. Specialization
- d. Foundations of Economic Analysis

Guidance: level 1

_____ is the practice of initiating, planning, executing, controlling, and closing the work of a team to achieve specific goals and meet specific success criteria at the specified time.

Exam Probability: **Low**

21. *Answer choices:*
(see index for correct answer)

- a. Planning
- b. Target culture
- c. Project management
- d. Law practice management

Guidance: level 1

" _____ s are the structural determinants of the cost of an activity, reflecting any linkages or interrelationships that affect it". Therefore we could assume that the _____ s determine the cost behavior within the activities, reflecting the links that these have with other activities and relationships that affect them.

Exam Probability: **Low**

22. *Answer choices:*

(see index for correct answer)

- a. RCA open-source application
- b. Variance
- c. Operating profit margin
- d. Cost driver

Guidance: level 1

:: Project management ::

_____ is a marketing activity that does an aggregate plan for the production process, in advance of 6 to 18 months, to give an idea to management as to what quantity of materials and other resources are to be procured and when, so that the total cost of operations of the organization is kept to the minimum over that period.

Exam Probability: **Medium**

23. *Answer choices:*

(see index for correct answer)

- a. Site survey
- b. Project
- c. Value of work done
- d. Aggregate planning

Guidance: level 1

:: ::

A _____ is a covering that is applied to the surface of an object, usually referred to as the substrate. The purpose of applying the _____ may be decorative, functional, or both. The _____ itself may be an all-over _____ , completely covering the substrate, or it may only cover parts of the substrate. An example of all of these types of _____ is a product label on many drinks bottles- one side has an all-over functional _____ and the other side has one or more decorative _____ s in an appropriate pattern to form the words and images.

Exam Probability: **Low**

24. *Answer choices:*
(see index for correct answer)

- a. hierarchical perspective
- b. imperative
- c. corporate values
- d. cultural

Guidance: level 1

:: Project management ::

_____ is a work methodology emphasizing the parallelisation of tasks , which is sometimes called simultaneous engineering or integrated product development using an integrated product team approach. It refers to an approach used in product development in which functions of design engineering, manufacturing engineering, and other functions are integrated to reduce the time required to bring a new product to market.

Exam Probability: **Medium**

25. *Answer choices:*
(see index for correct answer)

- a. Concurrent engineering
- b. Duration
- c. Project charter
- d. Axelos

Guidance: level 1

:: Natural materials ::

_____ is a finely-grained natural rock or soil material that combines one or more _____ minerals with possible traces of quartz , metal oxides and organic matter. Geologic _____ deposits are mostly composed of phyllosilicate minerals containing variable amounts of water trapped in the mineral structure. _____ s are plastic due to particle size and geometry as well as water content, and become hard, brittle and non–plastic upon drying or firing. Depending on the soil's content in which it is found, _____ can appear in various colours from white to dull grey or brown to deep orange-red.

Exam Probability: **Low**

26. *Answer choices:*
(see index for correct answer)

- a. Decomposed granite
- b. Bast fibre
- c. Perovskite
- d. Dry stone

Guidance: level 1

:: Building materials ::

_____ is an alloy of iron and carbon, and sometimes other elements. Because of its high tensile strength and low cost, it is a major component used in buildings, infrastructure, tools, ships, automobiles, machines, appliances, and weapons.

Exam Probability: **High**

27. *Answer choices:*
(see index for correct answer)

- a. Bioasphalt
- b. Fly ash brick
- c. Steel
- d. Cement render

Guidance: level 1

:: Management ::

_____ is a method of quality control which employs statistical methods to monitor and control a process. This helps to ensure that the process operates efficiently, producing more specification-conforming products with less waste . SPC can be applied to any process where the "conforming product" output can be measured. Key tools used in SPC include run charts, control charts, a focus on continuous improvement, and the design of experiments. An example of a process where SPC is applied is manufacturing lines.

Exam Probability: **Medium**

28. *Answer choices:*
(see index for correct answer)

- a. Business rule mining
- b. Corticon
- c. Statistical process control
- d. Economic order quantity

Guidance: level 1

:: Production and manufacturing ::

_____ was a management-led program to eliminate defects in industrial production that enjoyed brief popularity in American industry from 1964 to the early 1970s. Quality expert Philip Crosby later incorporated it into his "Absolutes of Quality Management" and it enjoyed a renaissance in the American automobile industry—as a performance goal more than as a program—in the 1990s. Although applicable to any type of enterprise, it has been primarily adopted within supply chains wherever large volumes of components are being purchased .

Exam Probability: **Low**

29. *Answer choices:*
(see index for correct answer)

- a. product lifecycle
- b. Advanced Manufacturing Software
- c. Changeover
- d. Order to cash

Guidance: level 1

:: ::

_____ is the process of finding an estimate, or approximation, which is a value that is usable for some purpose even if input data may be incomplete, uncertain, or unstable. The value is nonetheless usable because it is derived from the best information available. Typically, _____ involves "using the value of a statistic derived from a sample to estimate the value of a corresponding population parameter". The sample provides information that can be projected, through various formal or informal processes, to determine a range most likely to describe the missing information. An estimate that turns out to be incorrect will be an overestimate if the estimate exceeded the actual result, and an underestimate if the estimate fell short of the actual result.

Exam Probability: **Medium**

30. *Answer choices:*
(see index for correct answer)

- a. hierarchical perspective
- b. Estimation
- c. personal values
- d. process perspective

Guidance: level 1

:: Marketing ::

_____ or stock control can be broadly defined as "the activity of checking a shop's stock." However, a more focused definition takes into account the more science-based, methodical practice of not only verifying a business` inventory but also focusing on the many related facets of inventory management "within an organisation to meet the demand placed upon that business economically." Other facets of _____ include supply chain management, production control, financial flexibility, and customer satisfaction. At the root of _____ , however, is the _____ problem, which involves determining when to order, how much to order, and the logistics of those decisions.

Exam Probability: **Low**

31. *Answer choices:*
(see index for correct answer)

- a. Inventory control
- b. Customer insight

- c. Interruption marketing
- d. Content creation

Guidance: level 1

:: Manufacturing ::

_____ or lean production, often simply "lean", is a systematic method for the minimization of waste within a manufacturing system without sacrificing productivity, which can cause problems. Lean also takes into account waste created through overburden and waste created through unevenness in work loads . Working from the perspective of the client who consumes a product or service, "value" is any action or process that a customer would be willing to pay for.

Exam Probability: **Medium**

32. *Answer choices:*
(see index for correct answer)

- a. Lights out
- b. Lean manufacturing
- c. Acheson process
- d. Process manufacturing

Guidance: level 1

:: Industrial processes ::

_____ is a technique involving the condensation of vapors and the return of this condensate to the system from which it originated. It is used in industrial and laboratory distillations. It is also used in chemistry to supply energy to reactions over a long period of time.

Exam Probability: **High**

33. *Answer choices:*
(see index for correct answer)

- a. Calo tester
- b. Olefin metathesis
- c. Flue-gas stack
- d. Spin coating

Guidance: level 1

:: Asset ::

In financial accounting, an _____ is any resource owned by the business. Anything tangible or intangible that can be owned or controlled to produce value and that is held by a company to produce positive economic value is an _____ . Simply stated, _____ s represent value of ownership that can be converted into cash . The balance sheet of a firm records the monetary value of the _____ s owned by that firm. It covers money and other valuables belonging to an individual or to a business.

Exam Probability: **Medium**

34. *Answer choices:*
(see index for correct answer)

- a. Current asset
- b. Fixed asset

Guidance: level 1

:: Management ::

In organizational studies, _____ is the efficient and effective development of an organization's resources when they are needed. Such resources may include financial resources, inventory, human skills, production resources, or information technology and natural resources.

Exam Probability: **Low**

35. *Answer choices:*
(see index for correct answer)

- a. Evidence-based management
- b. Resource management
- c. Pareto analysis
- d. Management by exception

Guidance: level 1

:: Management ::

_____ is the identification, evaluation, and prioritization of risks followed by coordinated and economical application of resources to minimize, monitor, and control the probability or impact of unfortunate events or to maximize the realization of opportunities.

Exam Probability: **Low**

36. *Answer choices:*
(see index for correct answer)

- a. Risk management
- b. Managing stage boundaries
- c. Telescopic observations strategic framework
- d. Management buyout

Guidance: level 1

:: Gas technologies ::

A _____ is a device used to transfer heat between two or more fluids. _____ s are used in both cooling and heating processes. The fluids may be separated by a solid wall to prevent mixing or they may be in direct contact. They are widely used in space heating, refrigeration, air conditioning, power stations, chemical plants, petrochemical plants, petroleum refineries, natural-gas processing, and sewage treatment. The classic example of a _____ is found in an internal combustion engine in which a circulating fluid known as engine coolant flows through radiator coils and air flows past the coils, which cools the coolant and heats the incoming air. Another example is the heat sink, which is a passive _____ that transfers the heat generated by an electronic or a mechanical device to a fluid medium, often air or a liquid coolant.

Exam Probability: **Medium**

37. *Answer choices:*
(see index for correct answer)

- a. Air pump
- b. Vortex tube
- c. Heat exchanger
- d. Pressure swing adsorption

Guidance: level 1

:: Project management ::

In economics, _____ is the assignment of available resources to various uses. In the context of an entire economy, resources can be allocated by various means, such as markets or central planning.

Exam Probability: **High**

38. *Answer choices:*
(see index for correct answer)

- a. Bottleneck
- b. Mandated lead arranger
- c. Resource allocation
- d. Graphical Evaluation and Review Technique

Guidance: level 1

:: Industries ::

The _____ comprises the companies that produce industrial chemicals. Central to the modern world economy, it converts raw materials into more than 70,000 different products. The plastics industry contains some overlap, as most chemical companies produce plastic as well as other chemicals.

Exam Probability: **Low**

39. *Answer choices:*
(see index for correct answer)

- a. Chemical industry
- b. Space-based industry
- c. Radio industry
- d. New manufacturing economy

Guidance: level 1

:: Production and manufacturing ::

A BOM can define products as they are designed , as they are ordered , as they are built , or as they are maintained . The different types of BOMs depend on the business need and use for which they are intended. In process industries, the BOM is also known as the formula, recipe, or ingredients list. The phrase "bill of material" is frequently used by engineers as an adjective to refer not to the literal bill, but to the current production configuration of a product, to distinguish it from modified or improved versions under study or in test.

Exam Probability: **Medium**

40. *Answer choices:*
(see index for correct answer)

- a. Bill of materials
- b. Follow-the-sun
- c. Computer-aided process planning
- d. Foundation Fieldbus H1

Guidance: level 1

:: Materials ::

A _____ , also known as a feedstock, unprocessed material, or primary commodity, is a basic material that is used to produce goods, finished products, energy, or intermediate materials which are feedstock for future finished products. As feedstock, the term connotes these materials are bottleneck assets and are highly important with regard to producing other products. An example of this is crude oil, which is a _____ and a feedstock used in the production of industrial chemicals, fuels, plastics, and pharmaceutical goods; lumber is a _____ used to produce a variety of products including all types of furniture. The term "_____" denotes materials in minimally processed or unprocessed in states; e.g., raw latex, crude oil, cotton, coal, raw biomass, iron ore, air, logs, or water i.e. "...any product of agriculture, forestry, fishing and any other mineral that is in its natural form or which has undergone the transformation required to prepare it for internationally marketing in substantial volumes."

Exam Probability: **High**

41. *Answer choices:*
(see index for correct answer)

- a. Nordic Institute of Dental Materials
- b. Raw material
- c. Putty
- d. Samuel Peal

Guidance: level 1

:: ::

Catalysis is the process of increasing the rate of a chemical reaction by adding a substance known as a _____ , which is not consumed in the catalyzed reaction and can continue to act repeatedly. Because of this, only very small amounts of _____ are required to alter the reaction rate in principle.

Exam Probability: **High**

42. *Answer choices:*
(see index for correct answer)

- a. levels of analysis
- b. interpersonal communication
- c. cultural
- d. hierarchical perspective

Guidance: level 1

:: Business ::

The seller, or the provider of the goods or services, completes a sale in response to an acquisition, appropriation, requisition or a direct interaction with the buyer at the point of sale. There is a passing of title of the item, and the settlement of a price, in which agreement is reached on a price for which transfer of ownership of the item will occur. The seller, not the purchaser typically executes the sale and it may be completed prior to the obligation of payment. In the case of indirect interaction, a person who sells goods or service on behalf of the owner is known as a _____ man or _____ woman or _____ person, but this often refers to someone selling goods in a store/shop, in which case other terms are also common, including _____ clerk, shop assistant, and retail clerk.

Exam Probability: **High**

43. *Answer choices:*

(see index for correct answer)

- a. Business interoperability interface
- b. Organizational life cycle
- c. Sales
- d. Relationship Science

Guidance: level 1

:: Time management ::

_____ is the process of planning and exercising conscious control of time spent on specific activities, especially to increase effectiveness, efficiency, and productivity. It involves a juggling act of various demands upon a person relating to work, social life, family, hobbies, personal interests and commitments with the finiteness of time. Using time effectively gives the person "choice" on spending/managing activities at their own time and expediency.

Exam Probability: **Medium**

44. *Answer choices:*

(see index for correct answer)

- a. Time perception
- b. Time Trek
- c. Getting Things Done
- d. Time management

Guidance: level 1

:: Semiconductor companies ::

_____ Corporation is a Japanese multinational conglomerate corporation headquartered in Konan, Minato, Tokyo. Its diversified business includes consumer and professional electronics, gaming, entertainment and financial services. The company owns the largest music entertainment business in the world, the largest video game console business and one of the largest video game publishing businesses, and is one of the leading manufacturers of electronic products for the consumer and professional markets, and a leading player in the film and television entertainment industry. _____ was ranked 97th on the 2018 Fortune Global 500 list.

45. *Answer choices:*
(see index for correct answer)

- a. Sharp Corporation
- b. Diodes Incorporated
- c. Sony
- d. Hana Micron

Guidance: level 1

:: Information technology management ::

_____ within quality management systems and information technology systems is a process—either formal or informal—used to ensure that changes to a product or system are introduced in a controlled and coordinated manner. It reduces the possibility that unnecessary changes will be introduced to a system without forethought, introducing faults into the system or undoing changes made by other users of software. The goals of a _____ procedure usually include minimal disruption to services, reduction in back-out activities, and cost-effective utilization of resources involved in implementing change.

Exam Probability: **Low**

46. *Answer choices:*
(see index for correct answer)

- a. Change control
- b. Microsoft Operations Framework
- c. GESMES/TS
- d. Enterprise output management

Guidance: level 1

:: Marketing ::

_____ or stock is the goods and materials that a business holds for the ultimate goal of resale .

Exam Probability: **High**

47. *Answer choices:*
(see index for correct answer)

- a. Processing fluency
- b. Inventory
- c. European Information Technology Observatory
- d. Macromarketing

Guidance: level 1

:: Production and manufacturing ::

_____ is a theory of management that analyzes and synthesizes workflows. Its main objective is improving economic efficiency, especially labor productivity. It was one of the earliest attempts to apply science to the engineering of processes and to management. _____ is sometimes known as Taylorism after its founder, Frederick Winslow Taylor.

Exam Probability: **High**

48. *Answer choices:*
(see index for correct answer)

- a. Corrective and preventive action
- b. Scientific management
- c. Mockup
- d. PCR food testing

Guidance: level 1

:: Lean manufacturing ::

_____ is a scheduling system for lean manufacturing and just-in-time manufacturing . Taiichi Ohno, an industrial engineer at Toyota, developed _____ to improve manufacturing efficiency. _____ is one method to achieve JIT. The system takes its name from the cards that track production within a factory. For many in the automotive sector, _____ is known as the "Toyota nameplate system" and as such the term is not used by some other automakers.

Exam Probability: **Medium**

49. *Answer choices:*
(see index for correct answer)

- a. Production leveling
- b. Lean product development
- c. Andon

- d. Kanban

Guidance: level 1

:: Management ::

Business _____ is a discipline in operations management in which people use various methods to discover, model, analyze, measure, improve, optimize, and automate business processes. BPM focuses on improving corporate performance by managing business processes. Any combination of methods used to manage a company's business processes is BPM. Processes can be structured and repeatable or unstructured and variable. Though not required, enabling technologies are often used with BPM.

Exam Probability: **High**

50. *Answer choices:*
(see index for correct answer)

- a. Board of governors
- b. Process management
- c. Resource management
- d. Risk management

Guidance: level 1

:: Quality ::

The _____ , formerly the _____ Control , is a knowledge-based global community of quality professionals, with nearly 80,000 members dedicated to promoting and advancing quality tools, principles, and practices in their workplaces and communities.

Exam Probability: **High**

51. *Answer choices:*
(see index for correct answer)

- a. Market Driven Quality
- b. American Society for Quality
- c. Software Engineering Process Group
- d. Shigeo Shingo

Guidance: level 1

_____ is the process of creating, sharing, using and managing the knowledge and information of an organisation. It refers to a multidisciplinary approach to achieving organisational objectives by making the best use of knowledge.

Exam Probability: **Low**

52. *Answer choices:*

(see index for correct answer)

- a. FAO Country Profiles
- b. Content management system
- c. Knowledge management
- d. Master of Business Systems

Guidance: level 1

:: Business process ::

A committee is a body of one or more persons that is subordinate to a deliberative assembly. Usually, the assembly sends matters into a committee as a way to explore them more fully than would be possible if the assembly itself were considering them. Committees may have different functions and their type of work differ depending on the type of the organization and its needs.

Exam Probability: **Medium**

53. *Answer choices:*

(see index for correct answer)

- a. Sales process engineering
- b. Steering committee
- c. Intention mining
- d. Captive service

Guidance: level 1

:: ::

The _____ is a project plan of how the production budget will be spent over a given timescale, for every phase of a business project.

Exam Probability: **High**

54. *Answer choices:*
(see index for correct answer)

- a. Character
- b. Production schedule
- c. co-culture
- d. open system

Guidance: level 1

:: ::

A _____ or till is a mechanical or electronic device for registering and calculating transactions at a point of sale. It is usually attached to a drawer for storing cash and other valuables. A modern _____ is usually attached to a printer that can print out receipts for record-keeping purposes.

Exam Probability: **High**

55. *Answer choices:*
(see index for correct answer)

- a. cultural
- b. imperative
- c. corporate values
- d. Cash register

Guidance: level 1

:: Production and manufacturing ::

An _____ is a manufacturing process in which parts are added as the semi-finished assembly moves from workstation to workstation where the parts are added in sequence until the final assembly is produced. By mechanically moving the parts to the assembly work and moving the semi-finished assembly from work station to work station, a finished product can be assembled faster and with less labor than by having workers carry parts to a stationary piece for assembly.

Exam Probability: **Medium**

56. *Answer choices:*
(see index for correct answer)

- a. Enterprise control
- b. Assembly line
- c. Contract manufacturer
- d. ISO/IEC 17025

Guidance: level 1

:: Metals ::

A _____ is a material that, when freshly prepared, polished, or fractured, shows a lustrous appearance, and conducts electricity and heat relatively well. _____ s are typically malleable or ductile . A _____ may be a chemical element such as iron, or an alloy such as stainless steel.

Exam Probability: **High**

57. *Answer choices:*
(see index for correct answer)

- a. Metals of antiquity
- b. Tamahagane
- c. Metal
- d. Thulium

Guidance: level 1

:: Production and manufacturing ::

Automatic _____ in continuous production processes is a combination of control engineering and chemical engineering disciplines that uses industrial control systems to achieve a production level of consistency, economy and safety which could not be achieved purely by human manual control. It is implemented widely in industries such as oil refining, pulp and paper manufacturing, chemical processing and power generating plants.

Exam Probability: **Low**

58. *Answer choices:*
(see index for correct answer)

- a. Critical chain project management
- b. International Automotive Task Force
- c. Managed services
- d. Process control

Guidance: level 1

:: Information technology management ::

_____ concerns a cycle of organizational activity: the acquisition of information from one or more sources, the custodianship and the distribution of that information to those who need it, and its ultimate disposition through archiving or deletion.

Exam Probability: **Medium**

59. *Answer choices:*
(see index for correct answer)

- a. Electronic document and records management system
- b. ITIL security management
- c. Production support
- d. Information management

Guidance: level 1

Commerce

Commerce relates to "the exchange of goods and services, especially on a large scale." It includes legal, economic, political, social, cultural and technological systems that operate in any country or internationally.

:: ::

According to the philosopher Piyush Mathur , "Tangibility is the property that a phenomenon exhibits if it has and/or transports mass and/or energy and/or momentum".

Exam Probability: **Low**

1. *Answer choices:*

(see index for correct answer)

- a. open system
- b. hierarchical perspective
- c. functional perspective
- d. Tangible

Guidance: level 1

:: ::

A _____ or _____ s is a type of footwear and not a specific type of shoe. Most _____ s mainly cover the foot and the ankle, while some also cover some part of the lower calf. Some _____ s extend up the leg, sometimes as far as the knee or even the hip. Most _____ s have a heel that is clearly distinguishable from the rest of the sole, even if the two are made of one piece. Traditionally made of leather or rubber, modern _____ s are made from a variety of materials. _____ s are worn both for their functionality protecting the foot and leg from water, extreme cold, mud or hazards or providing additional ankle support for strenuous activities with added traction requirements , or may have hobnails on their undersides to protect against wear and to get better grip; and for reasons of style and fashion.

Exam Probability: **Low**

2. *Answer choices:*
(see index for correct answer)

- a. Boot
- b. process perspective
- c. open system
- d. personal values

Guidance: level 1

:: Service industries ::

_____ are the economic services provided by the finance industry, which encompasses a broad range of businesses that manage money, including credit unions, banks, credit-card companies, insurance companies, accountancy companies, consumer-finance companies, stock brokerages, investment funds, individual managers and some government-sponsored enterprises. _____ companies are present in all economically developed geographic locations and tend to cluster in local, national, regional and international financial centers such as London, New York City, and Tokyo.

Exam Probability: **Low**

3. *Answer choices:*
(see index for correct answer)

- a. Financial services
- b. Pension Administration

- c. Financial services in Japan
- d. Independent Financial Adviser

Guidance: level 1

:: ::

_____ is the collaborative effort of a team to achieve a common goal or to complete a task in the most effective and efficient way. This concept is seen within the greater framework of a team, which is a group of interdependent individuals who work together towards a common goal. Basic requirements for effective _____ are an adequate team size , available resources for the team to make use of , and clearly defined roles within the team in order for everyone to have a clear purpose. _____ is present in any context where a group of people are working together to achieve a common goal. These contexts include an industrial organization , athletics , a school , and the healthcare system . In each of these settings, the level of _____ and interdependence can vary from low , to intermediate , to high , depending on the amount of communication, interaction, and collaboration present between team members.

Exam Probability: **Medium**

4. *Answer choices:*
(see index for correct answer)

- a. Teamwork
- b. process perspective
- c. interpersonal communication
- d. functional perspective

Guidance: level 1

:: ::

In the broadest sense, _____ is any practice which contributes to the sale of products to a retail consumer. At a retail in-store level, _____ refers to the variety of products available for sale and the display of those products in such a way that it stimulates interest and entices customers to make a purchase.

Exam Probability: **High**

5. *Answer choices:*
(see index for correct answer)

- a. imperative
- b. corporate values
- c. cultural
- d. interpersonal communication

Guidance: level 1

:: Logistics ::

_____ is generally the detailed organization and implementation of a complex operation. In a general business sense, _____ is the management of the flow of things between the point of origin and the point of consumption in order to meet requirements of customers or corporations. The resources managed in _____ may include tangible goods such as materials, equipment, and supplies, as well as food and other consumable items. The _____ of physical items usually involves the integration of information flow, materials handling, production, packaging, inventory, transportation, warehousing, and often security.

Exam Probability: **Medium**

6. *Answer choices:*
(see index for correct answer)

- a. Low Altitude Parachute Extraction System
- b. StarShipIt
- c. Logistics
- d. Terminal Operating System

Guidance: level 1

:: ::

The _____ of 1990 is a civil rights law that prohibits discrimination based on disability. It affords similar protections against discrimination to Americans with disabilities as the Civil Rights Act of 1964, which made discrimination based on race, religion, sex, national origin, and other characteristics illegal. In addition, unlike the Civil Rights Act, the ADA also requires covered employers to provide reasonable accommodations to employees with disabilities, and imposes accessibility requirements on public accommodations.

Exam Probability: **Low**

7. *Answer choices:*
(see index for correct answer)

- a. co-culture
- b. similarity-attraction theory
- c. Americans with Disabilities Act
- d. hierarchical perspective

Guidance: level 1

:: Land value taxation ::

_____ , sometimes referred to as dry _____ , is the solid surface of Earth that is not permanently covered by water. The vast majority of human activity throughout history has occurred in _____ areas that support agriculture, habitat, and various natural resources. Some life forms have developed from predecessor species that lived in bodies of water.

Exam Probability: **High**

8. *Answer choices:*
(see index for correct answer)

- a. Land
- b. Harry Gunnison Brown
- c. Lands Valuation Appeal Court
- d. Land value tax

Guidance: level 1

:: ::

Regulatory economics is the economics of regulation. It is the application of law by government or independent administrative agencies for various purposes, including remedying market failure, protecting the environment, centrally-planning an economy, enriching well-connected firms, or benefiting politicians.

Exam Probability: **High**

9. *Answer choices:*
(see index for correct answer)

- a. hierarchical
- b. corporate values
- c. imperative
- d. deep-level diversity

Guidance: level 1

:: ::

A _____ consists of one people who live in the same dwelling and share meals. It may also consist of a single family or another group of people. A dwelling is considered to contain multiple _____ s if meals or living spaces are not shared. The _____ is the basic unit of analysis in many social, microeconomic and government models, and is important to economics and inheritance.

Exam Probability: **Medium**

10. *Answer choices:*
(see index for correct answer)

- a. functional perspective
- b. corporate values
- c. cultural
- d. Household

Guidance: level 1

:: ::

_____ Corporation is an American multinational technology company with headquarters in Redmond, Washington. It develops, manufactures, licenses, supports and sells computer software, consumer electronics, personal computers, and related services. Its best known software products are the _____ Windows line of operating systems, the _____ Office suite, and the Internet Explorer and Edge Web browsers. Its flagship hardware products are the Xbox video game consoles and the _____ Surface lineup of touchscreen personal computers. As of 2016, it is the world`s largest software maker by revenue, and one of the world`s most valuable companies. The word " _____ " is a portmanteau of "microcomputer" and "software". _____ is ranked No. 30 in the 2018 Fortune 500 rankings of the largest United States corporations by total revenue.

Exam Probability: **Medium**

11. *Answer choices:*
(see index for correct answer)

- a. interpersonal communication
- b. functional perspective
- c. process perspective
- d. Microsoft

Guidance: level 1

:: Auctioneering ::

A _____ is one of several similar kinds of auctions. Most commonly, it means an auction in which the auctioneer begins with a high asking price, and lowers it until some participant accepts the price, or it reaches a predetermined reserve price. This has also been called a clock auction or open-outcry descending-price auction. This type of auction is good for auctioning goods quickly, since a sale never requires more than one bid. Strategically, it`s similar to a first-price sealed-bid auction.

Exam Probability: **High**

12. *Answer choices:*
(see index for correct answer)

- a. Virginity auction
- b. Dutch auction
- c. Call for bids

- d. Auctionata

Guidance: level 1

:: Production economics ::

In microeconomics, _____ are the cost advantages that enterprises obtain due to their scale of operation , with cost per unit of output decreasing with increasing scale.

Exam Probability: **High**

13. *Answer choices:*
(see index for correct answer)

- a. Producer's risk
- b. Economies of scale
- c. Marginal cost of capital schedule
- d. Specialization

Guidance: level 1

:: ::

In Christian denominations that practice infant baptism, confirmation is seen as the sealing of Christianity created in baptism. Those being _____ are known as confirmands. In some denominations, such as the Anglican Communion and Methodist Churches, confirmation bestows full membership in a local congregation upon the recipient. In others, such as the Roman Catholic Church, Confirmation "renders the bond with the Church more perfect", because, while a baptized person is already a member, "reception of the sacrament of Confirmation is necessary for the completion of baptismal grace".

Exam Probability: **High**

14. *Answer choices:*
(see index for correct answer)

- a. open system
- b. interpersonal communication
- c. similarity-attraction theory
- d. functional perspective

Guidance: level 1

_____ is the percentage of a market accounted for by a specific entity. In a survey of nearly 200 senior marketing managers, 67% responded that they found the revenue- "dollar _____" metric very useful, while 61% found "unit _____" very useful.

Exam Probability: **Medium**

15. *Answer choices:*
(see index for correct answer)

- a. Profit chart
- b. Processing fluency theory of aesthetic pleasure
- c. Market share
- d. Price on application

Guidance: level 1

:: Auctioneering ::

An _____ is a process of buying and selling goods or services by offering them up for bid, taking bids, and then selling the item to the highest bidder. The open ascending price _____ is arguably the most common form of _____ in use today. Participants bid openly against one another, with each subsequent bid required to be higher than the previous bid. An _____ eer may announce prices, bidders may call out their bids themselves , or bids may be submitted electronically with the highest current bid publicly displayed. In a Dutch _____ , the _____ eer begins with a high asking price for some quantity of like items; the price is lowered until a participant is willing to accept the _____ eer's price for some quantity of the goods in the lot or until the seller's reserve price is met. While _____ s are most associated in the public imagination with the sale of antiques, paintings, rare collectibles and expensive wines, _____ s are also used for commodities, livestock, radio spectrum and used cars. In economic theory, an _____ may refer to any mechanism or set of trading rules for exchange.

Exam Probability: **High**

16. *Answer choices:*
(see index for correct answer)

- a. Auction

- b. Japanese auction
- c. Online auction
- d. Bid shading

Guidance: level 1

:: ::

In a supply chain, a _____ , or a seller, is an enterprise that contributes goods or services. Generally, a supply chain _____ manufactures inventory/stock items and sells them to the next link in the chain. Today, these terms refer to a supplier of any good or service.

Exam Probability: **High**

17. *Answer choices:*
(see index for correct answer)

- a. empathy
- b. personal values
- c. similarity-attraction theory
- d. Character

Guidance: level 1

:: Management accounting ::

_____ , or dollar contribution per unit, is the selling price per unit minus the variable cost per unit. "Contribution" represents the portion of sales revenue that is not consumed by variable costs and so contributes to the coverage of fixed costs. This concept is one of the key building blocks of break-even analysis.

Exam Probability: **High**

18. *Answer choices:*
(see index for correct answer)

- a. Entity-level controls
- b. Contribution margin
- c. Target income sales
- d. Invested capital

Guidance: level 1

A _____ exists when a specific person or enterprise is the only supplier of a particular commodity. This contrasts with a monopsony which relates to a single entity's control of a market to purchase a good or service, and with oligopoly which consists of a few sellers dominating a market. Monopolies are thus characterized by a lack of economic competition to produce the good or service, a lack of viable substitute goods, and the possibility of a high _____ price well above the seller's marginal cost that leads to a high _____ profit. The verb monopolise or monopolize refers to the process by which a company gains the ability to raise prices or exclude competitors. In economics, a _____ is a single seller. In law, a _____ is a business entity that has significant market power, that is, the power to charge overly high prices. Although monopolies may be big businesses, size is not a characteristic of a _____ . A small business may still have the power to raise prices in a small industry .

Exam Probability: **High**

19. *Answer choices:*
(see index for correct answer)

- a. Revenue-cap regulation
- b. Monopoly
- c. Chamberlinian monopolistic competition
- d. Patent

Guidance: level 1

To _____ is to make a deal between different parties where each party gives up part of their demand. In arguments, _____ is a concept of finding agreement through communication, through a mutual acceptance of terms—often involving variations from an original goal or desires.

Exam Probability: **High**

20. *Answer choices:*
(see index for correct answer)

- a. Transferable utility
- b. Signaling game

- c. Bargaining problem
- d. Continuous game

Guidance: level 1

:: ::

_____ is the social science that studies the production, distribution, and consumption of goods and services.

Exam Probability: **Low**

21. *Answer choices:*
(see index for correct answer)

- a. interpersonal communication
- b. functional perspective
- c. Economics
- d. imperative

Guidance: level 1

:: Mereology ::

_____ , in the abstract, is what belongs to or with something, whether as an attribute or as a component of said thing. In the context of this article, it is one or more components , whether physical or incorporeal, of a person's estate; or so belonging to, as in being owned by, a person or jointly a group of people or a legal entity like a corporation or even a society. Depending on the nature of the _____ , an owner of _____ has the right to consume, alter, share, redefine, rent, mortgage, pawn, sell, exchange, transfer, give away or destroy it, or to exclude others from doing these things, as well as to perhaps abandon it; whereas regardless of the nature of the _____ , the owner thereof has the right to properly use it , or at the very least exclusively keep it.

Exam Probability: **Low**

22. *Answer choices:*
(see index for correct answer)

- a. Gunk
- b. Simple
- c. Property

- d. Mereological essentialism

:: ::

_____ or accountancy is the measurement, processing, and communication of financial information about economic entities such as businesses and corporations. The modern field was established by the Italian mathematician Luca Pacioli in 1494. _____ , which has been called the "language of business", measures the results of an organization's economic activities and conveys this information to a variety of users, including investors, creditors, management, and regulators. Practitioners of _____ are known as accountants. The terms " _____ " and "financial reporting" are often used as synonyms.

Exam Probability: **High**

23. *Answer choices:*
(see index for correct answer)

- a. similarity-attraction theory
- b. corporate values
- c. empathy
- d. Accounting

:: ::

_____ are electronic transfer of money from one bank account to another, either within a single financial institution or across multiple institutions, via computer-based systems, without the direct intervention of bank staff.

Exam Probability: **High**

24. *Answer choices:*
(see index for correct answer)

- a. information systems assessment
- b. Electronic funds transfer
- c. personal values
- d. hierarchical perspective

:: E-commerce ::

_____ is a United States-based payment gateway service provider allowing merchants to accept credit card and electronic check payments through their website and over an Internet Protocol connection. Founded in 1996, _____ is now a subsidiary of Visa Inc. Its service permits customers to enter credit card and shipping information directly onto a web page, in contrast to some alternatives that require the customer to sign up for a payment service before performing a transaction.

Exam Probability: **Low**

25. *Answer choices:*
(see index for correct answer)

- a. CIPURSE
- b. Segundamano
- c. SwapSimple
- d. Notice and take down

:: Income ::

_____ is the application of disciplined analytics that predict consumer behaviour at the micro-market levels and optimize product availability and price to maximize revenue growth. The primary aim of _____ is selling the right product to the right customer at the right time for the right price and with the right pack. The essence of this discipline is in understanding customers' perception of product value and accurately aligning product prices, placement and availability with each customer segment.

Exam Probability: **High**

26. *Answer choices:*
(see index for correct answer)

- a. Trinity study
- b. Aggregate income
- c. Aggregate expenditure
- d. Income Per User

:: ::

_____ is "property consisting of land and the buildings on it, along with its natural resources such as crops, minerals or water; immovable property of this nature; an interest vested in this an item of real property, buildings or housing in general. Also: the business of _____ ; the profession of buying, selling, or renting land, buildings, or housing." It is a legal term used in jurisdictions whose legal system is derived from English common law, such as India, England, Wales, Northern Ireland, United States, Canada, Pakistan, Australia, and New Zealand.

Exam Probability: **Low**

27. *Answer choices:*
(see index for correct answer)

- a. hierarchical
- b. similarity-attraction theory
- c. Real estate
- d. interpersonal communication

:: ::

_____ , also referred to as orthostasis, is a human position in which the body is held in an upright position and supported only by the feet.

Exam Probability: **Low**

28. *Answer choices:*
(see index for correct answer)

- a. corporate values
- b. imperative
- c. interpersonal communication
- d. cultural

:: Economic globalization ::

_____ is an agreement in which one company hires another company to be responsible for a planned or existing activity that is or could be done internally,and sometimes involves transferring employees and assets from one firm to another.

Exam Probability: **Low**

29. *Answer choices:*
(see index for correct answer)

- a. reshoring
- b. Outsourcing

Guidance: level 1

:: Goods ::

In most contexts, the concept of _____ denotes the conduct that should be preferred when posed with a choice between possible actions. _____ is generally considered to be the opposite of evil, and is of interest in the study of morality, ethics, religion and philosophy. The specific meaning and etymology of the term and its associated translations among ancient and contemporary languages show substantial variation in its inflection and meaning depending on circumstances of place, history, religious, or philosophical context.

Exam Probability: **Low**

30. *Answer choices:*
(see index for correct answer)

- a. Good
- b. Superior good
- c. Giffen good
- d. Composite good

Guidance: level 1

:: E-commerce ::

_____ is a method of e-commerce where shoppers' friends become involved in the shopping experience. _____ attempts to use technology to mimic the social interactions found in physical malls and stores. With the rise of mobile devices, _____ is now extending beyond the online world and into the offline world of shopping.

Exam Probability: **Low**

31. *Answer choices:*
(see index for correct answer)

- a. Alternative currency
- b. Social shopping
- c. Information Systems Associates FZE
- d. Associate-O-Matic

Guidance: level 1

:: ::

A trade union is an association of workers forming a legal unit or legal personhood, usually called a "bargaining unit", which acts as bargaining agent and legal representative for a unit of employees in all matters of law or right arising from or in the administration of a collective agreement. Labour unions typically fund the formal organisation, head office, and legal team functions of the labour union through regular fees or union dues. The delegate staff of the labour union representation in the workforce are made up of workplace volunteers who are appointed by members in democratic elections.

Exam Probability: **Medium**

32. *Answer choices:*
(see index for correct answer)

- a. Labor union
- b. open system
- c. Character
- d. surface-level diversity

Guidance: level 1

:: Supply chain management ::

A _____ is a type of auction in which the traditional roles of buyer and seller are reversed. Thus, there is one buyer and many potential sellers. In an ordinary auction , buyers compete to obtain goods or services by offering increasingly higher prices. In contrast, in a _____ , the sellers compete to obtain business from the buyer and prices will typically decrease as the sellers underbid each other.

Exam Probability: **Medium**

33. *Answer choices:*

(see index for correct answer)

- a. Calculating demand forecast accuracy
- b. Dell Theory of Conflict Prevention
- c. Pacific Access
- d. Global supply-chain finance

Guidance: level 1

:: Warrants issued in Hong Kong Stock Exchange ::

_____ is a chemical element with symbol Ag and atomic number 47. A soft, white, lustrous transition metal, it exhibits the highest electrical conductivity, thermal conductivity, and reflectivity of any metal. The metal is found in the Earth`s crust in the pure, free elemental form , as an alloy with gold and other metals, and in minerals such as argentite and chlorargyrite. Most _____ is produced as a byproduct of copper, gold, lead, and zinc refining.

Exam Probability: **High**

34. *Answer choices:*

(see index for correct answer)

- a. Haitong Securities
- b. CITIC Pacific
- c. Sinofert Holdings
- d. Silver

Guidance: level 1

:: ::

_____ , in general use, is a devotion and faithfulness to a nation, cause, philosophy, country, group, or person. Philosophers disagree on what can be an object of _____ , as some argue that _____ is strictly interpersonal and only another human being can be the object of _____ . The definition of _____ in law and political science is the fidelity of an individual to a nation, either one`s nation of birth, or one`s declared home nation by oath .

Exam Probability: **Low**

35. *Answer choices:*
(see index for correct answer)

- a. Loyalty
- b. hierarchical perspective
- c. deep-level diversity
- d. surface-level diversity

Guidance: level 1

:: Workplace ::

_____ is asystematic determination of a subject`s merit, worth and significance, using criteria governed by a set of standards. It can assist an organization, program, design, project or any other intervention or initiative to assess any aim, realisable concept/proposal, or any alternative, to help in decision-making; or to ascertain the degree of achievement or value in regard to the aim and objectives and results of any such action that has been completed. The primary purpose of _____ , in addition to gaining insight into prior or existing initiatives, is to enable reflection and assist in the identification of future change.

Exam Probability: **Low**

36. *Answer choices:*
(see index for correct answer)

- a. Workplace deviance
- b. Emotions in the workplace
- c. Evaluation
- d. Workplace relationships

Guidance: level 1

_____ is the study and management of exchange relationships. _____ is the business process of creating relationships with and satisfying customers. With its focus on the customer, _____ is one of the premier components of business management.

Exam Probability: **Low**

37. *Answer choices:*
(see index for correct answer)

- a. similarity-attraction theory
- b. functional perspective
- c. Marketing
- d. cultural

Guidance: level 1

:: Consumer theory ::

A _____ is a technical term in psychology, economics and philosophy usually used in relation to choosing between alternatives. For example, someone prefers A over B if they would rather choose A than B.

Exam Probability: **Medium**

38. *Answer choices:*
(see index for correct answer)

- a. Business contract hire
- b. Consumption
- c. Revealed preference
- d. Preference

Guidance: level 1

:: Data interchange standards ::

_____ is the concept of businesses electronically communicating information that was traditionally communicated on paper, such as purchase orders and invoices. Technical standards for EDI exist to facilitate parties transacting such instruments without having to make special arrangements.

Exam Probability: **Medium**

39. *Answer choices:*
(see index for correct answer)

- a. Domain Application Protocol
- b. Electronic data interchange
- c. Uniform Communication Standard
- d. Interaction protocol

Guidance: level 1

:: Marketing ::

The _____ is a foundation model for businesses. The _____ has been defined as the "set of marketing tools that the firm uses to pursue its marketing objectives in the target market". Thus the _____ refers to four broad levels of marketing decision, namely: product, price, place, and promotion. Marketing practice has been occurring for millennia, but marketing theory emerged in the early twentieth century. The contemporary _____ , or the 4 Ps, which has become the dominant framework for marketing management decisions, was first published in 1960. In services marketing, an extended _____ is used, typically comprising 7 Ps, made up of the original 4 Ps extended by process, people, and physical evidence. Occasionally service marketers will refer to 8 Ps, comprising these 7 Ps plus performance.

Exam Probability: **Medium**

40. *Answer choices:*
(see index for correct answer)

- a. Marketing mix
- b. NauticExpo
- c. Ameritest
- d. customer-perceived value

Guidance: level 1

_____ , or auditory perception, is the ability to perceive sounds by detecting vibrations, changes in the pressure of the surrounding medium through time, through an organ such as the ear. The academic field concerned with _____ is auditory science.

Exam Probability: **Medium**

41. *Answer choices:*
(see index for correct answer)

- a. Hearing
- b. empathy
- c. Character
- d. functional perspective

Guidance: level 1

Advertising is a marketing communication that employs an openly sponsored, non-personal message to promote or sell a product, service or idea. Sponsors of advertising are typically businesses wishing to promote their products or services. Advertising is differentiated from public relations in that an advertiser pays for and has control over the message. It differs from personal selling in that the message is non-personal, i.e., not directed to a particular individual.Advertising is communicated through various mass media, including traditional media such as newspapers, magazines, television, radio, outdoor advertising or direct mail; and new media such as search results, blogs, social media, websites or text messages. The actual presentation of the message in a medium is referred to as an _____ , or "ad" or advert for short.

Exam Probability: **High**

42. *Answer choices:*
(see index for correct answer)

- a. Advertisement
- b. Character
- c. surface-level diversity
- d. personal values

Guidance: level 1

The _____ is a political and economic union of 28 member states that are located primarily in Europe. It has an area of 4,475,757 km2 and an estimated population of about 513 million. The EU has developed an internal single market through a standardised system of laws that apply in all member states in those matters, and only those matters, where members have agreed to act as one. EU policies aim to ensure the free movement of people, goods, services and capital within the internal market, enact legislation in justice and home affairs and maintain common policies on trade, agriculture, fisheries and regional development. For travel within the Schengen Area, passport controls have been abolished. A monetary union was established in 1999 and came into full force in 2002 and is composed of 19 EU member states which use the euro currency.

Exam Probability: **Low**

43. *Answer choices:*
(see index for correct answer)

- a. European Union
- b. hierarchical perspective
- c. information systems assessment
- d. functional perspective

Guidance: level 1

_____ , also known as flow production or continuous production, is the production of large amounts of standardized products, including and especially on assembly lines. Together with job production and batch production, it is one of the three main production methods.

Exam Probability: **High**

44. *Answer choices:*
(see index for correct answer)

- a. Mass production
- b. Reindustrialization
- c. Light industry
- d. Sexual division of labour

:: ::

_____ is the provision of service to customers before, during and after a purchase. The perception of success of such interactions is dependent on employees "who can adjust themselves to the personality of the guest". _____ concerns the priority an organization assigns to _____ relative to components such as product innovation and pricing. In this sense, an organization that values good _____ may spend more money in training employees than the average organization or may proactively interview customers for feedback.

Exam Probability: **Low**

45. *Answer choices:*
(see index for correct answer)

- a. empathy
- b. personal values
- c. Customer service
- d. Sarbanes-Oxley act of 2002

:: ::

_____ Holdings, Inc. is an American company operating a worldwide online payments system that supports online money transfers and serves as an electronic alternative to traditional paper methods like checks and money orders. The company operates as a payment processor for online vendors, auction sites, and many other commercial users, for which it charges a fee in exchange for benefits such as one-click transactions and password memory. _____ `s payment system, also called _____ , is considered a type of payment rail.

Exam Probability: **Medium**

46. *Answer choices:*
(see index for correct answer)

- a. empathy
- b. levels of analysis
- c. similarity-attraction theory
- d. PayPal

:: ::

An _____ is a systematic and independent examination of books, accounts, statutory records, documents and vouchers of an organization to ascertain how far the financial statements as well as non-financial disclosures present a true and fair view of the concern. It also attempts to ensure that the books of accounts are properly maintained by the concern as required by law. _____ ing has become such a ubiquitous phenomenon in the corporate and the public sector that academics started identifying an " _____ Society". The _____ or perceives and recognises the propositions before them for examination, obtains evidence, evaluates the same and formulates an opinion on the basis of his judgement which is communicated through their _____ ing report.

Exam Probability: **Low**

47. *Answer choices:*
<small>(see index for correct answer)</small>

- a. co-culture
- b. Audit
- c. personal values
- d. functional perspective

:: ::

A _____ is a structured form of play, usually undertaken for enjoyment and sometimes used as an educational tool. _____ s are distinct from work, which is usually carried out for remuneration, and from art, which is more often an expression of aesthetic or ideological elements. However, the distinction is not clear-cut, and many _____ s are also considered to be work or art .

Exam Probability: **Low**

48. *Answer choices:*
<small>(see index for correct answer)</small>

- a. open system
- b. corporate values
- c. empathy
- d. Game

Guidance: level 1

:: ::

_____ refers to a business or organization attempting to acquire goods or services to accomplish its goals. Although there are several organizations that attempt to set standards in the _____ process, processes can vary greatly between organizations. Typically the word " _____ " is not used interchangeably with the word "procurement", since procurement typically includes expediting, supplier quality, and transportation and logistics in addition to _____ .

Exam Probability: **Low**

49. *Answer choices:*
(see index for correct answer)

- a. hierarchical
- b. Purchasing
- c. similarity-attraction theory
- d. deep-level diversity

Guidance: level 1

:: Business ethics ::

_____ is a type of harassment technique that relates to a sexual nature and the unwelcome or inappropriate promise of rewards in exchange for sexual favors. _____ includes a range of actions from mild transgressions to sexual abuse or assault. Harassment can occur in many different social settings such as the workplace, the home, school, churches, etc. Harassers or victims may be of any gender.

Exam Probability: **Medium**

50. *Answer choices:*
(see index for correct answer)

- a. Salad Oil Scandal

- b. Workplace bullying
- c. Terror-free investing
- d. Sexual harassment

Guidance: level 1

:: ::

An _____ in international trade is a good or service produced in one country that is bought by someone in another country. The seller of such goods and services is an _____ er; the foreign buyer is an importer.

Exam Probability: **Low**

51. *Answer choices:*
(see index for correct answer)

- a. surface-level diversity
- b. empathy
- c. Export
- d. interpersonal communication

Guidance: level 1

:: Marketing analytics ::

_____ is a long-term, forward-looking approach to planning with the fundamental goal of achieving a sustainable competitive advantage. Strategic planning involves an analysis of the company's strategic initial situation prior to the formulation, evaluation and selection of market-oriented competitive position that contributes to the company's goals and marketing objectives.

Exam Probability: **High**

52. *Answer choices:*
(see index for correct answer)

- a. Sumall
- b. Mission-driven marketing
- c. Marketing strategy
- d. Perceptual map

Guidance: level 1

:: International trade ::

A _____ is a document issued by a carrier to acknowledge receipt of cargo for shipment. Although the term historically related only to carriage by sea, a _____ may today be used for any type of carriage of goods.

Exam Probability: **Low**

53. *Answer choices:*
(see index for correct answer)

- a. Bill of lading
- b. Trade Act of 1974
- c. Banyan merchants
- d. Quota share

Guidance: level 1

:: E-commerce ::

A _____ is a financial transaction involving a very small sum of money and usually one that occurs online. A number of _____ systems were proposed and developed in the mid-to-late 1990s, all of which were ultimately unsuccessful. A second generation of _____ systems emerged in the 2010s.

Exam Probability: **Medium**

54. *Answer choices:*
(see index for correct answer)

- a. Braintree
- b. Soldsie
- c. USAePay
- d. Video commerce

Guidance: level 1

:: Business models ::

A _____ , _____ company or daughter company is a company that is owned or controlled by another company, which is called the parent company, parent, or holding company. The _____ can be a company, corporation, or limited liability company. In some cases it is a government or state-owned enterprise. In some cases, particularly in the music and book publishing industries, subsidiaries are referred to as imprints.

Exam Probability: **Low**

55. *Answer choices:*
(see index for correct answer)

- a. Utility computing
- b. Subsidiary
- c. IASME
- d. Meta learning

Guidance: level 1

:: Stock market ::

_____ is freedom from, or resilience against, potential harm caused by others. Beneficiaries of _____ may be of persons and social groups, objects and institutions, ecosystems or any other entity or phenomenon vulnerable to unwanted change by its environment.

Exam Probability: **Low**

56. *Answer choices:*
(see index for correct answer)

- a. Delivery versus payment
- b. Ticker symbol
- c. Open outcry
- d. Security

Guidance: level 1

:: Cryptography ::

In cryptography, _____ is the process of encoding a message or information in such a way that only authorized parties can access it and those who are not authorized cannot. _____ does not itself prevent interference, but denies the intelligible content to a would-be interceptor. In an _____ scheme, the intended information or message, referred to as plaintext, is encrypted using an _____ algorithm – a cipher – generating ciphertext that can be read only if decrypted. For technical reasons, an _____ scheme usually uses a pseudo-random _____ key generated by an algorithm. It is in principle possible to decrypt the message without possessing the key, but, for a well-designed _____ scheme, considerable computational resources and skills are required. An authorized recipient can easily decrypt the message with the key provided by the originator to recipients but not to unauthorized users.

Exam Probability: **High**

57. *Answer choices:*
(see index for correct answer)

- a. Encryption
- b. plaintext
- c. ciphertext
- d. cryptosystem

Guidance: level 1

:: Scientific method ::

In the social sciences and life sciences, a _____ is a research method involving an up-close, in-depth, and detailed examination of a subject of study , as well as its related contextual conditions.

Exam Probability: **Medium**

58. *Answer choices:*
(see index for correct answer)

- a. explanatory research
- b. Preference test
- c. Case study
- d. Causal research

Guidance: level 1

Unlike sealed-bid auctions , an _____ is "open" or fully transparent, as the identity of all bidders is disclosed to each other during the auction. More generally, an auction mechanism is considered "English" if it involves an iterative process of adjusting the price in a direction that is unfavorable to the bidders . In contrast, a Dutch auction would adjust the price in a direction that favored the bidders .

Exam Probability: **High**

59. *Answer choices:*
(see index for correct answer)

- a. English auction
- b. Demsetz auction
- c. Vickrey auction
- d. Name Your Own Price

Guidance: level 1

Business ethics

Business ethics (also known as corporate ethics) is a form of applied ethics or professional ethics, that examines ethical principles and moral or ethical problems that can arise in a business environment. It applies to all aspects of business conduct and is relevant to the conduct of individuals and entire organizations. These ethics originate from individuals, organizational statements or from the legal system. These norms, values, ethical, and unethical practices are what is used to guide business. They help those businesses maintain a better connection with their stakeholders.

:: Utilitarianism ::

_____ is a school of thought that argues that the pursuit of pleasure and intrinsic goods are the primary or most important goals of human life. A hedonist strives to maximize net pleasure . However upon finally gaining said pleasure, happiness may remain stationary.

Exam Probability: **High**

1. *Answer choices:*
(see index for correct answer)

- a. Utilitarianism
- b. Mohism
- c. Preference utilitarianism
- d. Hedonism

Guidance: level 1

:: Confidence tricks ::

A _____ is a business model that recruits members via a promise of payments or services for enrolling others into the scheme, rather than supplying investments or sale of products. As recruiting multiplies, recruiting becomes quickly impossible, and most members are unable to profit; as such, _____ s are unsustainable and often illegal.

Exam Probability: **High**

2. *Answer choices:*

(see index for correct answer)

- a. Welsh Thrasher faith scam
- b. Pyramid scheme
- c. Spanish Prisoner
- d. The switch

Guidance: level 1

:: ::

A _____ is an organization, usually a group of people or a company, authorized to act as a single entity and recognized as such in law. Early incorporated entities were established by charter . Most jurisdictions now allow the creation of new _____ s through registration.

Exam Probability: **Medium**

3. *Answer choices:*

(see index for correct answer)

- a. imperative
- b. surface-level diversity
- c. hierarchical
- d. personal values

Guidance: level 1

:: ::

_____ or accountancy is the measurement, processing, and communication of financial information about economic entities such as businesses and corporations. The modern field was established by the Italian mathematician Luca Pacioli in 1494. _____ , which has been called the "language of business", measures the results of an organization`s economic activities and conveys this information to a variety of users, including investors, creditors, management, and regulators. Practitioners of _____ are known as accountants. The terms " _____ " and "financial reporting" are often used as synonyms.

Exam Probability: **High**

4. *Answer choices:*
(see index for correct answer)

- a. levels of analysis
- b. functional perspective
- c. empathy
- d. deep-level diversity

Guidance: level 1

:: Social responsibility ::

The United Nations Global Compact is a non-binding United Nations pact to encourage businesses worldwide to adopt sustainable and socially responsible policies, and to report on their implementation. The _____ is a principle-based framework for businesses, stating ten principles in the areas of human rights, labor, the environment and anti-corruption. Under the Global Compact, companies are brought together with UN agencies, labor groups and civil society. Cities can join the Global Compact through the Cities Programme.

Exam Probability: **High**

5. *Answer choices:*
(see index for correct answer)

- a. Footprints network
- b. UN Global Compact
- c. Collective impact
- d. Enterprise 2020

Guidance: level 1

_____ generally refers to a focus on the needs or desires of one's self. A number of philosophical, psychological, and economic theories examine the role of _____ in motivating human action.

Exam Probability: **Low**

6. *Answer choices:*

(see index for correct answer)

- a. information systems assessment
- b. Sarbanes-Oxley act of 2002
- c. Self-interest
- d. co-culture

Guidance: level 1

The Ethics & Compliance Initiative was formed in 2015 and consists of three nonprofit organizations: the Ethics Research Center, the Ethics & Compliance Association, and the Ethics & Compliance Certification Institute. Based in Arlington, Virginia, United States, ECI is devoted to the advancement of high ethical standards and practices in public and private institutions, and provides research about ethical standards, workplace integrity, and compliance practices and processes.

Exam Probability: **High**

7. *Answer choices:*

(see index for correct answer)

- a. empathy
- b. similarity-attraction theory
- c. information systems assessment
- d. Ethics Resource Center

Guidance: level 1

:: White-collar criminals ::

_____ refers to financially motivated, nonviolent crime committed by businesses and government professionals. It was first defined by the sociologist Edwin Sutherland in 1939 as "a crime committed by a person of respectability and high social status in the course of their occupation". Typical _____ s could include wage theft, fraud, bribery, Ponzi schemes, insider trading, labor racketeering, embezzlement, cybercrime, copyright infringement, money laundering, identity theft, and forgery. Lawyers can specialize in _____ .

Exam Probability: **Medium**

8. *Answer choices:*
(see index for correct answer)

- a. Tongsun Park
- b. White-collar crime

Guidance: level 1

:: ::

_____ is the collection of mechanisms, processes and relations by which corporations are controlled and operated. Governance structures and principles identify the distribution of rights and responsibilities among different participants in the corporation and include the rules and procedures for making decisions in corporate affairs. _____ is necessary because of the possibility of conflicts of interests between stakeholders, primarily between shareholders and upper management or among shareholders.

Exam Probability: **High**

9. *Answer choices:*
(see index for correct answer)

- a. Corporate governance
- b. interpersonal communication
- c. personal values
- d. Character

Guidance: level 1

:: ::

A _____ is a form of business network, for example, a local organization of businesses whose goal is to further the interests of businesses. Business owners in towns and cities form these local societies to advocate on behalf of the business community. Local businesses are members, and they elect a board of directors or executive council to set policy for the chamber. The board or council then hires a President, CEO or Executive Director, plus staffing appropriate to size, to run the organization.

Exam Probability: **Medium**

10. *Answer choices:*
(see index for correct answer)

- a. cultural
- b. similarity-attraction theory
- c. imperative
- d. personal values

Guidance: level 1

:: ::

Sustainability is the process of people maintaining change in a balanced environment, in which the exploitation of resources, the direction of investments, the orientation of technological development and institutional change are all in harmony and enhance both current and future potential to meet human needs and aspirations. For many in the field, sustainability is defined through the following interconnected domains or pillars: environment, economic and social, which according to Fritjof Capra is based on the principles of Systems Thinking. Sub-domains of _____ development have been considered also: cultural, technological and political. While _____ development may be the organizing principle for sustainability for some, for others, the two terms are paradoxical . _____ development is the development that meets the needs of the present without compromising the ability of future generations to meet their own needs. Brundtland Report for the World Commission on Environment and Development introduced the term of _____ development.

Exam Probability: **High**

11. *Answer choices:*
(see index for correct answer)

- a. Character
- b. similarity-attraction theory
- c. surface-level diversity
- d. Sustainable

Guidance: level 1

:: ::

The _____ of 1973 serves as the enacting legislation to carry out the provisions outlined in The Convention on International Trade in Endangered Species of Wild Fauna and Flora . Designed to protect critically imperiled species from extinction as a "consequence of economic growth and development untempered by adequate concern and conservation", the ESA was signed into law by President Richard Nixon on December 28, 1973. The law requires federal agencies to consult with the Fish and Wildlife Service &/or the NOAA Fisheries Service to ensure their actions are not likely to jeopardize the continued existence of any listed species or result in the destruction or adverse modification of designated critical habitat of such species. The U.S. Supreme Court found that "the plain intent of Congress in enacting" the ESA "was to halt and reverse the trend toward species extinction, whatever the cost." The Act is administered by two federal agencies, the United States Fish and Wildlife Service and the National Marine Fisheries Service .

Exam Probability: **High**

12. *Answer choices:*
(see index for correct answer)

- a. personal values
- b. Endangered Species Act
- c. cultural
- d. co-culture

Guidance: level 1

:: Toxicology ::

_____ or lead-based paint is paint containing lead. As pigment, lead chromate , Lead oxide, , and lead carbonate are the most common forms. Lead is added to paint to accelerate drying, increase durability, maintain a fresh appearance, and resist moisture that causes corrosion. It is one of the main health and environmental hazards associated with paint. In some countries, lead continues to be added to paint intended for domestic use, whereas countries such as the U.S. and the UK have regulations prohibiting this, although

_____ may still be found in older properties painted prior to the introduction of such regulations. Although lead has been banned from household paints in the United States since 1978, paint used in road markings may still contain it. Alternatives such as water-based, lead-free traffic paint are readily available, and many states and federal agencies have changed their purchasing contracts to buy these instead.

Exam Probability: **High**

13. *Answer choices:*
(see index for correct answer)

- a. Lethal dose
- b. Coliform index
- c. Toxicology
- d. Lead paint

Guidance: level 1

:: ::

_____ is a non-governmental environmental organization with offices in over 39 countries and an international coordinating body in Amsterdam, the Netherlands. _____ was founded in 1971 by Irving Stowe, and Dorothy Stowe, Canadian and US ex-pat environmental activists. _____ states its goal is to "ensure the ability of the Earth to nurture life in all its diversity" and focuses its campaigning on worldwide issues such as climate change, deforestation, overfishing, commercial whaling, genetic engineering, and anti-nuclear issues. It uses direct action, lobbying, research, and ecotage to achieve its goals. The global organization does not accept funding from governments, corporations, or political parties, relying on three million individual supporters and foundation grants. _____ has a general consultative status with the United Nations Economic and Social Council and is a founding member of the INGO Accountability Charter, an international non-governmental organization that intends to foster accountability and transparency of non-governmental organizations.

Exam Probability: **Medium**

14. *Answer choices:*
(see index for correct answer)

- a. Greenpeace
- b. surface-level diversity
- c. corporate values
- d. functional perspective

Guidance: level 1

:: Utilitarianism ::

_____ is a family of consequentialist ethical theories that promotes actions that maximize happiness and well-being for the majority of a population. Although different varieties of _____ admit different characterizations, the basic idea behind all of them is to in some sense maximize utility, which is often defined in terms of well-being or related concepts. For instance, Jeremy Bentham, the founder of _____, described utility as

Exam Probability: **Medium**

15. *Answer choices:*
(see index for correct answer)

- a. Global Happiness Organization
- b. Utilitarianism
- c. Act utilitarianism
- d. Felicific calculus

Guidance: level 1

:: Corporate crime ::

_____ LLP, based in Chicago, was an American holding company. Formerly one of the "Big Five" accounting firms , the firm had provided auditing, tax, and consulting services to large corporations. By 2001, it had become one of the world's largest multinational companies.

Exam Probability: **Medium**

16. *Answer choices:*
(see index for correct answer)

- a. Arthur Andersen LLP v. United States
- b. Tip and Trade
- c. Holdings of American International Group
- d. Walter Forbes

Guidance: level 1

:: Occupational safety and health ::

_____ is a chemical element with symbol Pb and atomic number 82. It is a heavy metal that is denser than most common materials. _____ is soft and malleable, and also has a relatively low melting point. When freshly cut, _____ is silvery with a hint of blue; it tarnishes to a dull gray color when exposed to air. _____ has the highest atomic number of any stable element and three of its isotopes are endpoints of major nuclear decay chains of heavier elements.

Exam Probability: **Medium**

17. *Answer choices:*
(see index for correct answer)

- a. Bernardino Ramazzini
- b. Seoul Declaration on Safety and Health at Work
- c. Safe Work Procedure
- d. Examinetics

:: Management ::

_____ or executive pay is composed of the financial compensation and other non-financial awards received by an executive from their firm for their service to the organization. It is typically a mixture of salary, bonuses, shares of or call options on the company stock, benefits, and perquisites, ideally configured to take into account government regulations, tax law, the desires of the organization and the executive, and rewards for performance.

Exam Probability: **Low**

18. *Answer choices:*
(see index for correct answer)

- a. Supply chain network
- b. Project management
- c. Executive compensation
- d. Reverse innovation

:: Water law ::

The _____ is the primary federal law in the United States governing water pollution. Its objective is to restore and maintain the chemical, physical, and biological integrity of the nation's waters; recognizing the responsibilities of the states in addressing pollution and providing assistance to states to do so, including funding for publicly owned treatment works for the improvement of wastewater treatment; and maintaining the integrity of wetlands. It is one of the United States' first and most influential modern environmental laws. As with many other major U.S. federal environmental statutes, it is administered by the U.S. Environmental Protection Agency , in coordination with state governments. Its implementing regulations are codified at 40 C.F.R. Subchapters D, N, and O .

Exam Probability: **High**

19. *Answer choices:*
(see index for correct answer)

- a. Water quality law

- b. Correlative rights doctrine
- c. Clean Water Act
- d. Return flow

Guidance: level 1

:: Leadership ::

_____ is leadership that is directed by respect for ethical beliefs and values and for the dignity and rights of others. It is thus related to concepts such as trust, honesty, consideration, charisma, and fairness.

Exam Probability: **High**

20. *Answer choices:*
(see index for correct answer)

- a. Transactional leadership
- b. The Intangibles of Leadership
- c. Three levels of leadership model
- d. Ethical leadership

Guidance: level 1

:: ::

A _____ is an astronomical body orbiting a star or stellar remnant that is massive enough to be rounded by its own gravity, is not massive enough to cause thermonuclear fusion, and has cleared its neighbouring region of _____ esimals.

Exam Probability: **Low**

21. *Answer choices:*
(see index for correct answer)

- a. co-culture
- b. corporate values
- c. hierarchical perspective
- d. Sarbanes-Oxley act of 2002

Guidance: level 1

:: ::

_____, O.S.A. was a German professor of theology, composer, priest, monk, and a seminal figure in the Protestant Reformation.

Exam Probability: **Medium**

22. *Answer choices:*
(see index for correct answer)

- a. hierarchical perspective
- b. surface-level diversity
- c. interpersonal communication
- d. Martin Luther

Guidance: level 1

:: ::

Competition law is a law that promotes or seeks to maintain market competition by regulating anti-competitive conduct by companies. Competition law is implemented through public and private enforcement. Competition law is known as " _____ law" in the United States for historical reasons, and as "anti-monopoly law" in China and Russia. In previous years it has been known as trade practices law in the United Kingdom and Australia. In the European Union, it is referred to as both _____ and competition law.

Exam Probability: **High**

23. *Answer choices:*
(see index for correct answer)

- a. similarity-attraction theory
- b. Antitrust
- c. cultural
- d. deep-level diversity

Guidance: level 1

:: United States law ::

The ABA _____ , created by the American Bar Association , are a set of rules that prescribe baseline standards of legal ethics and professional responsibility for lawyers in the United States. They were promulgated by the ABA House of Delegates upon the recommendation of the Kutak Commission in 1983. The rules are merely recommendations, or models, and are not themselves binding. However, having a common set of Model Rules facilitates a common discourse on legal ethics, and simplifies professional responsibility training as well as the day-to-day application of such rules. As of 2015, 49 states and four territories have adopted the rules in whole or in part, of which the most recent to do so was the Commonwealth of the Northern Mariana Islands in March 2015. California is the only state that has not adopted the ABA Model Rules, while Puerto Rico is the only U.S. jurisdiction outside of confederation has not adopted them but instead has its own Código de Ética Profesional.

Exam Probability: **Low**

24. *Answer choices:*

(see index for correct answer)

- a. Model Rules of Professional Conduct
- b. judgment notwithstanding the verdict

Guidance: level 1

:: ::

_____ is "property consisting of land and the buildings on it, along with its natural resources such as crops, minerals or water; immovable property of this nature; an interest vested in this an item of real property, buildings or housing in general. Also: the business of _____ ; the profession of buying, selling, or renting land, buildings, or housing." It is a legal term used in jurisdictions whose legal system is derived from English common law, such as India, England, Wales, Northern Ireland, United States, Canada, Pakistan, Australia, and New Zealand.

Exam Probability: **Medium**

25. *Answer choices:*

(see index for correct answer)

- a. open system
- b. information systems assessment

- c. similarity-attraction theory
- d. Real estate

Guidance: level 1

:: ::

_____ is a product prepared from the leaves of the _____ plant by curing them. The plant is part of the genus Nicotiana and of the Solanaceae family. While more than 70 species of _____ are known, the chief commercial crop is N. tabacum. The more potent variant N. rustica is also used around the world.

Exam Probability: **Low**

26. *Answer choices:*
(see index for correct answer)

- a. process perspective
- b. hierarchical
- c. Tobacco
- d. levels of analysis

Guidance: level 1

:: Minimum wage ::

The _____ are working people whose incomes fall below a given poverty line due to lack of work hours and/or low wages.Largely because they are earning such low wages, the _____ face numerous obstacles that make it difficult for many of them to find and keep a job, save up money, and maintain a sense of self-worth.

Exam Probability: **Medium**

27. *Answer choices:*
(see index for correct answer)

- a. Minimum wage in Taiwan
- b. Guaranteed minimum income
- c. Working poor
- d. National Anti-Sweating League

Guidance: level 1

A _____ or community development finance institution - abbreviated in both cases to CDFI - is a financial institution that provides credit and financial services to underserved markets and populations, primarily in the USA but also in the UK. A CDFI may be a community development bank, a community development credit union , a community development loan fund , a community development venture capital fund , a microenterprise development loan fund, or a community development corporation.

Exam Probability: **High**

28. *Answer choices:*
(see index for correct answer)

- a. Community development financial institution
- b. Principles for Responsible Investment
- c. GLS Bank
- d. Reliance Bank

Guidance: level 1

:: ::

_____ is the study and management of exchange relationships. _____ is the business process of creating relationships with and satisfying customers. With its focus on the customer, _____ is one of the premier components of business management.

Exam Probability: **High**

29. *Answer choices:*
(see index for correct answer)

- a. information systems assessment
- b. hierarchical perspective
- c. Marketing
- d. co-culture

Guidance: level 1

:: ::

The _____ was a severe worldwide economic depression that took place mostly during the 1930s, beginning in the United States. The timing of the _____ varied across nations; in most countries it started in 1929 and lasted until the late-1930s. It was the longest, deepest, and most widespread depression of the 20th century. In the 21st century, the _____ is commonly used as an example of how intensely the world's economy can decline.

Exam Probability: **High**

30. *Answer choices:*
(see index for correct answer)

- a. process perspective
- b. co-culture
- c. Character
- d. imperative

Guidance: level 1

:: Electronic feedback ::

_____ occurs when outputs of a system are routed back as inputs as part of a chain of cause-and-effect that forms a circuit or loop. The system can then be said to feed back into itself. The notion of cause-and-effect has to be handled carefully when applied to _____ systems.

Exam Probability: **High**

31. *Answer choices:*
(see index for correct answer)

- a. Positive feedback
- b. feedback loop

Guidance: level 1

:: ::

_____ is a bundle of characteristics, including ways of thinking, feeling, and acting, which humans are said to have naturally. The term is often regarded as capturing what it is to be human, or the essence of humanity. The term is controversial because it is disputed whether or not such an essence exists. Arguments about _____ have been a mainstay of philosophy for centuries and the concept continues to provoke lively philosophical debate. The concept also continues to play a role in science, with neuroscientists, psychologists and social scientists sometimes claiming that their results have yielded insight into _____ . _____ is traditionally contrasted with characteristics that vary among humans, such as characteristics associated with specific cultures. Debates about _____ are related to, although not the same as, debates about the comparative importance of genes and environment in development .

Exam Probability: **High**

32. *Answer choices:*
(see index for correct answer)

- a. Human nature
- b. cultural
- c. open system
- d. personal values

Guidance: level 1

:: ::

_____ Ltd. is the world's 2nd largest offshore drilling contractor and is based in Vernier, Switzerland. The company has offices in 20 countries, including Switzerland, Canada, United States, Norway, Scotland, India, Brazil, Singapore, Indonesia and Malaysia.

Exam Probability: **High**

33. *Answer choices:*
(see index for correct answer)

- a. interpersonal communication
- b. cultural
- c. deep-level diversity
- d. functional perspective

Guidance: level 1

In business management, _____ is a management style whereby a manager closely observes and/or controls the work of his/her subordinates or employees.

Exam Probability: **Medium**

34. *Answer choices:*

(see index for correct answer)

- a. Control freak
- b. Rat race
- c. Evaluation
- d. Micromanagement

Guidance: level 1

:: Labour relations ::

_____ is a field of study that can have different meanings depending on the context in which it is used. In an international context, it is a subfield of labor history that studies the human relations with regard to work – in its broadest sense – and how this connects to questions of social inequality. It explicitly encompasses unregulated, historical, and non-Western forms of labor. Here, _____ define "for or with whom one works and under what rules. These rules determine the type of work, type and amount of remuneration, working hours, degrees of physical and psychological strain, as well as the degree of freedom and autonomy associated with the work."

Exam Probability: **Medium**

35. *Answer choices:*

(see index for correct answer)

- a. Scranton Declaration
- b. Whipsaw strike
- c. Broad left
- d. Labor relations

Guidance: level 1

:: Production and manufacturing ::

_____ is a set of techniques and tools for process improvement. Though as a shortened form it may be found written as 6S, it should not be confused with the methodology known as 6S .

Exam Probability: **Medium**

36. *Answer choices:*
(see index for correct answer)

- a. Miniaturization
- b. Six Sigma
- c. Fieldbus Foundation
- d. Multi-Point Interface

Guidance: level 1

:: Timber industry ::

The _____ is an international non-profit, multi-stakeholder organization established in 1993 to promote responsible management of the world's forests. The FSC does this by setting standards on forest products, along with certifying and labeling them as eco-friendly.

Exam Probability: **Low**

37. *Answer choices:*
(see index for correct answer)

- a. Q-pit
- b. Forest Stewardship Council
- c. Ottawa River timber trade
- d. Lumber yard

Guidance: level 1

:: Trade unions ::

A _____ was a group formed of private citizens to administer law and order where they considered governmental structures to be inadequate. The term is commonly associated with the frontier areas of the American West in the mid-19th century, where groups attacked cattle rustlers and gangs, and people at gold mining claims. As non-state organizations no functioning checks existed to protect against excessive force or safeguard due process from the committees. In the years prior to the Civil War, some committees worked to free slaves and transport them to freedom.

Exam Probability: **Low**

38. *Answer choices:*
(see index for correct answer)

- a. Coordinating Committee of International Staff Unions and Associations of the United Nations System
- b. Independent union
- c. Vigilance committee
- d. Bump

Guidance: level 1

:: Business ::

_____ , or built-in obsolescence, in industrial design and economics is a policy of planning or designing a product with an artificially limited useful life, so that it becomes obsolete after a certain period of time. The rationale behind this strategy is to generate long-term sales volume by reducing the time between repeat purchases .

Exam Probability: **High**

39. *Answer choices:*
(see index for correct answer)

- a. American Environmental Assessment and Solutions Inc.
- b. Planned obsolescence
- c. Business partnering
- d. Citizenship for life

Guidance: level 1

:: Minimum wage ::

A _____ is the lowest remuneration that employers can legally pay their workers—the price floor below which workers may not sell their labor. Most countries had introduced _____ legislation by the end of the 20th century.

Exam Probability: **Low**

40. *Answer choices:*

(see index for correct answer)

- a. Guaranteed minimum income
- b. Minimum wage in the United States
- c. Minimum Wage Fairness Act
- d. Working poor

Guidance: level 1

:: United States federal defense and national security legislation ::

The USA _____ is an Act of the U.S. Congress that was signed into law by President George W. Bush on October 26, 2001. The title of the Act is a contrived three letter initialism preceding a seven letter acronym , which in combination stand for Uniting and Strengthening America by Providing Appropriate Tools Required to Intercept and Obstruct Terrorism Act of 2001. The acronym was created by a 23 year old Congressional staffer, Chris Kyle.

Exam Probability: **High**

41. *Answer choices:*

(see index for correct answer)

- a. Export Administration Act
- b. Patriot Act

Guidance: level 1

:: ::

Bernard Lawrence _____ is an American former market maker, investment advisor, financier, fraudster, and convicted felon, who is currently serving a federal prison sentence for offenses related to a massive Ponzi scheme. He is the former non-executive chairman of the NASDAQ stock market, the confessed operator of the largest Ponzi scheme in world history, and the largest financial fraud in U.S. history. Prosecutors estimated the fraud to be worth $64.8 billion based on the amounts in the accounts of _____ 's 4,800 clients as of November 30, 2008.

Exam Probability: **Low**

42. *Answer choices:*

(see index for correct answer)

- a. open system
- b. Sarbanes-Oxley act of 2002
- c. Madoff
- d. hierarchical

Guidance: level 1

:: Organizational structure ::

An _____ defines how activities such as task allocation, coordination, and supervision are directed toward the achievement of organizational aims.

Exam Probability: **Medium**

43. *Answer choices:*

(see index for correct answer)

- a. Organizational structure
- b. Organization of the New York City Police Department
- c. Followership
- d. Blessed Unrest

Guidance: level 1

:: Corporate governance ::

_____ refers to the practice of members of a corporate board of directors serving on the boards of multiple corporations. A person that sits on multiple boards is known as a multiple director. Two firms have a direct interlock if a director or executive of one firm is also a director of the other, and an indirect interlock if a director of each sits on the board of a third firm. This practice, although widespread and lawful, raises questions about the quality and independence of board decisions.

Exam Probability: **Low**

44. *Answer choices:*
(see index for correct answer)

- a. Chief innovation officer
- b. Interlocking directorate
- c. Gender representation on corporate boards of directors
- d. Short swing

Guidance: level 1

:: Offshoring ::

A _____ is the temporary suspension or permanent termination of employment of an employee or, more commonly, a group of employees for business reasons, such as personnel management or downsizing an organization. Originally, _____ referred exclusively to a temporary interruption in work, or employment but this has evolved to a permanent elimination of a position in both British and US English, requiring the addition of "temporary" to specify the original meaning of the word. A _____ is not to be confused with wrongful termination. Laid off workers or displaced workers are workers who have lost or left their jobs because their employer has closed or moved, there was insufficient work for them to do, or their position or shift was abolished . Downsizing in a company is defined to involve the reduction of employees in a workforce. Downsizing in companies became a popular practice in the 1980s and early 1990s as it was seen as a way to deliver better shareholder value as it helps to reduce the costs of employers . Indeed, recent research on downsizing in the U.S., UK, and Japan suggests that downsizing is being regarded by management as one of the preferred routes to help declining organizations, cutting unnecessary costs, and improve organizational performance. Usually a _____ occurs as a cost cutting measure.

45. *Answer choices:*

(see index for correct answer)

- a. TeleTech
- b. Advanced Contact Solutions
- c. Body shopping
- d. Offshoring Research Network

Guidance: level 1

:: ::

A _____ is a proceeding by a party or parties against another in the civil court of law. The archaic term "suit in law" is found in only a small number of laws still in effect today. The term " _____ " is used in reference to a civil action brought in a court of law in which a plaintiff, a party who claims to have incurred loss as a result of a defendant's actions, demands a legal or equitable remedy. The defendant is required to respond to the plaintiff's complaint. If the plaintiff is successful, judgment is in the plaintiff's favor, and a variety of court orders may be issued to enforce a right, award damages, or impose a temporary or permanent injunction to prevent an act or compel an act. A declaratory judgment may be issued to prevent future legal disputes.

46. *Answer choices:*

(see index for correct answer)

- a. Lawsuit
- b. interpersonal communication
- c. hierarchical
- d. cultural

Guidance: level 1

:: Public relations terminology ::

_____ , also called "green sheen", is a form of spin in which green PR or green marketing is deceptively used to promote the perception that an organization's products, aims or policies are environmentally friendly. Evidence that an organization is _____ often comes from pointing out the spending differences: when significantly more money or time has been spent advertising being "green", than is actually spent on environmentally sound practices. _____ efforts can range from changing the name or label of a product to evoke the natural environment on a product that contains harmful chemicals to multimillion-dollar marketing campaigns portraying highly polluting energy companies as eco-friendly.Publicized accusations of _____ have contributed to the term's increasing use.

Exam Probability: **Low**

47. *Answer choices:*
(see index for correct answer)

- a. Greenwashing
- b. Corporate pathos
- c. PR Gallery
- d. Photo op

Guidance: level 1

:: Parental leave ::

_____ , or family leave, is an employee benefit available in almost all countries. The term "_____" may include maternity, paternity, and adoption leave; or may be used distinctively from "maternity leave" and "paternity leave" to describe separate family leave available to either parent to care for small children. In some countries and jurisdictions, "family leave" also includes leave provided to care for ill family members. Often, the minimum benefits and eligibility requirements are stipulated by law.

Exam Probability: **High**

48. *Answer choices:*
(see index for correct answer)

- a. Cleveland Board of Education v. LaFleur
- b. Parental leave
- c. Pregnancy discrimination
- d. Equal Opportunities Commission v Secretary of State for Trade and Industry

:: Business ethics ::

_____ is an area of applied ethics which deals with the moral principles behind the operation and regulation of marketing. Some areas of _____ overlap with media ethics.

Exam Probability: **Low**

49. *Answer choices:*
(see index for correct answer)

- a. Resource Conservation and Recovery Act
- b. Voluntary compliance
- c. Marketing ethics
- d. Jewish business ethics

:: Business law ::

A _____ is an arrangement where parties, known as partners, agree to cooperate to advance their mutual interests. The partners in a _____ may be individuals, businesses, interest-based organizations, schools, governments or combinations. Organizations may partner to increase the likelihood of each achieving their mission and to amplify their reach. A _____ may result in issuing and holding equity or may be only governed by a contract.

Exam Probability: **High**

50. *Answer choices:*
(see index for correct answer)

- a. Hundi
- b. Business courts
- c. Enhanced use lease
- d. OHADA

:: Office work ::

_____ is the process and behavior in human interactions involving power and authority. It is also a tool to assess the operational capacity and to balance diverse views of interested parties. It is also known as office politics and organizational politics.It is the use of power and social networking within an organization to achieve changes that benefit the organization or individuals within it. Influence by individuals may serve personal interests without regard to their effect on the organization itself. Some of the personal advantages may include access to tangible assets, or intangible benefits such as status or pseudo-authority that influences the behavior of others. On the other hand, organizational politics can increase efficiency, form interpersonal relationships, expedite change, and profit the organization and its members simultaneously.Both individuals and groups may engage in office politics which can be highly destructive, as people focus on personal gains at the expense of the organization. "Self-serving political actions can negatively influence our social groupings, cooperation, information sharing, and many other organizational functions." Thus, it is vital to pay attention to organizational politics and create the right political landscape. "Politics is the lubricant that oils your organization`s internal gears." Office politics has also been described as "simply how power gets worked out on a practical, day-to-day basis."

Exam Probability: **Medium**

51. *Answer choices:*
(see index for correct answer)

- a. Workplace politics
- b. Copier service
- c. Executive suite
- d. Office humor

Guidance: level 1

:: Business ethics ::

_____ is a type of harassment technique that relates to a sexual nature and the unwelcome or inappropriate promise of rewards in exchange for sexual favors. _____ includes a range of actions from mild transgressions to sexual abuse or assault. Harassment can occur in many different social settings such as the workplace, the home, school, churches, etc. Harassers or victims may be of any gender.

Exam Probability: **Medium**

52. *Answer choices:*
(see index for correct answer)

- a. Sexual harassment
- b. Workplace bullying
- c. Foreign official
- d. Anti-consumerism

Guidance: level 1

:: ::

In regulatory jurisdictions that provide for it , _____ is a group of laws and organizations designed to ensure the rights of consumers as well as fair trade, competition and accurate information in the marketplace. The laws are designed to prevent the businesses that engage in fraud or specified unfair practices from gaining an advantage over competitors. They may also provides additional protection for those most vulnerable in society. _____ laws are a form of government regulation that aim to protect the rights of consumers. For example, a government may require businesses to disclose detailed information about products—particularly in areas where safety or public health is an issue, such as food.

Exam Probability: **High**

53. *Answer choices:*
(see index for correct answer)

- a. Consumer Protection
- b. information systems assessment
- c. personal values
- d. open system

Guidance: level 1

_____ is an ethical framework and suggests that an entity, be it an organization or individual, has an obligation to act for the benefit of society at large. _____ is a duty every individual has to perform so as to maintain a balance between the economy and the ecosystems. A trade-off may exist between economic development, in the material sense, and the welfare of the society and environment, though this has been challenged by many reports over the past decade. _____ means sustaining the equilibrium between the two. It pertains not only to business organizations but also to everyone whose any action impacts the environment. This responsibility can be passive, by avoiding engaging in socially harmful acts, or active, by performing activities that directly advance social goals. _____ must be intergenerational since the actions of one generation have consequences on those following.

Exam Probability: **Low**

54. *Answer choices:*

(see index for correct answer)

- a. Home economics
- b. Family and consumer science
- c. Euthenics
- d. Minnie Cumnock Blodgett

Guidance: level 1

:: ::

The _____ Group is a global financial investment management and insurance company headquartered in Des Moines, Iowa.

Exam Probability: **Medium**

55. *Answer choices:*

(see index for correct answer)

- a. cultural
- b. surface-level diversity
- c. Principal Financial
- d. imperative

Guidance: level 1

:: Anti-capitalism ::

_____ is a range of economic and social systems characterised by social ownership of the means of production and workers' self-management, as well as the political theories and movements associated with them. Social ownership can be public, collective or cooperative ownership, or citizen ownership of equity. There are many varieties of _____ and there is no single definition encapsulating all of them, with social ownership being the common element shared by its various forms.

Exam Probability: **Medium**

56. *Answer choices:*

(see index for correct answer)

- a. European Anti-Capitalist Left
- b. Anarchism
- c. New Anticapitalist Party
- d. Socialism

Guidance: level 1

:: False advertising law ::

The Lanham Act is the primary federal trademark statute of law in the United States. The Act prohibits a number of activities, including trademark infringement, trademark dilution, and false advertising.

Exam Probability: **High**

57. *Answer choices:*

(see index for correct answer)

- a. Rebecca Tushnet
- b. POM Wonderful LLC v. Coca-Cola Co.

Guidance: level 1

:: Business ethics ::

The _____ are the names of two corporate codes of conduct, developed by the African-American preacher Rev. Leon Sullivan, promoting corporate social responsibility.

Exam Probability: **High**

58. *Answer choices:*
(see index for correct answer)

- a. Unfree labour
- b. Resource Conservation and Recovery Act
- c. Interfaith Center on Corporate Responsibility
- d. Sullivan principles

Guidance: level 1

:: Culture ::

_____ is a society which is characterized by individualism, which is the prioritization or emphasis, of the individual over the entire group. _____ s are oriented around the self, being independent instead of identifying with a group mentality. They see each other as only loosely linked, and value personal goals over group interests. _____ s tend to have a more diverse population and are characterized with emphasis on personal achievements, and a rational assessment of both the beneficial and detrimental aspects of relationships with others. _____ s have such unique aspects of communication as being a low power-distance culture and having a low-context communication style. The United States, Australia, Great Britain, Canada, the Netherlands, and New Zealand have been identified as highly _____ s.

Exam Probability: **Low**

59. *Answer choices:*
(see index for correct answer)

- a. Intracultural
- b. Individualistic culture
- c. Low-context culture
- d. High-context

Guidance: level 1

Accounting

Accounting or accountancy is the measurement, processing, and communication of financial information about economic entities such as businesses and corporations. The modern field was established by the Italian mathematician Luca Pacioli in 1494. Accounting, which has been called the "language of business", measures the results of an organization's economic activities and conveys this information to a variety of users, including investors, creditors, management, and regulators.

:: ::

Accounts _____ is a legally enforceable claim for payment held by a business for goods supplied and/or services rendered that customers/clients have ordered but not paid for. These are generally in the form of invoices raised by a business and delivered to the customer for payment within an agreed time frame. Accounts _____ is shown in a balance sheet as an asset. It is one of a series of accounting transactions dealing with the billing of a customer for goods and services that the customer has ordered. These may be distinguished from notes _____ , which are debts created through formal legal instruments called promissory notes.

Exam Probability: **Low**

1. *Answer choices:*

(see index for correct answer)

- a. personal values
- b. process perspective
- c. Receivable
- d. deep-level diversity

Guidance: level 1

:: Accounting systems ::

In accounting, the controlling account is an account in the general ledger for which a corresponding subsidiary ledger has been created. The subsidiary ledger allows for tracking transactions within the controlling account in more detail. Individual transactions are posted both to the controlling account and the corresponding subsidiary ledger, and the totals for both are compared when preparing a trial balance to ensure accuracy.

Exam Probability: **Medium**

2. *Answer choices:*

(see index for correct answer)

- a. Unified ledger accounting
- b. Off-balance sheet
- c. Waste book
- d. Control account

Guidance: level 1

:: Legal terms ::

_____ is a state of prolonged public dispute or debate, usually concerning a matter of conflicting opinion or point of view. The word was coined from the Latin controversia, as a composite of controversus – "turned in an opposite direction," from contra – "against" – and vertere – to turn, or versus , hence, "to turn against."

Exam Probability: **Medium**

3. *Answer choices:*

(see index for correct answer)

- a. Controversy
- b. Adjudication
- c. Affray
- d. Motion to suppress

Guidance: level 1

:: Mathematical finance ::

In economics and finance, _____ , also known as present discounted value, is the value of an expected income stream determined as of the date of valuation. The _____ is always less than or equal to the future value because money has interest-earning potential, a characteristic referred to as the time value of money, except during times of negative interest rates, when the _____ will be more than the future value. Time value can be described with the simplified phrase, "A dollar today is worth more than a dollar tomorrow". Here, `worth more` means that its value is greater. A dollar today is worth more than a dollar tomorrow because the dollar can be invested and earn a day`s worth of interest, making the total accumulate to a value more than a dollar by tomorrow. Interest can be compared to rent. Just as rent is paid to a landlord by a tenant without the ownership of the asset being transferred, interest is paid to a lender by a borrower who gains access to the money for a time before paying it back. By letting the borrower have access to the money, the lender has sacrificed the exchange value of this money, and is compensated for it in the form of interest. The initial amount of the borrowed funds is less than the total amount of money paid to the lender.

Exam Probability: **Low**

4. *Answer choices:*
(see index for correct answer)

- a. Consumer math
- b. Stochastic discount factor
- c. AZFinText
- d. Lattice model

Guidance: level 1

:: Inventory ::

_____ is a system of inventory in which updates are made on a periodic basis. This differs from perpetual inventory systems, where updates are made as seen fit.

Exam Probability: **Low**

5. *Answer choices:*
(see index for correct answer)

- a. Periodic inventory
- b. GMROII

- c. Decomposition
- d. Buffer stock

Guidance: level 1

:: Finance ::

A _____ , publicly-traded company, publicly-held company, publicly-listed company, or public limited company is a corporation whose ownership is dispersed among the general public in many shares of stock which are freely traded on a stock exchange or in over-the-counter markets. In some jurisdictions, public companies over a certain size must be listed on an exchange. A _____ can be listed or unlisted .

Exam Probability: **High**

6. *Answer choices:*
(see index for correct answer)

- a. Non-operating income
- b. Public company
- c. Depletion
- d. Secured creditor

Guidance: level 1

:: Accounting journals and ledgers ::

_____ is a daybook or journal which is used to record transactions relating to adjustment entries, opening stock, accounting errors etc. The source documents of this prime entry book are journal voucher, copy of management reports and invoices.

Exam Probability: **High**

7. *Answer choices:*
(see index for correct answer)

- a. General journal
- b. Check register
- c. Cash receipts journal
- d. Sales journal

Guidance: level 1

A _____ or cheque, also called an image cash letter, clearing replacement document, or image replacement document, is a negotiable instrument used in electronic banking systems to represent a physical paper cheque. It may be wholly digital from payment initiation to clearing and settlement or it may be a digital reproduction of an original paper check.

Exam Probability: **Medium**

8. *Answer choices:*
(see index for correct answer)

- a. Substitute check
- b. Currence
- c. Ogone
- d. FreshBooks

Guidance: level 1

A _____ is the period used by governments for accounting and budget purposes, which varies between countries. It is also used for financial reporting by business and other organizations. Laws in many jurisdictions require company financial reports to be prepared and published on an annual basis, but generally do not require the reporting period to align with the calendar year. Taxation laws generally require accounting records to be maintained and taxes calculated on an annual basis, which usually corresponds to the _____ used for government purposes. The calculation of tax on an annual basis is especially relevant for direct taxation, such as income tax. Many annual government fees—such as Council rates, licence fees, etc.—are also levied on a _____ basis, while others are charged on an anniversary basis.

Exam Probability: **Medium**

9. *Answer choices:*
(see index for correct answer)

- a. hierarchical perspective
- b. information systems assessment
- c. cultural
- d. Fiscal year

:: Asset ::

In financial accounting, an _____ is any resource owned by the business. Anything tangible or intangible that can be owned or controlled to produce value and that is held by a company to produce positive economic value is an _____ . Simply stated, _____ s represent value of ownership that can be converted into cash . The balance sheet of a firm records the monetary value of the _____ s owned by that firm. It covers money and other valuables belonging to an individual or to a business.

Exam Probability: **Low**

10. *Answer choices:*
(see index for correct answer)

- a. Current asset
- b. Fixed asset

:: Loans ::

In finance, a _____ is the lending of money by one or more individuals, organizations, or other entities to other individuals, organizations etc. The recipient incurs a debt, and is usually liable to pay interest on that debt until it is repaid, and also to repay the principal amount borrowed.

Exam Probability: **High**

11. *Answer choices:*
(see index for correct answer)

- a. Equity loan
- b. Loan servicing
- c. Construction loan
- d. Loan

:: Expense ::

An _____ , operating expenditure, operational expense, operational expenditure or opex is an ongoing cost for running a product, business, or system. Its counterpart, a capital expenditure , is the cost of developing or providing non-consumable parts for the product or system. For example, the purchase of a photocopier involves capex, and the annual paper, toner, power and maintenance costs represents opex. For larger systems like businesses, opex may also include the cost of workers and facility expenses such as rent and utilities.

Exam Probability: **High**

12. *Answer choices:*
(see index for correct answer)

- a. Corporate travel
- b. Operating expense
- c. Stock option expensing
- d. Interest expense

Guidance: level 1

:: Tax avoidance ::

_____ s are any method of reducing taxable income resulting in a reduction of the payments to tax collecting entities, including state and federal governments. The methodology can vary depending on local and international tax laws.

Exam Probability: **High**

13. *Answer choices:*
(see index for correct answer)

- a. Tax shelter
- b. Salary packaging
- c. Perpetual traveler
- d. Double Irish arrangement

Guidance: level 1

:: Generally Accepted Accounting Principles ::

_____ is all a person's receipts and gains from all sources, before any deductions. The adjective "gross", as opposed to "net", generally qualifies a word referring to an amount, value, weight, number, or the like, specifying that necessary deductions have not been taken into account.

Exam Probability: **Medium**

14. *Answer choices:*

(see index for correct answer)

- a. Depreciation
- b. AICPA Statements of Position
- c. Gross income
- d. Expense

Guidance: level 1

:: ::

_____ science is the application of science to criminal and civil laws, mainly—on the criminal side—during criminal investigation, as governed by the legal standards of admissible evidence and criminal procedure.

Exam Probability: **Low**

15. *Answer choices:*

(see index for correct answer)

- a. hierarchical perspective
- b. Forensic
- c. co-culture
- d. Sarbanes-Oxley act of 2002

Guidance: level 1

:: Finance ::

The _____ of a corporation is the accumulated net income of the corporation that is retained by the corporation at a particular point of time, such as at the end of the reporting period. At the end of that period, the net income at that point is transferred from the Profit and Loss Account to the _____ account. If the balance of the _____ account is negative it may be called accumulated losses, retained losses or accumulated deficit, or similar terminology.

Exam Probability: **Medium**

16. *Answer choices:*
(see index for correct answer)

- a. Asset-backed commercial paper
- b. Signature line of credit
- c. Securities market
- d. Treasury company

Guidance: level 1

:: ::

A _____ is an entity that owes a debt to another entity. The entity may be an individual, a firm, a government, a company or other legal person. The counterparty is called a creditor. When the counterpart of this debt arrangement is a bank, the _____ is more often referred to as a borrower.

Exam Probability: **High**

17. *Answer choices:*
(see index for correct answer)

- a. levels of analysis
- b. functional perspective
- c. Sarbanes-Oxley act of 2002
- d. Debtor

Guidance: level 1

:: Project management ::

_____ is the widespread practice of collecting information and attempting to spot a pattern. In some fields of study, the term " _____ " has more formally defined meanings.

Exam Probability: **Medium**

18. *Answer choices:*

(see index for correct answer)

- a. Trend analysis
- b. Axelos
- c. Resource leveling
- d. Transfer of Burden

Guidance: level 1

:: Inventory ::

_____ is the maximum amount of goods, or inventory, that a company can possibly sell during this fiscal year. It has the formula.

Exam Probability: **Medium**

19. *Answer choices:*

(see index for correct answer)

- a. Stock demands
- b. Perpetual inventory
- c. Phantom inventory
- d. Inventory optimization

Guidance: level 1

:: Budgets ::

_____ is a method of budgeting in which all expenses must be justified and approved for each new period. Developed by Peter Pyhrr in the 1970s, _____ starts from a "zero base" at the beginning of every budget period, analyzing needs and costs of every function within an organization and allocating funds accordingly, regardless of how much money has previously been budgeted to any given line item.

20. *Answer choices:*

(see index for correct answer)

- a. Zero-based budgeting
- b. Public budgeting
- c. Personal budget
- d. Zero deficit budget

Guidance: level 1

:: Land value taxation ::

_____ , sometimes referred to as dry _____ , is the solid surface of Earth that is not permanently covered by water. The vast majority of human activity throughout history has occurred in _____ areas that support agriculture, habitat, and various natural resources. Some life forms have developed from predecessor species that lived in bodies of water.

Exam Probability: **High**

21. *Answer choices:*

(see index for correct answer)

- a. Georgism
- b. Henry George
- c. Prosper Australia
- d. Land

Guidance: level 1

:: ::

A _____ , in the word's original meaning, is a sheet of paper on which one performs work. They come in many forms, most commonly associated with children's school work assignments, tax forms, and accounting or other business environments. Software is increasingly taking over the paper-based _____ .

Exam Probability: **Low**

22. *Answer choices:*

(see index for correct answer)

- a. deep-level diversity
- b. Worksheet

- c. similarity-attraction theory
- d. co-culture

Guidance: level 1

:: Taxation in the United States ::

Basis , as used in United States tax law, is the original cost of property, adjusted for factors such as depreciation. When property is sold, the taxpayer pays/ taxes on a capital gain/ that equals the amount realized on the sale minus the sold property's basis.

Exam Probability: **Low**

23. *Answer choices:*
(see index for correct answer)

- a. Domestic international sales corporation
- b. Flip tax
- c. Cost basis
- d. Half-year convention

Guidance: level 1

:: Accounting software ::

_____ describes a type of application software that records and processes accounting transactions within functional modules such as accounts payable, accounts receivable, journal, general ledger, payroll, and trial balance. It functions as an accounting information system. It may be developed in-house by the organization using it, may be purchased from a third party, or may be a combination of a third-party application software package with local modifications. _____ may be on-line based, accessed anywhere at any time with any device which is Internet enabled, or may be desktop based. It varies greatly in its complexity and cost.

Exam Probability: **Low**

24. *Answer choices:*
(see index for correct answer)

- a. National Software
- b. TRAVERSE
- c. Accounting software

- d. ProSama 2010

Guidance: level 1

:: Management accounting ::

_____ , or dollar contribution per unit, is the selling price per unit minus the variable cost per unit. "Contribution" represents the portion of sales revenue that is not consumed by variable costs and so contributes to the coverage of fixed costs. This concept is one of the key building blocks of break-even analysis.

Exam Probability: **High**

25. *Answer choices:*
(see index for correct answer)

- a. Revenue center
- b. Invested capital
- c. Backflush accounting
- d. Investment center

Guidance: level 1

:: Personal taxes ::

A _____ is the completion of documentation that calculates an entity's income earned with the amount of tax payable to the government, government organisations or to potential taxpayers.

Exam Probability: **Low**

26. *Answer choices:*
(see index for correct answer)

- a. Grantor retained annuity trust
- b. Tax return
- c. Lay Tithes
- d. Church tax

Guidance: level 1

:: Accounting terminology ::

_____ or capital expense is the money a company spends to buy, maintain, or improve its fixed assets, such as buildings, vehicles, equipment, or land. It is considered a _____ when the asset is newly purchased or when money is used towards extending the useful life of an existing asset, such as repairing the roof.

Exam Probability: **High**

27. *Answer choices:*
(see index for correct answer)

- a. Capital surplus
- b. Share premium
- c. Mark-to-market
- d. Statement of financial position

Guidance: level 1

:: Real estate ::

Amortisation is paying off an amount owed over time by making planned, incremental payments of principal and interest. To amortise a loan means "to kill it off". In accounting, amortisation refers to charging or writing off an intangible asset's cost as an operational expense over its estimated useful life to reduce a company's taxable income.

Exam Probability: **High**

28. *Answer choices:*
(see index for correct answer)

- a. Amortization
- b. Shea Properties
- c. Green belt
- d. Real estate pricing

Guidance: level 1

:: Competition (economics) ::

In taxation and accounting, _____ refers to the rules and methods for pricing transactions within and between enterprises under common ownership or control. Because of the potential for cross-border controlled transactions to distort taxable income, tax authorities in many countries can adjust intragroup transfer prices that differ from what would have been charged by unrelated enterprises dealing at arm's length . The OECD and World Bank recommend intragroup pricing rules based on the arm's-length principle, and 19 of the 20 members of the G20 have adopted similar measures through bilateral treaties and domestic legislation, regulations, or administrative practice. Countries with _____ legislation generally follow the OECD _____ Guidelines for Multinational Enterprises and Tax Administrations in most respects, although their rules can differ on some important details.

Exam Probability: **High**

29. *Answer choices:*
(see index for correct answer)

- a. Leapfrogging
- b. Currency competition
- c. Transfer pricing
- d. Competition

Guidance: level 1

:: Pharmaceutical industry ::

A _____ is a document in which data collected for a clinical trial is first recorded. This data is usually later entered in the case report form. The International Conference on Harmonisation of Technical Requirements for Registration of Pharmaceuticals for Human Use guidelines define _____ s as "original documents, data, and records." _____ s contain source data, which is defined as "all information in original records and certified copies of original records of clinical findings, observations, or other activities in a clinical trial necessary for the reconstruction and evaluation of the trial."

Exam Probability: **Medium**

30. *Answer choices:*
(see index for correct answer)

- a. Innovative Medicines Initiative
- b. Boxed warning

- c. Source document
- d. Drug Master File

Guidance: level 1

:: ::

_____ is the field of accounting concerned with the summary, analysis and reporting of financial transactions related to a business. This involves the preparation of financial statements available for public use. Stockholders, suppliers, banks, employees, government agencies, business owners, and other stakeholders are examples of people interested in receiving such information for decision making purposes.

Exam Probability: **Low**

31. *Answer choices:*
(see index for correct answer)

- a. levels of analysis
- b. Financial accounting
- c. open system
- d. co-culture

Guidance: level 1

:: Generally Accepted Accounting Principles ::

An _____ or profit and loss account is one of the financial statements of a company and shows the company's revenues and expenses during a particular period.

Exam Probability: **High**

32. *Answer choices:*
(see index for correct answer)

- a. Income statement
- b. Earnings before interest, taxes, depreciation, and amortization
- c. Indian Accounting Standards
- d. Chinese accounting standards

Guidance: level 1

:: Costs ::

The _____ is computed by dividing the total cost of goods available for sale by the total units available for sale. This gives a weighted-average unit cost that is applied to the units in the ending inventory.

Exam Probability: **High**

33. *Answer choices:*
(see index for correct answer)

- a. Cost reduction
- b. Cost competitiveness of fuel sources
- c. Cost curve
- d. Average cost

Guidance: level 1

:: ::

The _____ is an American stock exchange located at 11 Wall Street, Lower Manhattan, New York City, New York. It is by far the world's largest stock exchange by market capitalization of its listed companies at US$30.1 trillion as of February 2018. The average daily trading value was approximately US$169 billion in 2013. The NYSE trading floor is located at 11 Wall Street and is composed of 21 rooms used for the facilitation of trading. A fifth trading room, located at 30 Broad Street, was closed in February 2007. The main building and the 11 Wall Street building were designated National Historic Landmarks in 1978.

Exam Probability: **Medium**

34. *Answer choices:*
(see index for correct answer)

- a. levels of analysis
- b. Character
- c. co-culture
- d. hierarchical

Guidance: level 1

:: Value theory ::

Within philosophy, it can be known as ethics or axiology. Early philosophical investigations sought to understand good and evil and the concept of "the good". Today, much of _____ aspires to the scientifically empirical, recording what people do value and attempting to understand why they value it in the context of psychology, sociology, and economics.

Exam Probability: **Medium**

35. *Answer choices:*
(see index for correct answer)

- a. Law of value
- b. Subjective theory of value
- c. Intrinsic theory of value
- d. Value theory

Guidance: level 1

:: Taxation ::

_____ is a type of tax law that allows a person to give assets to his or her spouse with reduced or no tax imposed upon the transfer. Some _____ laws even apply to transfers made postmortem. The right to receive property conveys ownership for tax purposes. A decree of divorce transfers the right to that property by reason of the marriage and is also a transfer within a marriage. It makes no difference whether the property itself or equivalent compensation is transferred before, or after the decree dissolves the marriage. There is no U.S. estate and gift tax on transfers of any amount between spouses, whether during their lifetime or at death. There is an important exceptions for non-citizens. The U.S. federal Estate and gift tax _____ is only available if the surviving spouse is a U.S. citizen. For a surviving spouse who is not a U.S. citizen a bequest through a Qualified Domestic Trust defers estate tax until principal is distributed by the trustee, a U.S. citizen or corporation who also withholds the estate tax. Income on principal distributed to the surviving spouse is taxed as individual income. If the surviving spouse becomes a U.S. citizen, principal remaining in a Qualifying Domestic Trust may then be distributed without further tax.

Exam Probability: **High**

36. *Answer choices:*
(see index for correct answer)

- a. Income tax and gambling losses
- b. Marital deduction
- c. Fair market value
- d. East African School of Taxation

Guidance: level 1

:: International accounting organizations ::

The _____ is the global organization for the accountancy profession. Founded in 1977, IFAC has more than 175 members and associates in more than 130 countries and jurisdictions, representing nearly 3 million accountants employed in public practice, industry and commerce, government, and academe. The organization supports the development, adoption and implementation of international standards for accounting education, ethics, and the public sector as well as audit and assurance. It supports four independent standard-setting boards, which establish international standards on ethics, auditing and assurance, accounting education, and public sector accounting. It also issues guidance to encourage high quality performance by professional accountants in business and small and medium accounting practices.

Exam Probability: **Medium**

37. *Answer choices:*
(see index for correct answer)

- a. World Congress of Accountants
- b. Forum of Firms
- c. International Federation of Accountants
- d. International Accounting Standards Committee

Guidance: level 1

:: Financial accounting ::

A _____ is an ownership interest in a corporation with enough voting stock shares to prevail in any stockholders' motion. A majority of voting shares is always a _____ . When a party holds less than the majority of the voting shares, other present circumstances can be considered to determine whether that party is still considered to hold a controlling ownership interest.

Exam Probability: **High**

38. *Answer choices:*

(see index for correct answer)

- a. Associate company
- b. Controlling interest
- c. Intellectual capital
- d. Hidden asset

Guidance: level 1

:: Pricing ::

_____ is a pricing strategy in which the selling price is determined by adding a specific amount markup to a product's unit cost. An alternative pricing method is value-based pricing.

Exam Probability: **Low**

39. *Answer choices:*

(see index for correct answer)

- a. Martingale pricing
- b. Lerner index
- c. Cost-plus pricing
- d. Invoice price

Guidance: level 1

:: ::

An _____ is a contingent motivator. Traditional _____ s are extrinsic motivators which reward actions to yield a desired outcome. The effectiveness of traditional _____ s has changed as the needs of Western society have evolved. While the traditional _____ model is effective when there is a defined procedure and goal for a task, Western society started to require a higher volume of critical thinkers, so the traditional model became less effective. Institutions are now following a trend in implementing strategies that rely on intrinsic motivations rather than the extrinsic motivations that the traditional _____ s foster.

Exam Probability: **Low**

40. *Answer choices:*

(see index for correct answer)

- a. Incentive
- b. surface-level diversity
- c. empathy
- d. cultural

Guidance: level 1

:: Business law ::

A _____ is a form of partnership similar to a general partnership except that while a general partnership must have at least two general partners , a _____ must have at least one GP and at least one limited partner.

Exam Probability: **Low**

41. *Answer choices:*
(see index for correct answer)

- a. Limited partnership
- b. Agency in English law
- c. Power harassment
- d. Voidable floating charge

Guidance: level 1

:: Investment ::

_____ , and investment appraisal, is the planning process used to determine whether an organization's long term investments such as new machinery, replacement of machinery, new plants, new products, and research development projects are worth the funding of cash through the firm's capitalization structure . It is the process of allocating resources for major capital, or investment, expenditures. One of the primary goals of _____ investments is to increase the value of the firm to the shareholders.

Exam Probability: **Low**

42. *Answer choices:*
(see index for correct answer)

- a. Price return
- b. Capital budgeting
- c. Value premium
- d. William Spell

:: Management accounting ::

An _____ is a classification used for business units within an enterprise. The essential element of an _____ is that it is treated as a unit which is measured against its use of capital, as opposed to a cost or profit center, which are measured against raw costs or profits.

Exam Probability: **High**

43. *Answer choices:*

(see index for correct answer)

- a. Investment center
- b. Direct material total variance
- c. Certified Management Accountants of Canada
- d. Cost accounting

:: Generally Accepted Accounting Principles ::

Financial statements prepared and presented by a company typically follow an external standard that specifically guides their preparation. These standards vary across the globe and are typically overseen by some combination of the private accounting profession in that specific nation and the various government regulators. Variations across countries may be considerable, making cross-country evaluation of financial data challenging.

Exam Probability: **Medium**

44. *Answer choices:*

(see index for correct answer)

- a. Closing entries
- b. Generally Accepted Accounting Principles
- c. Depreciation
- d. Operating income

:: Pricing ::

_____ is the difference between a lower selling price and a higher purchase price, resulting in a financial loss for the seller.

Exam Probability: **Medium**

45. *Answer choices:*
(see index for correct answer)

- a. Base point pricing
- b. Capital loss
- c. Fire sale
- d. indifference pricing

Guidance: level 1

:: Generally Accepted Accounting Principles ::

_____ is a measure of a fixed or current asset`s worth when held in inventory, in the field of accounting. NRV is part of the Generally Accepted Accounting Principles and International Financial Reporting Standards that apply to valuing inventory, so as to not overstate or understate the value of inventory goods. _____ is generally equal to the selling price of the inventory goods less the selling costs . Therefore, it is expected sales price less selling costs . NRV prevents overstating or understating of an assets value. NRV is the price cap when using the Lower of Cost or Market Rule.

Exam Probability: **High**

46. *Answer choices:*
(see index for correct answer)

- a. Fin 48
- b. Net realizable value
- c. Standard Business Reporting
- d. Cost pool

Guidance: level 1

:: Financial statements ::

_____ s - are the "Financial statements of a group in which the assets, liabilities, equity, income, expenses and cash flows of the parent company and its subsidiaries are presented as those of a single economic entity", according to International Accounting Standard 27 "Consolidated and separate financial statements", and International Financial Reporting Standard 10 " _____ s".

Exam Probability: **High**

47. *Answer choices:*
(see index for correct answer)

- a. Financial report
- b. Statement on Auditing Standards No. 55
- c. Consolidated financial statement
- d. Financial statement

Guidance: level 1

:: Insolvency ::

_____ is the process in accounting by which a company is brought to an end in the United Kingdom, Republic of Ireland and United States. The assets and property of the company are redistributed. _____ is also sometimes referred to as winding-up or dissolution, although dissolution technically refers to the last stage of _____ . The process of _____ also arises when customs, an authority or agency in a country responsible for collecting and safeguarding customs duties, determines the final computation or ascertainment of the duties or drawback accruing on an entry.

Exam Probability: **Low**

48. *Answer choices:*
(see index for correct answer)

- a. United Kingdom insolvency law
- b. Bankruptcy
- c. Liquidation
- d. George Samuel Ford

Guidance: level 1

:: ::

_____ is the income that is gained by governments through taxation. Taxation is the primary source of income for a state. Revenue may be extracted from sources such as individuals, public enterprises, trade, royalties on natural resources and/or foreign aid. An inefficient collection of taxes is greater in countries characterized by poverty, a large agricultural sector and large amounts of foreign aid.

Exam Probability: **Low**

49. *Answer choices:*
(see index for correct answer)

- a. information systems assessment
- b. corporate values
- c. levels of analysis
- d. Character

Guidance: level 1

:: Management accounting ::

In _____ or managerial accounting, managers use the provisions of accounting information in order to better inform themselves before they decide matters within their organizations, which aids their management and performance of control functions.

Exam Probability: **High**

50. *Answer choices:*
(see index for correct answer)

- a. Management accounting
- b. Management control system
- c. Direct material total variance
- d. Target costing

Guidance: level 1

:: Credit cards ::

The _____ Company, also known as Amex, is an American multinational financial services corporation headquartered in Three World Financial Center in New York City. The company was founded in 1850 and is one of the 30 components of the Dow Jones Industrial Average. The company is best known for its charge card, credit card, and traveler's cheque businesses.

Exam Probability: **High**

51. *Answer choices:*
(see index for correct answer)

- a. Black Card
- b. Visa Black Card
- c. Smiley v. Citibank
- d. American Express

Guidance: level 1

:: Accounting source documents ::

_____ is a letter sent by a customer to a supplier to inform the supplier that their invoice has been paid. If the customer is paying by cheque, the _____ often accompanies the cheque. The advice may consist of a literal letter or of a voucher attached to the side or top of the cheque.

Exam Probability: **High**

52. *Answer choices:*
(see index for correct answer)

- a. Credit memo
- b. Parcel audit
- c. Credit memorandum
- d. Remittance advice

Guidance: level 1

:: Types of business entity ::

A sole _____ , also known as the sole trader, individual entrepreneurship or _____ , is a type of enterprise that is owned and run by one person and in which there is no legal distinction between the owner and the business entity. A sole trader does not necessarily work `alone`—it is possible for the sole trader to employ other people.

Exam Probability: **Medium**

53. *Answer choices:*
(see index for correct answer)

- a. Proprietorship
- b. Delaware General Corporation Law
- c. Joint-stock company
- d. Intermediary corporation

Guidance: level 1

:: ::

_____ or accountancy is the measurement, processing, and communication of financial information about economic entities such as businesses and corporations. The modern field was established by the Italian mathematician Luca Pacioli in 1494. _____ , which has been called the "language of business", measures the results of an organization's economic activities and conveys this information to a variety of users, including investors, creditors, management, and regulators. Practitioners of _____ are known as accountants. The terms " _____ " and "financial reporting" are often used as synonyms.

Exam Probability: **Medium**

54. *Answer choices:*
(see index for correct answer)

- a. levels of analysis
- b. Accounting
- c. corporate values
- d. interpersonal communication

Guidance: level 1

:: Basic financial concepts ::

In finance, maturity or _____ refers to the final payment date of a loan or other financial instrument, at which point the principal is due to be paid.

Exam Probability: **Low**

55. *Answer choices:*
(see index for correct answer)

- a. Lodgement
- b. balloon payment
- c. Inflation
- d. Maturity date

Guidance: level 1

:: Accounting ::

_____ are key sources of information and evidence used to prepare, verify and/or audit the financial statements. They also include documentation to prove asset ownership for creation of liabilities and proof of monetary and non monetary transactions.

Exam Probability: **Low**

56. *Answer choices:*
(see index for correct answer)

- a. Accounting records
- b. Morison International
- c. Russian GAAP
- d. Efficiency-based absorption costing

Guidance: level 1

:: Money ::

In economics, _____ is money in the physical form of currency, such as banknotes and coins. In bookkeeping and finance, _____ is current assets comprising currency or currency equivalents that can be accessed immediately or near-immediately . _____ is seen either as a reserve for payments, in case of a structural or incidental negative _____ flow or as a way to avoid a downturn on financial markets.

Exam Probability: **Low**

57. *Answer choices:*
(see index for correct answer)

- a. Token money
- b. Key money
- c. Standard of deferred payment
- d. Money creation

Guidance: level 1

:: Income taxes ::

An _____ is a tax imposed on individuals or entities that varies with respective income or profits . _____ generally is computed as the product of a tax rate times taxable income. Taxation rates may vary by type or characteristics of the taxpayer.

Exam Probability: **High**

58. *Answer choices:*
(see index for correct answer)

- a. Income tax in Singapore
- b. Income tax
- c. Income tax in Australia
- d. Rouanet Law

Guidance: level 1

:: Finance ::

_____ is the ability of a bank customer in the United States and Canada to deposit a check into a bank account from a remote location, such as an office or home, without having to physically deliver the check to the bank. This is typically accomplished by scanning a digital image of a check into a computer, then transmitting that image to the bank. The practice became legal in the United States in 2004 when the Check Clearing for the 21st Century Act took effect, though not all banks have implemented the system.

Exam Probability: **Low**

59. *Answer choices:*
(see index for correct answer)

- a. Senior stretch loan
- b. SUGAM ITR-4S
- c. Securities market
- d. Remote deposit

Guidance: level 1

INDEX: Correct Answers

Foundations of Business

1. c: Interview

2. c: Dimension

3. d: Cultural

4. a: Total quality management

5. : INDEX

6. a: Reputation

7. : Corporate governance

8. c: Organizational structure

9. d: Solution

10. d: Import

11. c: Number

12. d: Free trade

13. a: Limited liability

14. a: Sales

15. a: Risk management

16. c: Recession

17. b: Quality control

18. d: Industry

19. c: Credit card

20. c: Image

21. c: Opportunity cost

22. d: Arthur Andersen

23. : Money

24. : Six Sigma

25. a: Stock

26. : Financial services

27. b: Cooperative

28. c: Raw material

29. b: Bias

30. b: Ownership

31. a: Building

32. d: Buyer

33. b: Marketing strategy

34. b: Bankruptcy

35. a: Advertising

36. c: Marketing mix

37. c: Utility

38. d: Internal Revenue Service

39. c: Threat

40. c: Consumer Protection

41. a: Bank

42. b: Loan

43. c: Availability

44. b: Sony

45. a: Insurance

46. a: Land

47. d: Frequency

48. b: Perception

49. a: Credit

50. : Variable cost

51. c: Industrial Revolution

52. c: Trade agreement

53. c: Officer

54. d: Technology

55. : Financial crisis

56. b: Logistics

57. b: Contract

58. : Preferred stock

59. b: Meeting

Management

1. b: Organizational structure

2. b: Customer

3. b: Market research

4. a: Change management

5. : Cash flow

6. b: Questionnaire

7. d: Expatriate

8. c: Intranet

9. c: Individualism

10. a: Dilemma

11. b: Virtual team

12. b: Policy

13. : Quality control

14. d: Efficiency

15. a: Small business

16. c: Negotiation

17. d: Job description

18. a: Variable cost

19. a: Philosophy

20. b: Management by objectives

21. : Collaboration

22. b: Committee

23. c: Forecasting

24. b: Management process

25. a: Delegation

26. a: Benchmarking

27. b: Resource

28. c: Innovation

29. a: Strategy

30. c: Labor relations

31. c: Analysis

32. a: Best practice

33. : Business process

34. c: Argument

35. : Ratio

36. : Organizational learning

37. d: Contingency theory

38. d: Size

39. b: Corporate governance

40. a: Inventory control

41. a: Performance management

42. b: Reason

43. d: Compromise

44. a: Vertical integration

45. a: Autonomy

46. a: Training and development

47. a: Market share

48. a: Strategic alliance

49. c: Cost leadership

50. b: Corporation

51. b: General manager

52. : Resource allocation

53. d: Integrity

54. d: Income

55. d: Accounting

56. c: Referent power

57. a: Employment

58. d: Strategic management

59. d: Project manager

Business law

1. : Labor relations

2. d: Security interest

3. d: Board of directors

4. d: Lease

5. c: Punitive damages

6. d: Commerce Clause

7. : Securities and Exchange Commission

8. a: Forgery

9. c: Criminal procedure

10. b: Personal property

11. : Accounting

12. c: Berne Convention

13. b: Assignee

14. d: Administrative law

15. b: Real property

16. b: Merger

17. b: Corporate governance

18. : Management

19. : Probate

20. a: Affirmative action

21. c: Trial

22. b: Disclaimer

23. d: Treaty

24. d: Securities Act

25. a: Antitrust

26. c: White-collar crime

27. b: Respondeat superior

28. b: Security agreement

29. a: Brand

30. b: Jurisdiction

31. c: Insurable interest

32. b: Regulation

33. a: Cause of action

34. : Federal Arbitration Act

35. b: Dividend

36. : Duty of care

37. c: Puffery

38. b: Prohibition

39. d: Licensee

40. d: Preference

41. c: Holder in due course

42. d: Tangible

43. a: Statutory Law

44. : Service mark

45. c: Subsidiary

46. : Economic espionage

47. a: Arbitration clause

48. b: Option contract

49. c: Shares

50. d: Writ

51. d: Comparative negligence

52. b: Standing

53. : Defamation

54. c: Consumer credit

55. : Partnership

56. c: Operation of law

57. d: Plaintiff

58. c: Health insurance

59. d: Real estate

Finance

1. d: Capital asset

2. c: Derivative

3. : Enron

4. a: Firm

5. d: Common stock

6. : Sinking fund

7. a: Net present value

8. : Mutual fund

9. d: Government bond

10. a: Saving

11. d: Income tax

12. c: Capital budgeting

13. d: Social security

14. c: Security

15. d: Face

16. b: Total cost

17. c: Insurance

18. : Retirement

19. : Sole proprietorship

20. a: Commercial bank

21. a: Net worth

22. a: Certified Public Accountant

23. : Chief financial officer

24. a: Raw material

25. d: Market price

26. a: Internal rate of return

27. a: Budget

28. b: Merchandising

29. b: Financial market

30. d: Cash equivalent

31. c: Bank account

32. : Accrual

33. : Variable cost

34. : Gross margin

35. c: Indirect costs

36. : Income statement

37. d: Financial instrument

38. b: Return on investment

39. : Liquidation

40. d: Volume

41. b: Absorption costing

42. c: Cost

43. c: Brand

44. : Cash management

45. b: Interest expense

46. d: Specific identification

47. a: Debenture

48. d: Audit

49. c: Double taxation

50. : Need

51. a: Periodic inventory

52. c: Stock exchange

53. : Municipal bond

54. b: Inventory

55. c: Intangible asset

56. d: Stockholder

57. a: Pension

58. d: Public company

59. : Accounts receivable

Human resource management

1. c: Employee Polygraph Protection Act

2. b: Empowerment

3. c: Psychological contract

4. c: Outplacement

5. b: Worker Adjustment and Retraining Notification Act

6. b: Fair Labor Standards Act

7. b: Job satisfaction

8. d: Cross-training

9. b: Material safety data sheet

10. : Human resources

11. a: Offshoring

12. b: Unemployment insurance

13. : McDonnell Douglas Corp. v. Green

14. c: Work ethic

15. b: Employee stock

16. b: Concurrent validity

17. a: Profession

18. : Recruitment

19. c: Person Analysis

20. b: Six Sigma

21. d: Wage curve

22. : Cost leadership

23. d: Skill

24. a: Needs analysis

25. c: Unemployment

26. : Internal consistency

27. c: Substance abuse

28. c: International Brotherhood of Teamsters

29. c: Workplace violence

30. c: Census

31. a: Control group

32. c: Needs assessment

33. b: Wage

34. d: Sick leave

35. d: Employee assistance program

36. b: Job security

37. a: Compa-ratio

38. d: Training

39. b: Works council

40. : Schedule

41. : Eustress

42. d: Employee stock ownership plan

43. : Labor relations

44. d: Culture shock

45. b: Goal setting

46. b: Equal Employment Opportunity Commission

47. b: Social networking

48. : E-learning

49. b: Job enlargement

50. b: Enforcement

51. c: Evidence-based

52. : Knowledge worker

53. c: Love contract

54. c: Predictive validity

55. a: Severance package

56. d: Executive compensation

57. c: Sexual harassment

58. d: Social loafing

59. b: Nearshoring

Information systems

1. c: Internet

2. d: Information

3. c: Zynga

4. : Security management

5. c: Threat

6. c: Geographic information system

7. d: Database management system

8. a: Social commerce

9. b: Copyright

10. c: Strategic planning

11. b: Positioning system

12. a: Electronic data interchange

13. b: Debit card

14. c: Spamming

15. a: Star

16. : Data center

17. d: Online analytical processing

18. b: BitTorrent

19. d: Computer security

20. : Critical success factor

21. d: Metadata

22. c: Text mining

23. c: Personalization

24. b: Market share

25. c: Domain Name System

26. d: Government-to-citizen

27. d: Domain name

28. a: Packet switching

29. : PageRank

30. d: Second Life

31. a: Authentication protocol

32. : Web content

33. d: Network management

34. c: Google

35. c: Entity-relationship

36. a: Spyware

37. b: Network interface card

38. c: Supply chain

39. a: Tacit knowledge

40. d: Affiliate marketing

41. : Data integrity

42. a: ICANN

43. a: Mozy

44. a: Intranet

45. d: QR code

46. : E-commerce

47. a: Verisign

48. a: Digital rights management

49. c: Asset

50. d: Telnet

51. a: Backup

52. c: Password

53. : Disaster recovery plan

54. c: Data analysis

55. c: Government-to-business

56. c: Mouse

57. : Automation

58. : Security controls

59. b: Byte

Marketing

1. a: Firm

2. : Distribution channel

3. a: Information technology

4. c: Census

5. d: Inflation

6. c: Relationship marketing

7. c: Target market

8. a: Argument

9. d: Integrated marketing

10. a: Goal

11. b: Unique selling proposition

12. d: Customer experience

13. b: Manufacturing

14. d: Monopoly

15. a: Exchange rate

16. : Technology

17. a: Price

18. b: Convenience

19. : Demand

20. d: Market share

21. : Planning

22. : Social media

23. : Department store

24. d: Telemarketing

25. b: Presentation

26. : Selling

27. d: Stock

28. d: Evolution

29. d: Warehouse

30. : Cost

31. : Creativity

32. d: Life

33. c: Audit

34. b: Competition

35. d: Consultant

36. a: Global marketing

37. d: Project

38. c: Adoption

39. : Standing

40. d: Market segments

41. b: Qualitative research

42. c: Customer value

43. c: Policy

44. : Universal Product Code

45. : Investment

46. c: Industry

47. c: Total Quality Management

48. b: Return on investment

49. a: American Express

50. b: Product development

51. a: Public

52. b: Advertising

53. : Publicity

54. b: Comparative advertising

55. b: Tangible

56. a: Raw material

57. b: Appeal

58. : Market segmentation

59. c: Corporation

Manufacturing

1. a: Thomas Register

2. c: Customer

3. d: Durability

4. a: DMAIC

5. c: Minitab

6. b: Supply chain risk management

7. c: Quality function deployment

8. c: Sunk costs

9. c: Certification

10. a: Workflow

11. : Purchasing process

12. : Solution

13. a: Check sheet

14. a: Value engineering

15. a: Natural resource

16. b: Remanufacturing

17. c: Strategic planning

18. d: Inspection

19. a: Obsolescence

20. : Synergy

21. c: Project management

22. d: Cost driver

23. d: Aggregate planning

24. : Coating

25. a: Concurrent engineering

26. : Clay

27. c: Steel

28. c: Statistical process control

29. : Zero Defects

30. b: Estimation

31. a: Inventory control

32. b: Lean manufacturing

33. : Reflux

34. c: Asset

35. b: Resource management

36. a: Risk management

37. c: Heat exchanger

38. c: Resource allocation

39. a: Chemical industry

40. a: Bill of materials

41. b: Raw material

42. : Catalyst

43. c: Sales

44. d: Time management

45. c: Sony

46. a: Change control

47. b: Inventory

48. b: Scientific management

49. d: Kanban

50. b: Process management

51. b: American Society for Quality

52. c: Knowledge management

53. b: Steering committee

54. b: Production schedule

55. d: Cash register

56. b: Assembly line

57. c: Metal

58. d: Process control

59. d: Information management

Commerce

1. d: Tangible

2. a: Boot

3. a: Financial services

4. a: Teamwork

5. : Merchandising

6. c: Logistics

7. c: Americans with Disabilities Act

8. a: Land

9. : Economic regulation

10. d: Household

11. d: Microsoft

12. b: Dutch auction

13. b: Economies of scale

14. : Confirmed

15. c: Market share

16. a: Auction

17. : Vendor

18. b: Contribution margin

19. b: Monopoly

20. : Compromise

21. c: Economics

22. c: Property

23. d: Accounting

24. b: Electronic funds transfer

25. : Authorize.Net

26. : Revenue management

27. c: Real estate

28. : Standing

29. b: Outsourcing

30. a: Good

31. b: Social shopping

32. a: Labor union

33. : Reverse auction

34. d: Silver

35. a: Loyalty

36. c: Evaluation

37. c: Marketing

38. d: Preference

39. b: Electronic data interchange

40. a: Marketing mix

41. a: Hearing

42. a: Advertisement

43. a: European Union

44. a: Mass production

45. c: Customer service

46. d: PayPal

47. b: Audit

48. d: Game

49. b: Purchasing

50. d: Sexual harassment

51. c: Export

52. c: Marketing strategy

53. a: Bill of lading

54. : Micropayment

55. b: Subsidiary

56. d: Security

57. a: Encryption

58. c: Case study

59. a: English auction

Business ethics

1. d: Hedonism

2. b: Pyramid scheme

3. : Corporation

4. : Accounting

5. b: UN Global Compact

6. c: Self-interest

7. d: Ethics Resource Center

8. b: White-collar crime

9. a: Corporate governance

10. : Chamber of Commerce

11. d: Sustainable

12. b: Endangered Species Act

13. d: Lead paint

14. a: Greenpeace

15. b: Utilitarianism

16. : Arthur Andersen

17. : Lead

18. c: Executive compensation

19. c: Clean Water Act

20. d: Ethical leadership

21. : Planet

22. d: Martin Luther

23. b: Antitrust

24. a: Model Rules of Professional Conduct

25. d: Real estate

26. c: Tobacco

27. c: Working poor

28. a: Community development financial institution

29. c: Marketing

30. : Great Depression

31. c: Feedback

32. a: Human nature

33. : Transocean

34. d: Micromanagement

35. d: Labor relations

36. b: Six Sigma

37. b: Forest Stewardship Council

38. c: Vigilance committee

39. b: Planned obsolescence

40. : Minimum wage

41. b: Patriot Act

42. c: Madoff

43. a: Organizational structure

44. b: Interlocking directorate

45. : Layoff

46. a: Lawsuit

47. a: Greenwashing

48. b: Parental leave

49. c: Marketing ethics

50. : Partnership

51. a: Workplace politics

52. a: Sexual harassment

53. a: Consumer Protection

54. : Social responsibility

55. c: Principal Financial

56. d: Socialism

57. c: Lanham Act

58. d: Sullivan principles

59. b: Individualistic culture

Accounting

1. c: Receivable

2. d: Control account

3. a: Controversy

4. : Present value

5. a: Periodic inventory

6. b: Public company

7. a: General journal

8. a: Substitute check

9. d: Fiscal year

10. c: Asset

11. d: Loan

12. b: Operating expense

13. a: Tax shelter

14. c: Gross income

15. b: Forensic

16. : Retained earnings

17. d: Debtor

18. a: Trend analysis

19. : Cost of goods available for sale

20. a: Zero-based budgeting

21. d: Land

22. b: Worksheet

23. c: Cost basis

24. c: Accounting software

25. : Contribution margin

26. b: Tax return

27. : Capital expenditure

28. a: Amortization

29. c: Transfer pricing

30. c: Source document

31. b: Financial accounting

32. a: Income statement

33. d: Average cost

34. : New York Stock Exchange

35. d: Value theory

36. b: Marital deduction

37. c: International Federation of Accountants

38. b: Controlling interest

39. c: Cost-plus pricing

40. a: Incentive

41. a: Limited partnership

42. b: Capital budgeting

43. a: Investment center

44. b: Generally Accepted Accounting Principles

45. b: Capital loss

46. b: Net realizable value

47. c: Consolidated financial statement

48. c: Liquidation

49. : Tax revenue

50. a: Management accounting

51. d: American Express

52. d: Remittance advice

53. a: Proprietorship

54. b: Accounting

55. d: Maturity date

56. a: Accounting records

57. : Cash

58. b: Income tax

59. d: Remote deposit

CPSIA information can be obtained
at www.ICGtesting.com
Printed in the USA
LVHW041330301019
635717LV00008B/967/P